THE COMPLETE
BRITISH
MOTORCYCLE

THE CLASSICS FROM 1907 TO THE PRESENT

THE COMPLETE
BRITISH
MOTORCYCLE

THE CLASSICS FROM 1907 TO THE PRESENT

JOHN CARROLL

PUBLISHED BY
SALAMANDER BOOKS LIMITED
LONDON

This edition published in 2001
by Salamander Books Limited
8, Blenheim Court,
Brewery Road,
London N7 9NT

A member of the Chrysalis Group plc

© 2001 Salamander Books
Limited

9 8 7 6 5 4 3 2 1

ISBN 1-84065-253-5

Credits

Photographer
Neil Sutherland

Editor
Philip de Ste. Croix

Designer
Roger Hyde

Photograph coordinator
Steve Kirkby

Index
Richard O'Neill

Salamander Books Ltd
Art Director
John Heritage
Editorial Directors
Will Steeds, Charlotte Davies

Colour reproduction
Studio Tec, Leeds, England

Printed in Hong Kong

Credits

The motorcycles pictured here come to you courtesy of their owners. Our thanks to all of them for their kindness and cooperation, without which there would be no book. The majority of the machines illustrated in these pages were photographed at two locations: the National Motorcycle Museum in Birmingham and the A.R. East collection at A.R.E. Ltd in Farnham. Our warm thanks go to N.M.M. founder Mr W.R. Richards and Tony East who respectively permitted the photography of their outstanding collections, and to the two men who so tirelessly helped to organize the actual motorcycles for photography – Dave Roach at the N.M.M. and Brian at A.R.E. Ltd who showed never-ending patience as they expertly handled the chosen bikes. Thanks also to Carl Rosner for allowing us to photograph the new Triumph Tiger and Thunderbird at his dealership in Sanderstead, South Croydon and to Bavanar Products Ltd, Therapia Trading Estate, Croydon for making an Indian Royal Enfield Bullet available for photography.

We recognize that some words – model names and designations, for example – mentioned herein are the property of the trademark holders. We use them for identification purposes only. This is not an official publication.

The information in this book is true and complete to the best of our knowledge. All recommendations are made without any guarantee on the part of the author or Publisher, who also disclaim any liability incurred in connection with the use of these data or specific details.

The Author

John Carroll is a long-time motorcycle enthusiast whose first real motorcycle was a '71 Triumph Daytona which he still regrets having sold. He has worked full time and freelanced for a variety of two- and four-wheeled publications including a spell editing *Back Street Heroes*, the cult English custom bike magazine. He has written a number of books on Indian and Harley-Davidson motorcycles, as well as about machines with more than two wheels. He is a Geography graduate and lives in Yorkshire, England.

DEDICATION
This book is dedicated to all the working men who ever rode a motorcycle to work in the pouring rain on a November morning including Sid Davies, Alex McLennan, Tommy Carroll and Ken Jellicoe.

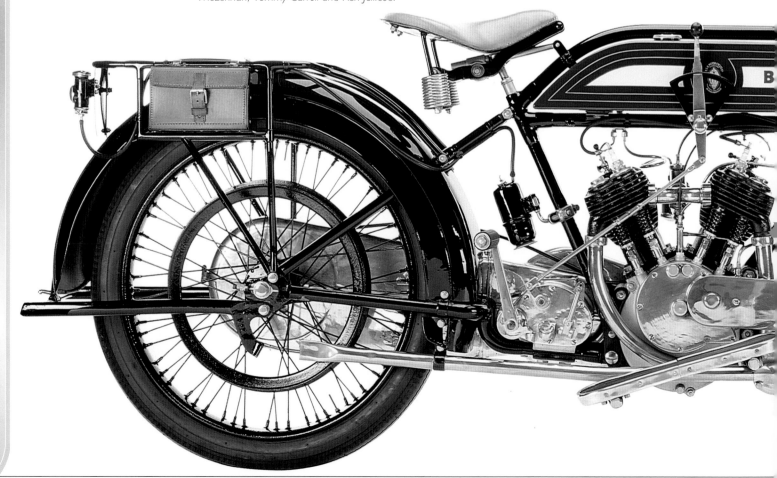

CONTENTS

INTRODUCTION

To many motorcyclists the very words "British bikes" conjure up images of the halcyon days of yore when the British were the largest producers of motorcycles in the world and race winners were always seated on a motorcycle made by any one of several world-class British companies. To others, more cynical, it brings to mind only oily, unreliable two-wheelers made by companies that were outclassed and outdated. The reality is that both recollections are often accurate, but date from different decades.

In common with the history of motorcycle manufacture around the world, the first British machines were derived from bicycles. In the early days it usually seemed that British manufacturers could do no wrong and a huge variety of companies flourished. However, world wars and economic depression took their toll of makers and despite huge sales in the fondly remembered 1950s and 1960s, the contraction of the industry had already begun. Several companies did not resume production after World War Two and others, such as Sunbeam, were acquired by larger manufacturers in the prewar years and sold again during the war years. It was, however, the 1970s which witnessed the real decimation of the industry for reasons which have been the subject of endless speculation and numerous books. Suffice to say that in little more than ten years the British motorcycle industry was reduced to almost nothing.

There followed a fitful period during which a few small companies attempted to produce motorcycles, including Hesketh, Norton and the co-operative at Triumph, but none could be described as major producers. When Triumph's assets were auctioned in 1983, it was easy to believe that the British motorcycle industry could be consigned to the pages of history books and that motorcycle manufacture was now primarily the province of the Japanese. It was not to be the case, however, and an upturn in motorcycling saw a revival in the fortunes of some European factories, a rags-to-riches tale for Harley-Davidson in the USA and, perhaps most unexpectedly, the revival of the Triumph name from a new Midlands factory in Hinckley.

The new Triumphs are sports bikes that stand comparison with the best from Japan, and yet follow the tradition of sporting motorcycles made by British companies, such as the Brough Superior and the Vincent Black Shadow. Although there have always been luxury sports motorcycles manufactured in Britain, far more numerous were the commuter motorcycles on which working men made their way to their offices, factories and shops. The Japanese motorcycles may

INTRODUCTION

have finished off the last of the large-capacity motorcycles made in Britain, but it was the cheap family car – the Morris Minor and the Ford Popular – that vastly reduced the number of two-wheeled commuters and made the sidecar outfit obsolete in the 1960s.

This book attempts to chronicle the rise and fall and recent revival of the British motorcycle industry from its first, almost experimental, machines to its present generation of liquid-cooled four-cylinder superbikes. On the following pages are a selection of motorcycles included to illustrate the sheer diversity of the products made by the once massive industry. There are both humble commuter machines and gentlemen's sporting motorcycles, the completely conventional and the truly innovative, as well as the successes and failures. There are a selection of motorcycles from the troubled days of the early 1940s when the British factories turned their production towards assisting the military effort to defeat fascism, a number of significant racing bikes, and even a British motorcycle manufactured far beyond Britain's shores . . .

John Carroll, 2000

AJS MODEL D

SPECIFICATIONS
Year: 1915
Engine type: V-twin
Engine cycle: Four-stroke
Capacity: 748cc (45.62cu in)
Bore & stroke: 74 x 87mm
Horsepower: n/a
Top speed: n/a
Compression ratio: n/a
Carburettor: Amac
Transmission: 3-speed
Brakes: F. Stirrup. R. Drum
Ignition: Magneto
Frame: Steel diamond
Suspension: F. Sprung girders.
R. None
Wheelbase: n/a
Weight: 276lb (125kg)
Fuel: n/a
Oil: Total loss
Tyres: n/a

AJS MODEL D (1915)

The AJS Model D was typical of many of the larger-capacity motorcycles of its day – the V-twin was a popular engine configuration before the trend towards singles and, later, vertical twins. The Model D was launched by AJS in 1912 and was one of a series of AJS V-twins that ran until 1940 when the 1000cc (61cu in) Model 2 was last produced. Production was interrupted when the company stopped making motorcycles in order to make munitions during World War One.

The Model D was initially launched as a 698cc machine, but by the time this motorcycle was made in 1915, the capacity had been increased to 748cc. While the first cylinder heads had been removable, those on the larger machine were integral with the casting of the cylinder barrels. A single Amac carburettor was connected to both cylinders through a T-shaped inlet manifold and the Splitdorf magneto for the ignition was positioned horizontally, forward of the front cylinder. The side-valve engine was connected to a 3-speed countershaft gearbox by a primary chain and drove the rear wheel with another – fully enclosed – chain. All-chain drive in this manner was advanced for the time, although it subsequently became commonplace.

The engine was started by using the kickstarter mounted at the rear of the transmission. The engine and transmission were fitted into a tubular steel frame that clearly showed the bicycle origins of the motorcycle. The

Above: The Model D was AJS's heavyweight V-twin of the 1910s. Such machines were popular for use in conjunction with sidecars.

Right: The Model D was AJS's heavyweight V-twin of the 1910s. Such machines were popular for use in conjunction with sidecars.

Above: The final drive chain was enclosed and drove the rear wheel from the 3-speed gearbox via the clutch.

frame was diamond-shaped like a pedal cycle, devoid of rear suspension and only slightly altered to suit the installation of an engine. The front brake was of the bicycle-type stirrup design while the rear was of the drum type. The forks were sprung and of a proprietary brand known as Brampton Bi-Flex, an allusion to their springing. Sprung bicycle-style saddles, as fitted here, were popular to compensate for the lack of rear suspension.

Fuel and lubricating oils were carried in a compartmentalized tank below the top tube of the frame. The fuel simply flowed down a tube to the carburettor, but the lubrication system was altogether more complicated. The engine featured what is known as total-loss lubrication meaning that the lubricant was not recirculated but "lost" through the engine whilst in motion. The rider was expected to keep the engine lubricated by pumping in oil by means of the hand pump mounted on the side of the tank at necessary intervals. A sight glass was available to allow the rider to check on the amount of oil remaining in the tank. The lever mounted on the tank behind the oil pump was to allow the rider to change gear in conjunction with the handlebar-mounted clutch lever adjacent to the left-hand grip. The other handlebar levers were for the operation of front and rear brakes while the twistgrip operated the throttle by means of a cable to the carburettor.

This machine was manufactured before electric lights were the norm for motorcycles and it was equipped with acetylene lights front and rear. These lights relied on the reaction between water and calcium carbide to give off acetylene gas that burns with a bright flame and, with a reflector, could be used for a light.

Below: The hand gearshift and engine oil hand pump were located on the right side of the sculptured fuel tank to facilitate their being used by the rider while the motorcycle was in motion.

Left: Acetylene lights that relied on the reaction between water and calcium carbide were fitted to the front and rear of motorcycles until electric lights became practical.

Above: The array of levers to be operated by the rider included throttle, brakes, ignition advance/retard, gear levers and oil pump.

Above: The V-twin engine was of a side-valve design and displaced 748cc through a bore and stroke of 74 x 87mm. The valves can be seen in the sides of the cylinder barrel castings.

AJS R7

SPECIFICATIONS

Year: 1930
Engine type: Ohc single
Engine cycle: Four-stroke
Capacity: 346cc (21cu in)
Bore & stroke: 70 x 90mm
Horsepower: n/a
Top speed: n/a
Compression ratio: n/a
Carburettor: n/a
Transmission: 4-speed
Brakes: F & R. Drum
Ignition: Magneto
Frame: Tubular steel
Suspension: F. Sprung girders.
R. None
Wheelbase: n/a
Weight: 290lb (132kg)
Fuel: n/a
Oil: n/a
Tyres: F. 21in R. n/a

Right: The unusual design of exhaust silencer was known as a Brooklands Can and was fitted to bikes raced at Brooklands to minimize noise so as to avoid complaints from residents who lived near the race circuit.

AJS R7 (1930)

The AJS company was founded in Wolverhampton by Albert John Stevens and his brothers in 1911. They had already for some time been producing engines for other manufacturers. The first AJS machine was a 2.5hp single-cylinder-engined motorcycle although the company soon went on to produce V-twins. AJS then became involved in the production of racing motorcycles and, from 1927 onwards, following the lead of Norton and Velocette, it produced overhead-camshaft singles for this purpose. In 1930 the family took the decision to diversify their manufacturing business using the skills from motorcycle and sidecar production. They sought to establish themselves as car, lorry and bus manufacturers. They also saw potential for their woodworking facility to produce furniture and cabinets for radiograms. The onset of the Great Depression meant that the new venture did not go as well as expected, however, and in 1931 the bank foreclosed on the company. The family settled its debts and the AJS name and assets were purchased by Matchless and moved to down to Woolwich in London.

When designating its motorcycles, the company used an alphabetical prefix to indicate the year of manufacture – R was 1930, S was 1931 etc. and a number to signify the capacity – 7 indicated a 350cc. From 1933 onwards the year was indicated by its last two digits, i.e. 33 for 1933. The 1930 AJS range included nine different motorcycles ranging from the R2, a 998cc side-valve V-twin, to the R12, a 249cc twin-port single. In

between came the R7 and R10, overhead-camshaft models of 346cc and 495cc respectively. Like all overhead-camshaft AJS machines, these motorcycles had the camshaft chain driven on the right and the case for it reached from the crankcase to the cambox. The same case also extended forward to the end of the magneto which was mounted forward of the vertical cylinder barrel. The oil pump was sited on the outside of this case as the overhead-camshaft AJS had dry-sump lubrication. The oil tank was bolted to the frame under the seat. The foot-change transmission was a proprietary 4-speed unit manufactured by Burman.

As the AJS R7 was primarily built for racing, it did not come equipped with lights or a front mudguard as standard. A minimal rear mudguard covered just sufficient of the rear tyre and acted as the mount for the pillion pad onto which the rider could slide in order to adopt a more streamlined position while racing. The handlebars were cranked downwards and the foot pegs located well back on the frame's lower tubes for the same reason. The frame was devoid of rear suspension and rider comfort depended on the springing of the saddle and the sprung girder forks and friction damping.

Following the acquisition of the company by Matchless, the move to Woolwich went smoothly and had little effect on the production of AJS machines in general. The range was manufactured pretty much as before. The exception was in the production of the overhead-camshaft singles. The two models for 1931 would have been the S7 and S10, but few, if any, of these motorcycles were built for at least two years.

Below: The pillion pad was mounted on the rear mudguard as close to the saddle as possible. It was not intended for a pillion passenger but to allow the rider to sit further back when racing.

Above: The 4-speed transmission and chain final drive were conventional and proven motorcycle components by the 1930s.

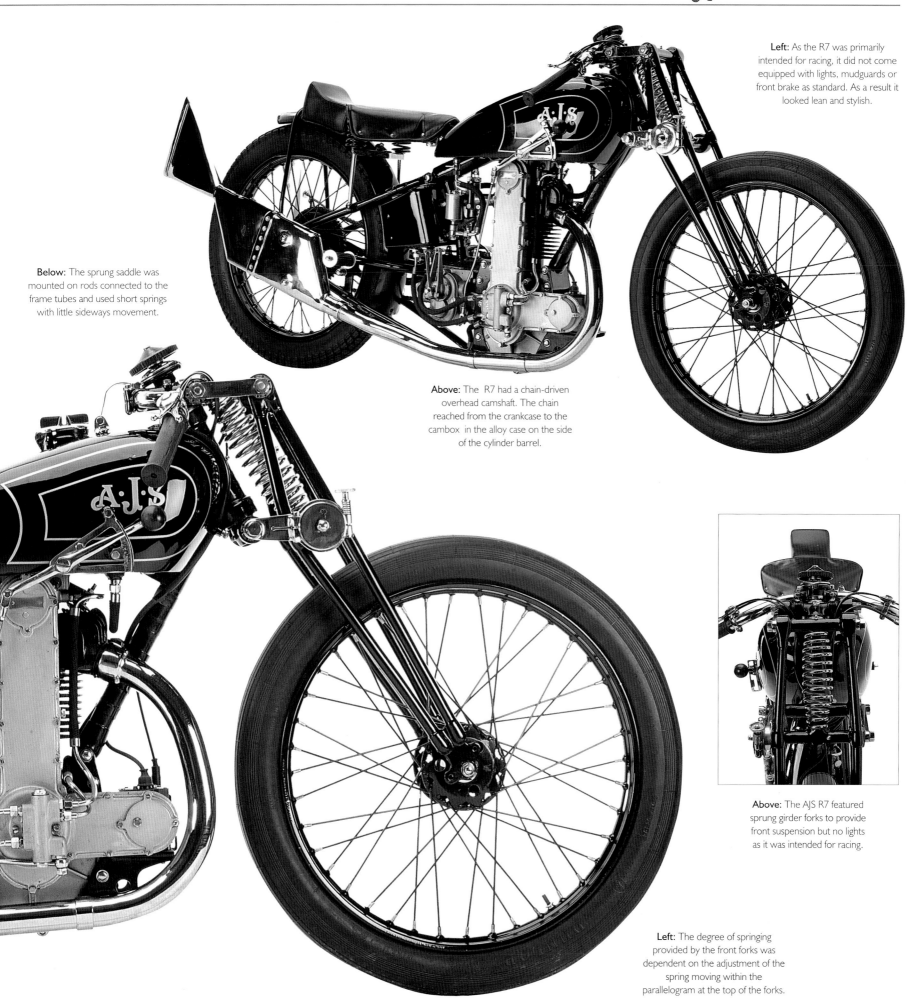

Left: As the R7 was primarily intended for racing, it did not come equipped with lights, mudguards or front brake as standard. As a result it looked lean and stylish.

Below: The sprung saddle was mounted on rods connected to the frame tubes and used short springs with little sideways movement.

Above: The R7 had a chain-driven overhead camshaft. The chain reached from the crankcase to the cambox in the alloy case on the side of the cylinder barrel.

Above: The AJS R7 featured sprung girder forks to provide front suspension but no lights as it was intended for racing.

Left: The degree of springing provided by the front forks was dependent on the adjustment of the spring moving within the parallelogram at the top of the forks.

AJS PORCUPINE E95

SPECIFICATIONS

Year: 1954
Engine type: Dohc parallel twin
Engine cycle: Four-stroke
Capacity: 499cc (30.37cu in)
Bore & stroke: 68 x 68.5mm
Horsepower: 55bhp @ 7600rpm
Top speed: n/a
Compression ratio: n/a
Carburettor: Twin Amals
Transmission: 4-speed
Brakes: F & R. Drum
Ignition: Magneto
Frame: Steel duplex cradle
Suspension: F. Telescopic forks. R. Swingarm and shock absorbers
Wheelbase: n/a
Weight: n/a
Fuel: n/a
Oil: 1.5 gallons (6.82lit)
Tyres: n/a

Right: The AJS Porcupine was designed solely for racing as a supercharged motorcycle. However, the interruption to the sport caused by World War Two and a change of rules concerning superchargers meant that it never realized its full potential.

AJS PORCUPINE (1954)

The AJS Porcupine was a British bike designed for a specific purpose, namely racing, but it was made almost obsolete from the word go by a change of circumstances. It was a supercharged design but before it could be used in its blown – supercharged – form the rules for motorcycle racing were changed to outlaw superchargers. This change in the regulations meant that the induction system of the AJS had to redesigned before it could be raced in normally aspirated form.

During the 1930s certain marques, such as BMW and Gilera, raced 500cc supercharged motorcycles to great effect in international motorcycle sport and it was these machines that inspired the engineers and designers at AJS. Motorcycle racing had, of course, been interrupted by the outbreak of World War Two, but during the war years the company sought to design a motorcycle in anticipation of postwar events. It was to be supercharged. For this reason the cylinders were laid flat, to maximize air cooling, and a supercharger cradle was cast into the top of the gearbox. The fins on the flat cylinders were spiked in design and were the inspiration for the motorcycle's Porcupine nickname. A prototype was

constructed immediately after the war, but in the aftermath of the ban on superchargers all AJS's engineers could do to improve performance was to increase the compression ratio significantly and redesign the inlet manifolds.

The 1947 version of the Porcupine produced 40bhp and this was gradually increased as a result of painstaking development work to 55bhp by the mid-1950s. The handling of the machine required development too. It had been designed with a low centre of gravity but it experienced problems with suspension damping. However, factory policy forbade a move to non-AJS shock absorbers. Despite the problems the Porcupine was competitive at times. Les Graham, for example, won the 1949 World Championship aboard one despite a magneto failure two miles from the finish while leading the 1949 Senior Isle of Man TT which required him to push the bike home to tenth position. Later TT events saw the Porcupine finish in the top five for the next four years, usually behind the works Nortons.

The design of the engine was strong as it was intended to withstand the extra stresses brought about by supercharging. It featured a one-piece forged crankshaft, supported in roller bearings at each end and a 1.75in

Below: The large-capacity saddle tank style of petrol tank provided sufficient fuel for long races.

Above: Although the various designs of engine used in the Porcupine were innovative, much of the remainder of the machine was conventional, including a 4-speed transmission and chain final drive.

(44mm) plain bearing in the centre. The con rods were made from RR56 aluminium alloy while the crankcase, gearbox and sump were cast from the magnesium alloy elektron. The spike-finned alloy cylinders were cast separately and capped with a one-piece cylinder head. The "porcupine" fins were later discontinued, as this 1954 model shows, but the name stuck.

The camshafts were hollow forgings supported in roller bearings and gear-driven. The oil pump and magneto above the crankcase were also gear-driven and the pump circulated the lubricant at a rate of 45 gallons per hour @ 7000rpm. The main feeds were to the centre main bearing and cam boxes. The chain was lubricated by a bleed line to drillings in the

sprocket off the scavenge line from the sump. The primary drive was by means of a pair of spur gears and the clutch was ventilated because of the speeds the machine was expected to achieve. Final drive was from the opposite side of the gearbox to the primary and all the pions and shafts ran on roller bearings because of the torque expected from a super-charged engine.

Through the years AJS engineers experimented with design improvements. These included moving the cylinders from horizontal to 45 degrees, using normally finned castings, increasing the sump capacity, fitting a chain drive to the magneto, as well as numerous frame and tank alterations.

Below: The Porcupine did suffer from handling problems on occasions, but the manufacturers insisted on the fitment of their own brand of shock absorbers rather than specialist proprietary items.

Above: The rider's eye view of the machine forwards through the aero screen takes in the businesslike clip-on handlebars, racing filler cap, race number, top fork yoke and speedo.

Above: The unusual protrusion from the front of the engine seen here is the large-capacity sump for the lubrication oil. It was positioned here to keep the centre of gravity as low as possible.

Left: The Porcupine nickname came about as a result of the number of fins cast into the engine to aid cooling. The name stuck even when these fins were later discontinued.

AJS MODEL 18S

SPECIFICATIONS
Year: 1950
Engine type: Ohv single
Engine cycle: Four-stroke
Capacity: 497cc (30.3cu in)
Bore & stroke: 82.5 x 93mm
Horsepower: 23bhp @ 5400rpm
Top speed: 84mph (135kph)
Compression ratio: 5.9:1
Carburettor: Amal
Transmission: 4-speed
Brakes: F & R. Drum
Ignition: Magneto
Frame: Steel cradle
Suspension: F. Telescopic forks. R. Swingarm and candlestick dampers
Wheelbase: 55.25in (1403mm)
Weight: 387lb (176kg)
Fuel: 3.5 gallons (15.9lit) est.
Oil: 6 pints (3.4lit) est.
Tyres: 3.25 x 19in

Right: By 1950, when this AJS Model 18S was made, the company had long been part of Associated Motorcycles, and Matchless and AJS machines differed only in their badges and magneto position.

AJS MODEL 18S (1950)

AJS and Matchless had merged as one company – AMC or Associated Motor Cycles – in 1937 and gradually their products came to be simply badge-engineered versions of one another's range. This process was slowed by the outbreak of World War Two but accelerated again after peace was concluded. The two marques' machines were built on the same Woolwich production line using most of the same parts, but despite this uniformity the company promoted the two brands with separate advertising campaigns and different competition riders racing on the two makes. The only significant difference, and one that persisted until 1951, was the position of the magneto.

The postwar range announced in 1945 included two new models, the 16M and 18. These two machines, closely based on the wartime G3L, were almost identical except for the diameter of the cylinder bore and the type of exhausts pipes fitted. The 16M featured a 69mm bore while the 18 had an 82.5mm bore. These dimensions, in conjunction with a stroke of 93mm, gave the engines displacements of 348 and 497cc respectively. The machines were typical of British single-cylinder motorcycles of the period, being constructed with a built-up crankshaft, a vertically split crankcase, an iron barrel and iron head. The magneto on the AJS was

Above: On AJS engines the magneto was mounted forward of the cylinder barrel, while it went behind on Matchless models.

Right: Despite the presence of a swingarm and rear shock absorbers, the solo saddle is sprung while the pillion pad is not.

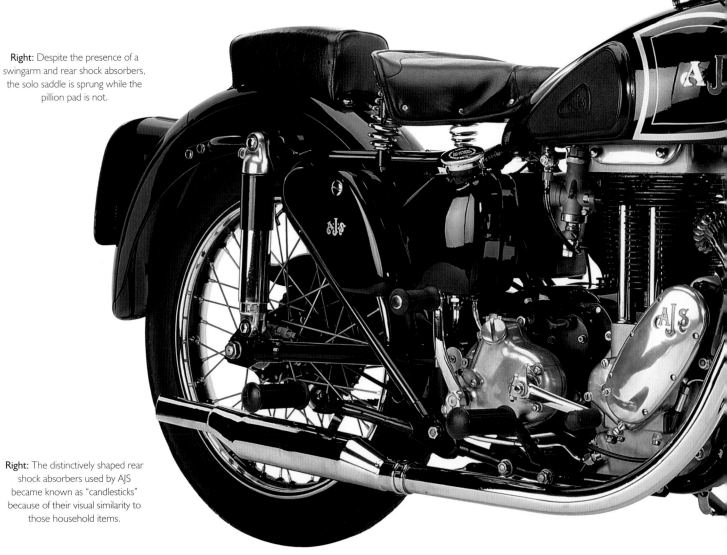

Right: The distinctively shaped rear shock absorbers used by AJS became known as "candlesticks" because of their visual similarity to those household items.

Above: The 497cc overhead-valve single achieved this displacement through a bore and stroke of 82.5 x 93mm. It produced 23bhp @ 5400rpm.

Right: This is the 497cc AJS Model 18S, the smaller-capacity version was the 348cc 16MS. These corresponded to the G80 and G3LS Matchless machines.

Below: The widespread use of telescopic forks meant that headlamps could be mounted to sleeves fitted around the length of fork tube between the top and bottom fork yokes.

Above: The postwar single-cylinder motorcycles from AMC evolved only gradually from the wartime models, because in the days of "export or die" continuous production was all-important.

positioned forward of the cylinder and was chain-driven from the exhaust camshaft. The two machines formed the basis of AJS's postwar range for some years, while a range of competition variants was announced in the spring of 1946. These were given a C suffix, the two models being known as the 16MC and 18C.

The immediate postwar years saw British industry driving to achieve exports to help Britain's economic position in the wake of the war – "export or die" was the catchphrase of the time – so little change was made to successful machines such as the 16M and 18 AJS. Uninterrupted production was paramount. The range expanded for 1949 when AMC introduced sprung frames and twin-cylinder engines. The 16M and 18 singles were upgraded with the new frame becoming the 16MS and 18S.

Unlike many contemporary manufacturers AMC never used a plunger-style frame – one with a sprung axle in a rigid frame – but moved from rigid ones to a swinging-arm-and-shock-absorbers system. The company manufactured its own rear dampers which were nicknamed candlesticks because of their distinctive shape. The rigid-framed models remained in production and, in fact, the two models were made alongside one another with bolt-together frames. Rigid frames received one type of rear section while the swingarm models received another. The front sections incorporating the engine cradle were identical. The Matchless variants were known as the G3L and G80 with rigid frames, while with swingarms they were styled the G3LS and G80S.

Little change was made to the roadgoing range for 1950 although the competition models were refined somewhat. It was similar story for 1951, although the Matchless magneto was finally moved to the same position forward of the engine as that on the AJS. The candlestick dampers were replaced by stronger ones that subsequently became known as jam-pots, again a reference to their distinctive shape. The singles ran on in various forms until 1963, and they are often best remembered as trials and scrambles machines when they were equipped with alloy fuel tanks and other competition-developed components, rather than clothed in the more mundane roadgoing trim seen here.

ARIEL RED HUNTER

SPECIFICATIONS

Year: 1937
Engine type: Ohv single
Engine cycle: Four-stroke
Capacity: 346cc (21.1cu in)
Bore & stroke: 72 x 85mm
Horsepower: 17bhp @ 5600rpm
Top speed: 80mph (129kph)
Compression ratio: n/a
Carburettor: Amal
Transmission: 4-speed
Brakes: F. & R. Drum
Ignition: Magneto
Frame: Tubular steel
Suspension: F. Sprung girders. R. None
Wheelbase: 56in (1422mm)
Weight: 320lb (145kg)
Fuel: 3.5 gallons (15.9lit)
Oil: 6 pints (3.4lit)
Tyres: F. 3.25 x 20in.
R. 3.50 x 19in

Above: Ariel's logo was plain and unadorned, unlike some others of the time.

Right: Unusual exhausts of this shape had their origins in the famed "Brooklands Can" – a racing exhaust designed to minimize noise at the English circuit. These were intended to add sporting flair to a road machine.

ARIEL RED HUNTER NH (1937)

The basic line of single-cylinder motorcycles made by Ariel was established by Val Page when he joined the company in the autumn of 1925. For the 1927 models he moved the magneto behind the engine and used chain drive from the camshaft to operate it. This basic design lasted for 30 years. By 1931 the company was producing a 346cc displacement single with overhead valves although its cylinder barrel was inclined forward 30 degrees. The Red Hunter name first appeared in 1932 on a sporting 499cc single with four overhead valves and a vertical cylinder. In the same year the company ran into financial difficulties which led to a reorganization under the direction of Jack Sangster whose family had a long association with the company. Edward Turner was given charge of the design department and he decided to slim down the range.

In order to make savings, all sloping engines were discontinued and only vertical engines remained in production. The vertical engine configuration was developed and the Red Hunter range expanded to include 248 and 346cc versions. The model designation indicated both capacity and model; L signified 249cc, N 346cc and V 499cc. The letter F signified a standard model, G a deluxe machine, and H a Red Hunter. A number of variations were available, single- and twin-port heads could be specified, as could high- or low-level exhausts pipes and different Burman gearboxes. In these forms the single-cylinder machines continued in production through 1937 when this motorcycle was manufactured. It features a twin-port head necessitating two exhaust pipes – high-level pipes, as used for competition, are fitted.

The Red Hunter NH in this form was a completely conventional motorcycle of its time; the 350cc displacement was a popular size in British motorcycling, and single-cylinder engines were the norm, as were a rigid frame and girder forks. The instruments were located on top of the fuel tank and a sprung solo seat offered a degree of comfort to the rider. The Red Hunter was a proven motorcycle by 1937, and with Edward Turner's addition of red paint and chrome on the fuel tank an attractive one at that. It attracted a loyal band of enthusiasts which ensured production would continue into the 1950s.

Production was interrupted during the war years although Ariel Motors, as the firm had become in 1936, produced the W/NG for service use. In the last year before the outbreak of war Ariel experimented with a spring frame intended to give a constant chain tension. It used a complex arrangement of pivots which tended to wear quickly in use and

limited wheel movement. After the war rear suspension came in the form of a plunger frame as did telescopic forks which were introduced during 1946. The Ariel Square Four was considered by many to be Ariel's flag-ship model and in line with the postwar shift to vertical twins, Ariel introduced the Huntmaster. It was powered by a 647cc overhead-valve twin that was in fact a disguised BSA Golden Flash engine. In attempting to follow market trends, in 1958 Ariel discontinued their four-stroke machines – including the venerable singles – in order to concentrate on the innovative Ariel Leader.

Below: Ariel's model designations were indicative of both displacement and model. This NH of 1937 was a 350 – N and a Red Hunter – H.

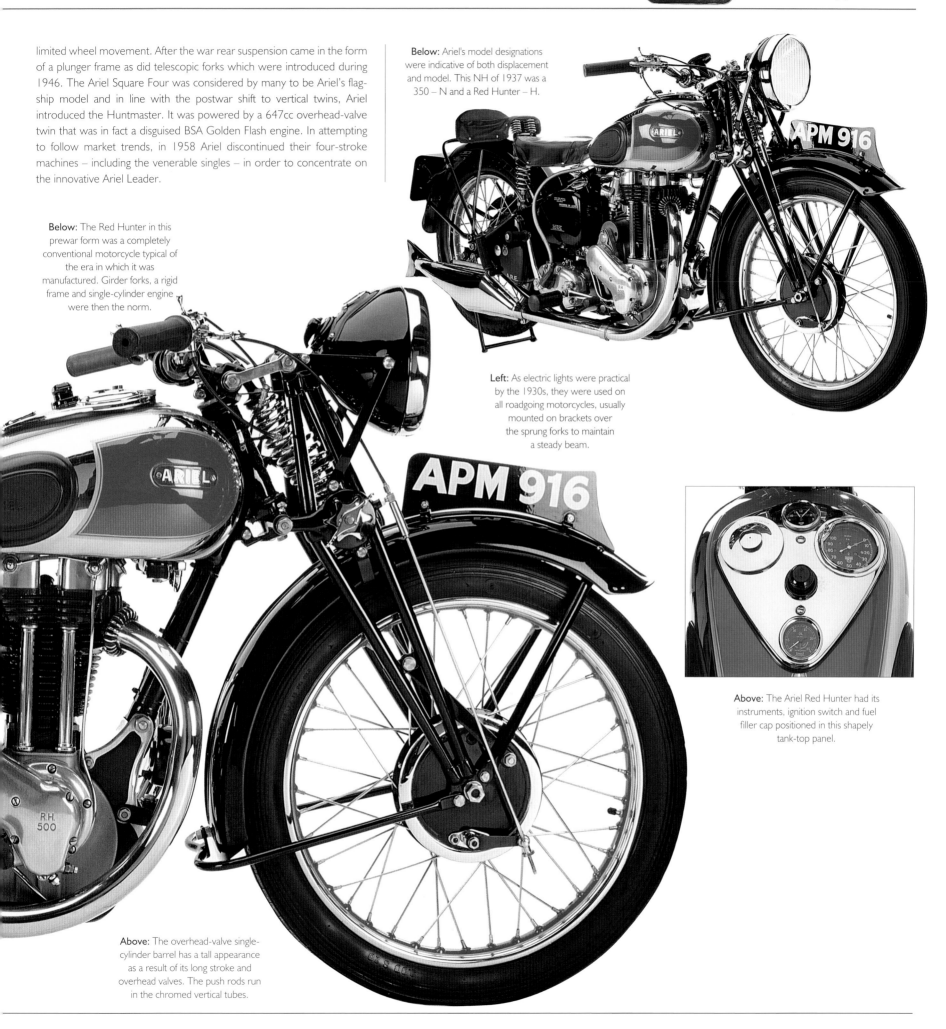

Below: The Red Hunter in this prewar form was a completely conventional motorcycle typical of the era in which it was manufactured. Girder forks, a rigid frame and single-cylinder engine were then the norm.

Left: As electric lights were practical by the 1930s, they were used on all roadgoing motorcycles, usually mounted on brackets over the sprung forks to maintain a steady beam.

Above: The Ariel Red Hunter had its instruments, ignition switch and fuel filler cap positioned in this shapely tank-top panel.

Above: The overhead-valve single-cylinder barrel has a tall appearance as a result of its long stroke and overhead valves. The push rods run in the chromed vertical tubes.

ARIEL 4G SQUARE FOUR

SPECIFICATIONS
Year: 1949
Engine type: Square four
Engine cycle: Four-stroke
Capacity: 995cc (60.7cu in)
Bore & stroke: 65 x 75mm
Horsepower: 34 @ 5400rpm
Top speed: 90mph (145kph)
Compression ratio: n/a
Carburettor: Solex
Transmission: 4-speed
Brakes: F. & R. Drum
Ignition: Coil
Frame: Tubular steel
Suspension: F. Telescopic forks.
R. Plunger suspension
Wheelbase: 56in (1422mm)
Weight: 430lb (195kg)
Fuel: 3.875 gallons (17.6lit)
Oil: n/a
Tyres: F. 3.25 x 19in.
R. 4.00 x 18in.

Above: The instruments, ignition switch and fuel filler cap were integrated into the tank-top panel of the Square Four.

Right: The Ariel Square Four caused a sensation at its 1931 introduction and soon gained its "Squariel" nickname because of its engine configuration – the cylinders were arranged in two pairs.

ARIEL SQUARE FOUR (1949)

Ariel introduced an impressive new motorcycle in 1931 with a unique engine. It was a four-cylinder machine with the cylinders arranged vertically in two pairs. It quickly gained the nickname of Squariel. Edward Turner had designed the engine which, in its first incarnation, incorporated a unit-construction 3-speed gearbox. The prototype engine was of a particularly compact design because the crankshafts were connected by gears which also drove the transmission. This proved too costly for economic production, so the first production machines featured a more conventional drive from the rear crankshaft. These first Square Fours displaced 498cc through a cylinder bore and stroke of 51 x 61mm but by 1932 the company was also producing a 601cc version. The increased capacity was achieved by overboring the cylinders to 56mm. The two models were designated the 4F/5.32 and 4F/6.32 respectively. Within a couple of years the smaller displacement model had been discontinued in favour if the larger one, and production continued until the machine was significantly redesigned for 1937.

The engine was altered from overhead-camshaft configuration to overhead valve and it was increased in displacement to 995cc with a bore and stroke of 65 x 75mm. The camshaft was chain-driven from the rear crankshaft which was connected through spur gears to the forward one. The crankshafts were steel forgings while the con rods were alloy. These were all contained within an iron block and cylinder head. The redesigned version was to stay in production for a number of years as the 4G, although in 1938 a more basic version was manufactured and tagged the 4H, while a smaller-capacity version displacing 599cc was known as the 4F. Production of Fours was interrupted by World War Two.

The prewar model was reintroduced in July 1945 little changed from the 1939 version. It still had girder forks, a rigid frame and a 4-speed Burman gearbox. The entire Ariel range was fitted with telescopic forks for 1947, and production continued until the Squariel was again redesigned in 1948. The new version made its first appearance in 1949. Ariel's engineers had changed to an all-alloy engine in an attempt to reduce the overall weight of the Four. They had also changed from magneto to coil and skew gear-driven points ignition with a distributor and dynamo. This, coupled with the rear plunger suspension, added up to what is considered to be the best Ariel Square Four. Finish was generally red and chrome on the petrol tank with matching wheel rims. The

Squariel in this form was reputed to be fast for its day and endowed with good handling characteristics, albeit prone to weaving on rough roads at speed. However, it was more at home on surfaced main roads.

Production of the Square Four continued into the 1950s and another version was introduced as the Mark II, which still featured plunger rear suspension. Production continued until 1959 with the final Square Four being known as the 4GII model (see overleaf).

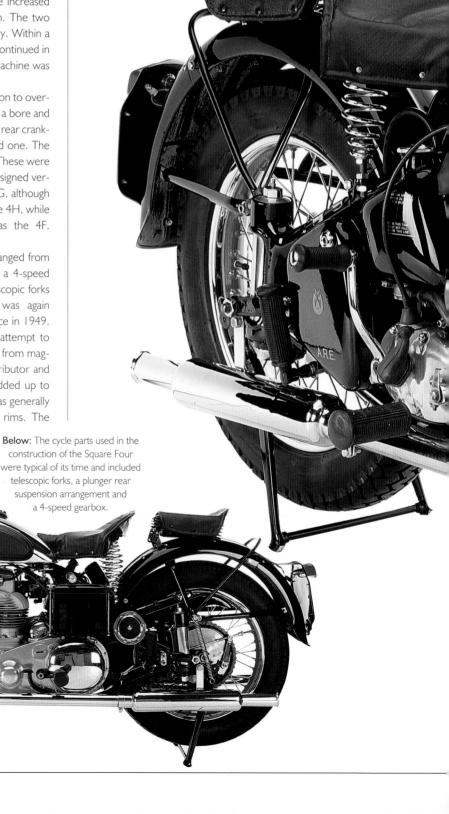

Below: The cycle parts used in the construction of the Square Four were typical of its time and included telescopic forks, a plunger rear suspension arrangement and a 4-speed gearbox.

Above: The four cylinders of the engine were arranged in a square configuration, when viewed from above, which remains unusual even to this day.

Left: Hydraulic telescopic forks were fitted across the Ariel range from 1947, superseding the prewar-type of sprung girder forks.

Above: The engine was revised several times during the production run. In 1949 it was an all-alloy unit of 995cc displacement with a bore and stroke of 65 x 75mm.

Right: A drum half-width hub front brake laced to a 19-inch front wheel and partially enclosed by a valance mudguard was a conventional and widely used arrangement in the late 1940s and early 1950s.

ARIEL NH HUNTER

SPECIFICATIONS
Year: 1949
Engine type: Ohv single
Engine cycle: Four-stroke
Capacity: 346cc (21.1cu in)
Bore & stroke: 72 x 85mm
Horsepower: 19bhp
Top speed: 75mph (121kph)
Compression ratio: n/a
Carburettor: Amal
Transmission: 4-speed
Brakes: F. & R. Drum
Ignition: Magneto
Frame: Tubular steel
Suspension: F. Telescopic forks.
R. Plunger frame
Wheelbase: 56in (1422mm)
Weight: 365lb (166kg)
Fuel: 3.75 gallons (17lit)
Oil: 6 pints (3.4lit)
Tyres: 3.25 x 19in

ARIEL 4GII SQUARE FOUR

SPECIFICATIONS
Year: 1956
Engine type: Vertical ohv
square four
Engine cycle: Four-stroke
Capacity: 995cc (60.7cu in)
Bore & stroke: 65 x 75mm
Horsepower: 40bhp @
5600rpm
Top speed: 105mph (169kph)
Compression ratio: 6.45:1
Carburettor: SU
Transmission: 4-speed
Brakes: F. SLS drum. R. Drum
Ignition: Coil and points
Frame: Steel cradle
Suspension: F.Telescopic forks.
R. Swingarm and shock absorbers
Wheelbase: 56in (1422mm)
Weight: 465lb (211kg)
Fuel: 5 gallons (22.7lit)
Oil: 6 pints (3.4lit)
Tyres: F. 3.25 x 19in.
R. 4.00 x 18in

ARIEL NH HUNTER (1949)

Ariel manufactured a considerable number of their 350cc ohv single-cylin-der-engined motorcycles for the war effort; these were known as the W/NG. At the war's end the company simply redirected the production of this proven machine to civilian markets. In civilian trim the motorcycle became known as the NG model. It was one of five single-cylinder machines listed by the company from 1945 onwards. The VG was a 499cc overhead-valve model and the VB a side-valve 600. The NH and VH were the sporting Red Hunter singles in the 350cc and 500cc classes respectively. The basis of these engines stretched back to Val Page's 1926 design when the magneto was moved to a position behind the vertical cylinder barrel.

The basic single was an engine typical of British motorcycles of the time, comprising a vertically split alloy crankcase and a built-up crankshaft. The cylinder head and barrel were cast iron. The production of all the singles continued in this basic form for several years although telescopic forks were fitted and later a plunger frame offered rear suspension. The singles were somewhat overshadowed by the more glamorous four-cylinder models – the Squariels – and from 1948 onwards the twins which were designated with a K prefix. The transmission, cycle parts and finish of the twins and singles were similar. The transmission was a 4-speed item dri-ven by a primary chain via a dry clutch. Final drive was also by chain.

These traditional motorcycles had a long production run: the NH sin-gle was not discontinued until 1959 when the company switched to its modern enclosed two-strokes, such as the Leader. The NH and VH sin-gles were also the basis of a number of off-road competition models such as the VCH Hunter which featured an all-alloy engine in a rigid frame.

Above: The 350cc single-cylinder engine was completely typical of its time and powered a commuter's motorcycle rather than an out-and-out sports bike. The engine produced 19bhp.

Below: The Ariel NH Hunter was essentially a postwar version of the 350cc machine made by Ariel for the war effort and the wartime machine was itself a militarized version of the prewar civilian machine. The NH Hunter had evolved rather than been specifically designed.

ARIEL 4GII SQUARE FOUR (1956)

The long-running Ariel 4G Square Four became the 4GII at the end of the 1953 season. The reason for the redesignation was because the model was partially redesigned. The major change was the shift from plunger rear suspension to a swingarm. The Solex carburettor was also replaced by an SU, but little in terms of the styling changed until the headlamp was enclosed in a cowl for 1956 and the front hub was changed for a full-width alloy item. In this form the Ariel Square Four was revealed in its last incarnation as it was finally discontinued in 1959.

Four-cylinder motorcycles were later popularized by the various Japanese manufacturers who offered in-line rather than square fours, with the engines mounted transversely in the frame, approximately a decade after the demise of the Ariel Square Four. The discontinuation of the Square Four and other Ariel models with the exception of the two-stroke Leader and its derivatives signalled the beginning of the end for the com-

pany. Ariel had been owned by BSA since 1944 and indeed Ariel's 646cc parallel twin was in reality a badge-engineered BSA A10. The Leader, acknowledged as the last real Ariel, was only produced for a few more years before BSA, who had also owned Triumph since 1951, halted its production. The British motorcycle industry was starting to contract in response to a changing market and the process would continue for more than another decade. The Ariel name would briefly surface one more time as British companies tried, albeit too little too late, to move with the times.

Below: The Square Four was redesignated the 4GII in 1953 after a partial redesign of the cycle parts, including the provision of plunger rear suspension as well as a change in the make of carburettor fitted.

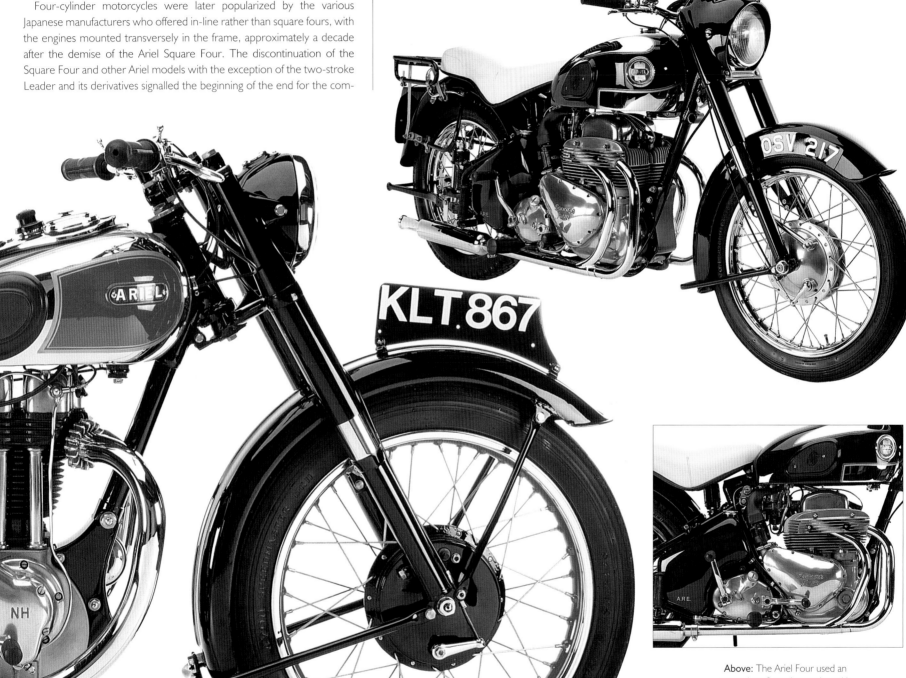

Above: This 1949 NH Hunter was built to what was in reality a "prewar specification". Rigid frames, half-width hub brakes, tank-mounted instruments and switches, even solo saddles and chromed petrol tanks were all soon superseded.

Above: The Ariel Four used an unusual configuration engine with four vertical cylinders arranged in a square. The engine remained in production for many years, although it was partially redesigned during the production run.

ARIEL FH HUNTMASTER

SPECIFICATIONS

Year: 1958
Engine type: Vertical twin
Engine cycle: Four-stroke
Capacity: 647cc (39.5cu in)
Bore & stroke: 70 x 84mm
Horsepower: 34bhp @ 5750rpm
Top speed: 100mph (161kph)
Compression ratio: 6.5:1
Carburettor: Amal
Transmission: 4-speed
Brakes: F. & R. Drum
Ignition: Magneto
Frame: Duplex cradle
Suspension: F. Telescopic forks. R. Swingarm and shock absorbers
Wheelbase: 56in (1422mm)
Weight: 365lb (166kg)
Fuel: 4 gallons (18.2lit)
Oil: 6 pints (3.4lit)
Tyres: F. 3.25 x 19in. R. 3.50 x 19in

Right: The lines of the FH Huntmaster might appear traditional but the 1950s had seen motorcycles incorporate much new technology. Telescopic forks, rear swingarm and shock absorber suspension, full-width hub brakes and dual seats had all become the norm throughout much of the industry.

ARIEL FH HUNTMASTER (1958)

The trend for vertical parallel twins that was established by Edward Turner's design for Triumph in the last years before World War Two took off in the late 1940s. Each British manufacturer of large displacement motorcycles wanted at least one twin in its range. It is, therefore, ironic that Ariel, on whose payroll Edward Turner had previously been, had to make do with a badge-engineered BSA twin as one of its offerings. Jack Sangster, the owner of Ariel, had purchased Triumph in 1936 and transferred Edward Turner from Ariel to Triumph. BSA later bought both these companies, acquiring Ariel in 1944 and Triumph in 1951.

Ariel's first twins were the 499cc KG and KH models introduced in 1948. These were followed by the ohv 650cc FH twin of 1954. This machine was known as the Huntmaster and its engine was in fact a BSA Golden Flash unit, rather than a larger capacity version of Ariel's own 499cc twin. The BSA engine was used with a few changes made in order to camouflage the fact that it was not an Ariel product. The changes were, in the main, to the timing chest and rocker cover. The former had "twin" cast into it in script. The BSA engine was installed in a cradle frame with swinging-arm rear suspension. The Ariel used its own style of petrol tank and a Burman gearbox which also helped disguise the BSA origins of the

Above: The Ariel twin engine was bolted into a steel tubular cradle frame, but the swingarm was manufactured from welded steel pressings. The engine and 4-speed gearbox were not of unit construction.

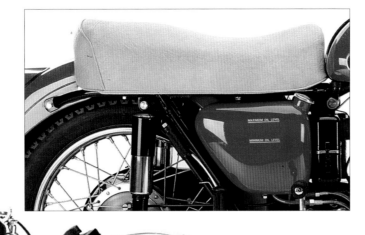

Left: Edward Turner's design for Triumph had begun the trend away from single-cylinder engines to parallel twins, to the extent that most other British manufacturers wanted a twin in their range. The NH Hunter used a rebadged BSA twin engine.

Right: The provision of rear suspension for motorcycles enabled manufacturers to replace a sprung solo saddle with a dual seat which offered more comfort, especially for the pillion passenger, and changed the appearance of motorcycles.

engine. Ariel also used the new frame for the smaller displacement twin. The swingarm was made up from steel pressings welded together – quite unlike the tubular swingarms favoured by other manufacturers. Accompanying the new frame was a dual seat as standard and some new cycle parts. The Huntmaster was a wholly conventional motorcycle with large mudguards and a solid appearance. In this late 1950s form the FH Huntmaster was primarily intended for sidecar work, although the potential for sales in this market was already declining.

As the Huntmaster was a new model, it went into 1955 almost unchanged except for the use of an Amal Monobloc carburettor. The majority of Ariel's motorcycles, including the Huntmaster, were redesigned for 1956. Changes included the provision of a headlamp cowl and alloy wheel hubs. In 1957 the KH twin was dropped from the model range as the Ariel company prepared for a radical new motorcycle for the next decade. This new machine was, of course, the two-stroke Ariel Leader with its pressed-steel frame. The success of this machine, which was launched in 1958, quickly encouraged Ariel to discontinue their more traditional four-stroke motorcycles. Some were dropped at the beginning of 1959 and the remainder in the autumn of the same year, with one exception. This was the FH 650cc twin, built as the Cyclone for the American market, which stayed in production until 1960. The two-strokes lasted another five years after this before the BSA-Triumph group that owned Ariel stopped production altogether and closed the factory.

Left: The Huntmaster in this form was intended in the main for sidecar use, although, due to the increasing availability of cheap family cars, sales to this market were already in decline by the late 1950s and would continue to contract until it eventually disappeared.

Left: British road traffic legislation in the 1950s required that motorcycles should have front number plates. Some of those with valanced mudguards had one plate affixed to either side as here.

ARIEL LEADER

SPECIFICATIONS
Year: 1964
Engine type: Twin
Engine cycle: Two-stroke
Capacity: 249cc (15cu in)
Bore & stroke: 54 x 54mm
Horsepower: 17.5bhp @ 7000rpm
Top speed: 70mph (113kph)
Compression ratio: 10:1
Carburettor: Amal
Transmission: 4-speed
Brakes: F & R. Drum
Ignition: Coil
Frame: Pressed-steel hollow beam
Suspension: F. Trailing link forks. R. Swingarm and shock absorbers
Wheelbase: 51in (1295mm)
Weight: 310lb (141kg)
Fuel: 2.5 gallons (11.4lit)
Oil: Mixed with fuel
Tyres: 3.25 x 16in

ARIEL 3

SPECIFICATIONS
Year: 1970
Engine type: Single
Engine cycle: Two-stroke
Capacity: 49cc (2.99cu in)
Bore & stroke: n/a
Horsepower: n/a
Top speed: n/a
Compression ratio: n/a
Carburettor: n/a
Transmission: Single-speed
Brakes: F. Drum. R. Drum
Ignition: n/a
Frame: Pressed steel
Suspension: F. Single sided fork.
Wheelbase: n/a
Weight: n/a
Fuel: 1.5 gallons (6.8lit)
Oil: Mixed with fuel
Tyres: 2.00 x 12in

Right: Because the Leader was intended for commuter use, it was given equipment to increase its practicality, such as hard panniers and combined windscreen and legshields that offered a degree of weather protection.

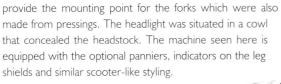

ARIEL LEADER (1964)

The use of pressed-steel frames for motorcycles was not new; many German motorcycles of the 1930s had been constructed around such a frame, but it was never a common design feature of British motorcycles. Nor was scooter-like enclosed bodywork. One notable experiment that included both these features was the Ariel Leader. Ariel's slogan proclaimed the company as producer of "the modern motorcycle" and the Leader was created in response to the massive popularity of Italian motor scooters in Britain in the 1950s.

The first Leaders were designed by Val Page and unveiled in 1958. Leg shields and a windscreen offered weather protection equal to that of a scooter, while enclosed bodywork both concealed the motorcycle's mechanical components and looked stylish and modern. The new machine was well received by both press and public and sales were sufficient to justify a production run that continued until 1965. A sports version was offered from 1960 – it was less enclosed but otherwise similar – and these were later followed by the Golden Arrow and a 200cc version.

Behind the pressed-steel panels were a 249cc motorcycle engine and 4-speed gearbox fitted to a pressed-steel beam frame. Small-diameter wheels gave the machine more scooter-like proportions and parts of the bodywork doubled as storage space. What appeared to be the petrol tank was in fact a storage compartment, while the fuel and oil tank was accommodated by the frame pressing. The pressing extended forwards to provide the mounting point for the forks which were also made from pressings. The headlight was situated in a cowl that concealed the headstock. The machine seen here is equipped with the optional panniers, indicators on the leg shields and similar scooter-like styling.

Below: The fuel and oil mixture for the two-stroke engine was actually carried in the pressed steel frame tubes, while what appears to be the petrol tank is a storage compartment.

Below: Much of the styling of the Leader drew its inspiration from the Italian scooters popular in the early 1960s. The two-stroke engine remained in the position considered conventional for a motorcycle, but it was enclosed like a scooter.

Right: The panniers seen fitted either side of the rear wheel of this machine were an optional extra aimed at further increasing the practical application of the Leader as a commuter's motorcycle.

Above: The Leader was fitted with a 250cc motorcycle engine, but the scooter-inspired enclosed bodywork meant that its mechanical components were hidden from view.

Left: Plastic windshields such as this offer the rider more weather protection than their appearance might suggest.

Right: The Ariel 3 was another attempt to offer a functional machine to the British public, rather than something styled as a motorcycle. It was novel but unsuccessful.

Below: The Ariel 3 was hinged to allow it to corner without lifting a rear wheel. This endowed it with handling characteristics that were distinctly unusual.

Above: The procedures for starting the Ariel 3 were such that it was not straightforward to use. This factor may explain why the machine did not sell in any numbers to motorcyclists or non-motorcyclists.

Above: The Ariel Leader used a variety of new ideas in its construction, such as the use of trailing link front forks assembled from steel pressings which concealed much of the wheel.

ARIEL 3 (1970)

The Ariel 3 – a three-wheeled shopper's moped – is included in this book simply to give an indication of how massive the decline of the British motorcycle industry was, and yet how the fascination with new technology characteristic of the latter days could conceivably have led to something. At first glance it seems ironic that the name of a company which was noted for engineering motorcycles such as the Square Four should appear on a diminutive motorized tricycle manufactured by the once massive company celebrated for the Rocket Gold Star and the Rocket III. However, it is equally ironic that Sochiro Honda underpinned the entire Honda empire with the not dissimilar Honda Cub, a step-through design of moped, albeit a two-wheeler. While motorcycles such as the Honda CB750/4 were competing for sales with the last large capacity British bikes, such as Triumph Tridents, the Honda Cub was being mass-produced for the world market to the extent that more examples of it have been manufactured than any other two-wheeler in history.

The Ariel 3 was not a success in sales terms, the statistic that mattered most, and it is possible to speculate endlessly as to why. The Ariel 3 may have been too little, too late, but it is more likely that it was inadequately designed for its target market. Primarily aimed at women shoppers, the Ariel 3 had a complex pedal-start procedure that required a dog to be engaged in the rear wheel. Its flexible design, which allowed both rear wheels to remain in contact with the road while cornering, and the system of drive to only one rear wheel endowed it with unusual handling characteristics and it was reputedly dangerous to ride in wet conditions because of this. At least one test rider was hospitalized while demonstrating it to BSA management, and other test riders at Umberslade Hall only rode it under sufferance and, reportedly, as a penance for crashing a bigger capacity test machine. The Ariel 3's target market, non-motorcyclists, demanded something more straightforward and less unorthodox, and very few were ever sold.

ARMSTRONG MT500

SPECIFICATIONS
Year: 1985
Engine type: Ohc single
Engine cycle: Two-stroke
Capacity: 485cc (29.6cu in)
Bore & stroke: n/a
Horsepower: 32bhp @ 6200rpm
Top speed: 95mph (153kph)
Compression ratio: n/a
Carburettor: n/a
Transmission: n/a
Brakes: F. & R. Drum
Ignition: n/a
Frame: Steel cradle
Suspension: F. Telescopic forks. R. Swingarm and shock absorbers
Wheelbase: n/a
Weight: 355lb (161kg)
Fuel: n/a
Oil: In frame
Tyres: F. 90/90.21. R. tba

Above: The Armstrong MT500 has a neat instrument binnacle which contains the speedometer and warning lights for engine functions such as ignition and oil pressure.

BEARDMORE PRECISION MODEL C

SPECIFICATIONS
Year: 1924
Engine type: Side-valve single
Engine cycle: Four-stroke
Capacity: 598cc (36.5cu in)
Bore & stroke: 89 x 96mm
Horsepower: 4.5 hp
Top speed: n/a
Compression ratio: n/a
Carburettor: n/a
Transmission: 3-speed
Brakes: F & R. Contracting band
Ignition: Magneto
Frame: Tubular steel
Suspension: F & R. Leaf-sprung
Wheelbase: 54.5in (1384mm)
Weight: 300lb (136kg)
Fuel: n/a
Oil: n/a
Tyres: 26 x 3in

ARMSTRONG MT500 (1985)

In 1980 Armstrong, a manufacturer of automotive components, moved into motorcycle production through the acquisition of Cotton, a company which had intermittently produced motorcycles since 1919 including Rotax-powered machines from 1976. Armstrong subsequently acquired CCM – Clews Competition Motorcycles – in 1981. The new company produced Rotax-powered roadracers, off-road competition machines and military motorcycles.

The military machines were based on the off-road competition bikes as the thinking behind the design of military motorcycles had changed radically. Previously military motorcycles were essentially militarized versions of roadgoing singles and twins, but by the time Armstrong came to supply military machines, the advantages of a lighter off-road type of machine had been perceived. The design of off-road bikes had progressed rapidly during the 1970s, so the Armstrong MT500 bore little resemblance to the BSAs and Nortons ridden by previous generations of soldiers.

The MT500 looked like a modern motocrosser painted green, which in many ways is exactly what it was. The engine was an Austrian-made Rotax unit fitted to a steel cradle frame with a box-section steel swingarm rear suspension assembly giving good ground clearance. The forks were long-travel telescopic items and there was ample clearance between the mudguards and tyres. Like the mudguards, the fuel tank was made from plastic and the rectangular headlight was housed in the front of the instrument binnacle. Substantial frames for capacious panniers and a luggage rack were fitted.

Armstrong withdrew from motorcycle manufacture in 1987, although Harley-Davidson acquired rights in the design of the MT500 and went on to produce a machine that was very similar to this for military use. Motorcycles such as these saw action in the Gulf War of 1991 where their design proved able to cope with hard desert going.

Above: The Armstrong MT500 was powered by a 485cc two-stroke engine that gave it a top speed of around 95mph (153kph). The whole machine was designed to be simple and rugged.

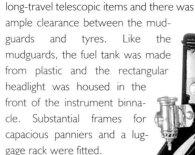

Right: The Beardmore Precision employed a rear stand typical of many British bikes of the period. It lifted the rear wheel off the ground when in use, and clipped to the mudguard when not.

Above: The rear suspension of the machine, like the front, relied on leaf springs in a triangulated arrangement, which is something other manufacturers later used with varying degrees of success.

BEARDMORE PRECISION MODEL C (1924)

This Beardmore Precision motorcycle, like many motorcycles from the interwar years of motorcycling, featured numerous components of unusual or unorthodox design. The suspension was an example of this, both front and rear suspension being of a leaf-sprung design. This, in itself, was not uncommon, but the L-shaped design of the front spring most certainly was. Another unusual feature was the way in which the mudguard stays acted as mounting points for parts of the suspension arrangement. Equally notable was the manner in which the pressed-steel fuel tank was integral to the frame tube, to the extent that it acted as a stressed part of the frame. Later designs of major components would become much more standardized – forks, for example, would become primarily sprung girders, then hydraulic telescopics.

Beardmore Precision motorcycles were made by F.E. Baker Ltd of King's Norton, Birmingham with backing from the Beardmore firm of shipbuilders. From 1910 onwards Baker's Precision company supplied engines, both singles and V-twins, to other manufacturers. It first made a complete motorcycle in 1912. In 1919 the company secured financial backing from the Beardmore shipbuilding concern and accordingly changed its name to Beardmore Precision. Its first machine was a 350cc two-stroke; then four-strokes, such as this model C, entered the range. Despite its original and innovative designs, sales were not impressive, and after a poor performance in the 1924 Isle of Man TT, the company folded. Baker went on to produce a range of small-capacity, Villiers-engined, two-stroke motorcycles under his own name between 1926 and 1930 when the company was taken over by James.

Below: The Beardmore Precision utilized an unusual arrangement of quarter elliptic springs to provide front suspension.

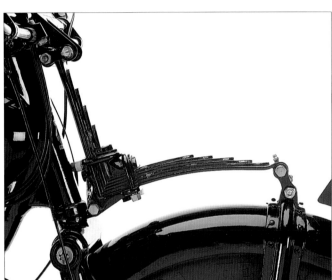

Left: Motorcycles like the Beardmore Precision that used numerous innovative and unorthodox ideas were common during the 1920s, but few survived long in a competitive commercial market.

Below: The Beardmore's single-cylinder engine displaced 598cc. The magneto was located behind the cylinder barrel.

BROUGH SUPERIOR SS100

SPECIFICATIONS
Year: 1930
Engine type: Ohv V-twin
Engine cycle: Four-stroke
Capacity: 995cc (60.7cu in)
Bore & stroke: 80 x 99mm
Horsepower: 45bhp @ 4800rpm
Top speed: 100mph (161kph)
Compression ratio: n/a
Carburettor: Amal
Transmission: 4-speed
Brakes: F. & R. Drum
Ignition: Magneto
Frame: Steel cradle
Suspension: F. Sprung Castle forks. R. Pivoted fork
Wheelbase: 58in (1473mm)
Weight: 370lb (168kg)
Fuel: 4.25 gallons (19.3lit)
Oil: n/a
Tyres: 3.5 x 21in

Above: Brough Superior was the eponymous name that George Brough gave to the motorcycle manufacturing company he set up in Nottingham in 1921.

Right: Only 384 Brough Superior SS100s were made and the war ended production as the company moved into specialist machining.

BROUGH SUPERIOR SS100 (1930)

William E. Brough designed and built motorcycles of both single and V-twin engine configuration from 1908 onwards. With the co-operation of Granville Bradshaw, he then concentrated his attention on the use of flat-twin engines, first one of Bradshaw's own design, a 496cc ABC engine and later similar configuration engines of 496cc, 692cc and 810cc displacement. Production of motorcycles continued until 1926. Brough's son, George, did not favour flat-twins, however, and he left the family business to start his own motorcycle company in 1921.

Brough Superior was the name George Brough gave to the company he set up in 1921 in Nottingham, England. His machines were built to the highest standards almost regardless of cost. The motorcycles built by this new company were in the main constructed around V-twin engines supplied by other British manufacturers, including Matchless, JAP and MAG. Brough built motorcycles that he personally liked to ride and he was famed for competing aboard one nicknamed Old Bill during the 1920s.

George Brough had a reputation for being both a talented engineer and a perfectionist, and he assembled his motorcycles completely to make sure that everything was functioning correctly before stripping them again for painting and plating. One of the distinguishing features of the Brough range was the style of the fuel tank. Each one was made from hand-formed pieces of metal soldered together.

Right: Broughs were built to the highest specification from components of the highest quality. This meant they were expensive machines and is why they became known as "the Rolls-Royce of motorcycles".

Brough knew that he could charge high prices for individually-built quality motorcycles but that he also had to keep his customers happy through prompt dispatch of spare parts.

The SS100 was one of the Brough Superior machines that was assembled to the highest of standards; only 384 were made. It used an overhead V-twin type 8/50 engine from JAP, a Sturmey-Archer gearbox and featured both front and rear suspension. The SS100 was boosted for 1934 with the fitment of an engine with two magnetos, two carburettors and two double oil pumps. The new version was capable of 110mph (177kph) but was unreliable. A Matchless-engined SS100 was announced in 1936. Smaller displacement motorcycles in the firm's range were the 680 and SS80 of 677cc and 981cc respectively.

Undoubtedly Brough's most famous customer for the machines advertised as the Rolls-Royce of motorcycles was T.E. Lawrence, better known as Lawrence of Arabia. Lawrence owned a succession of Brough motorcycles that he nicknamed George I to George VII. The enigmatic desert

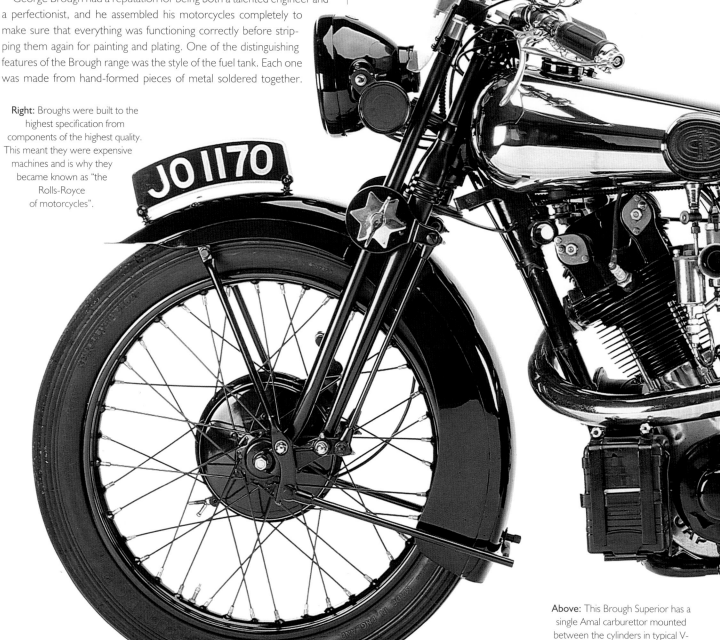

Above: This Brough Superior has a single Amal carburettor mounted between the cylinders in typical V-twin practice although a later version had a carburettor per cylinder.

warrior was tragically killed in 1935 in an accident on a Brough Superior near his home in Bovington, Dorset.

Production of Brough Superiors continued until 1940 but did not resume after World War Two because Brough did not consider that any of the engines then available were suitable for his motorcycles. George Brough had also experimented with flat-twin-, flat-four-, V-four- and in-line four-engined motorcycles, examples of which were displayed at motorcycle shows in the late 1920s and 1930s. The company undertook machine work for Rolls-Royce during World War Two, such as the precision machining of Merlin aero-engine crankshafts.

Left: The SS100 was powered by an overhead-valve V-twin engine made by JAP. It was fitted with an Amal carb and magneto ignition, and was capable of exceeding the magic 100mph (161kph) barrier.

Below: The sprung solo saddle was mounted from the frame right behind the streamlined, soldered and chrome-plated fuel tank.

Above: The Brough Superior was made famous by George Brough competing on a version that he nicknamed "Old Bill". Also T.E. Lawrence – Lawrence of Arabia – was a regular customer for Broughs.

Above: The Brough frame was unusual for the time and had rear suspension provided by a fork design whereby the triangular rear section of the frame pivoted.

BSA MODEL E

Above: The company logo proudly proclaimed BSA's origins as a manufacturer of guns.

Right: The Model E was one of only two motorcycles listed by BSA for 1921. Iit was powered by a 770cc side-valve V-twin engine.

BSA MODEL E (1921)

The BSA initials stand for Birmingham Small Arms. Long before they manufactured motorcycles, this company mass-produced rifles and other weapons. This is why the BSA logo features three rifles arranged in a pyramid formation with their barrels crossed. The company was founded by a group of craftsmen gunsmiths who saw the benefits of mass-production in an age when wars were requiring more and more weaponry. BSA produced its first motorcycle in 1910 – it was single-cylinder machine with belt drive, and from this humble beginning BSA went on to great things. By 1920 there were three models in the range. This included the Model E V-twin of 770cc displacement which was seen as an ideal mount for pulling sidecars – indeed the frame featured integral sidecar lugs for this purpose.

The Model E was one of only two motorcycles listed by BSA for 1921 and was the forerunner of a series of solid and reliable BSA motorcycles. The company built a number of side-valve V-twins between the wars. As installed in the Model E, the side-valve 50-degree V-twin engine featured a front-mounted Lucas magneto and an Amac carburettor. It was connected to a 3-speed gearbox and both primary and final drive chains were enclosed in aluminium cases. These major components were installed in a tubular-steel diamond frame with two parallel horizontal top tubes between which the almost rectangular petrol tank was fitted. Cantilever sprung forks provided front suspension and in the absence of rear sus-

pension the solo saddle was sprung. Brakes were rubber blocks which were applied to dummy rims mounted on the spoked road wheels. The wheels were partially covered by steel mudguards finished in black, like the frame, rather than in the green and white of the tank. While most of these components were unremarkable at the time, the key to BSA's success lay in producing motorcycles that were generally considered reliable and value for money.

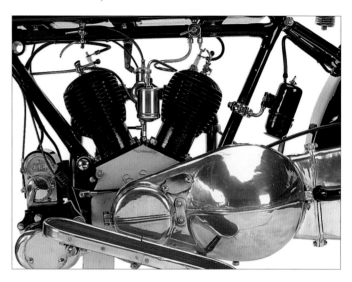

Above right: The side-valve V-twin displaced 770cc through a bore and stroke of 76 x 85mm and produced 6hp. Primary drive was by chain.

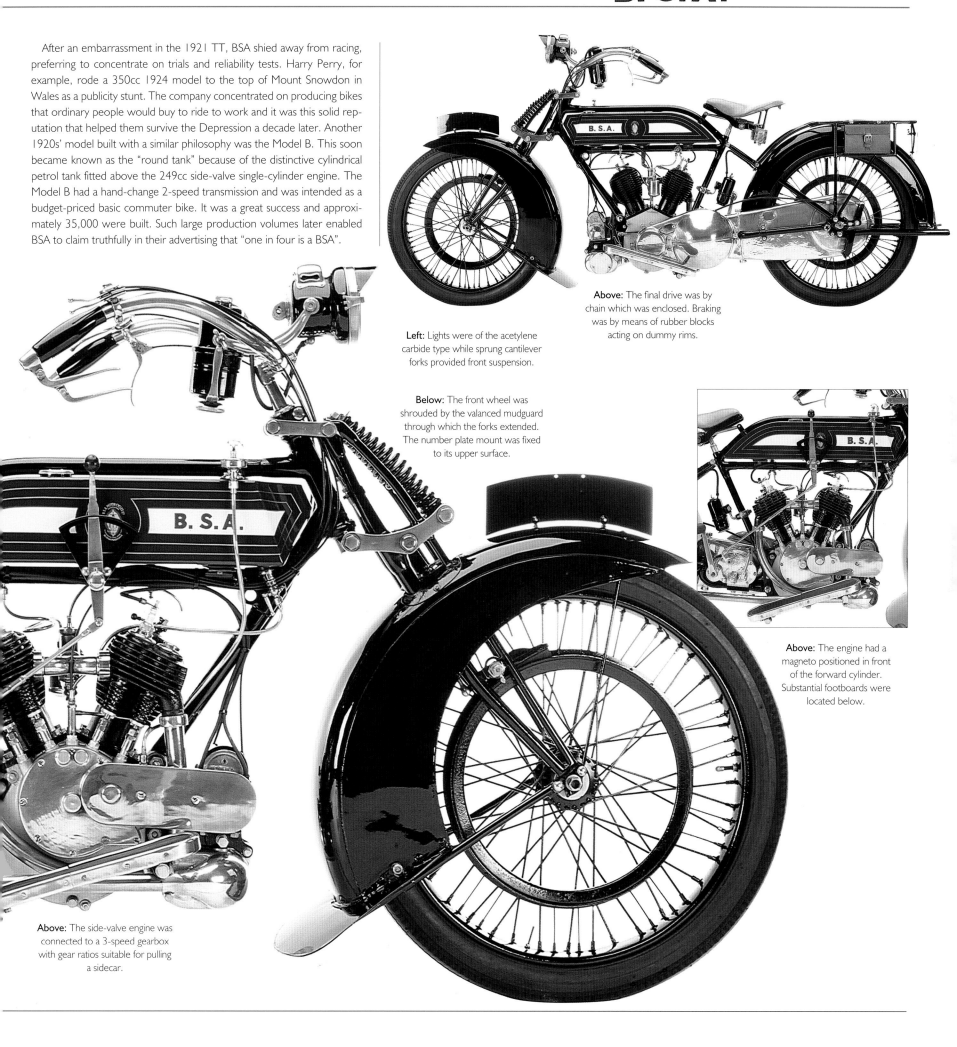

After an embarrassment in the 1921 TT, BSA shied away from racing, preferring to concentrate on trials and reliability tests. Harry Perry, for example, rode a 350cc 1924 model to the top of Mount Snowdon in Wales as a publicity stunt. The company concentrated on producing bikes that ordinary people would buy to ride to work and it was this solid reputation that helped them survive the Depression a decade later. Another 1920s' model built with a similar philosophy was the Model B. This soon became known as the "round tank" because of the distinctive cylindrical petrol tank fitted above the 249cc side-valve single-cylinder engine. The Model B had a hand-change 2-speed transmission and was intended as a budget-priced basic commuter bike. It was a great success and approximately 35,000 were built. Such large production volumes later enabled BSA to claim truthfully in their advertising that "one in four is a BSA".

Above: The final drive was by chain which was enclosed. Braking was by means of rubber blocks acting on dummy rims.

Left: Lights were of the acetylene carbide type while sprung cantilever forks provided front suspension.

Below: The front wheel was shrouded by the valanced mudguard through which the forks extended. The number plate mount was fixed to its upper surface.

Above: The engine had a magneto positioned in front of the forward cylinder. Substantial footboards were located below.

Above: The side-valve engine was connected to a 3-speed gearbox with gear ratios suitable for pulling a sidecar.

BSA SLOPER

SPECIFICATIONS
Year: 1927
Engine type: Ohv single
Engine cycle: Four-stroke
Capacity: 493cc (30.08cu in)
Bore & stroke: 80 x 98mm
Horsepower: 20bhp
Top speed: 75mph
(121kph) est.
Compression ratio: n/a
Carburettor: Amal
Transmission: 3-speed
Brakes: F. & R. Drum
Ignition: Magneto
Frame: Tubular steel
Suspension: F. Sprung girders.
R. None
Wheelbase: n/a
Weight: 337lb (153kg)
Fuel: 2.75 gallons (12.5lit)
Oil: n/a
Tyres: 3.25 x 19in

Above: BSA stands for
Birmingham Small Arms. The
company was founded by a
group of gunsmiths, hence the
three rifles used in the logo
that appears on the tank.

Right: The BSA Sloper was so
named simply because the
cylinder barrel of the single-
cylinder engine sloped
forwards. The machine was
given an S prefix by its maker.

BSA S27 SLOPER (1927)

The BSA Sloper with its inclined engine was introduced by BSA in 1927
as a 500cc overhead-valve single with an S prefix to its numerical year
designation. The S was generally accepted to indicate that it was a
"sloper", in other words that the single cylinder of the engine was inclined
forwards. This was not necessarily the purpose of the S prefix, but for all
that it stuck fast and set a trend for the naming of inclined engines. The
Sloper became a firm favourite amongst the BSA range and through
annual upgrades remained in BSA's range until the mid-1930s.

The S27 featured a twin downtube frame between which tubes the
exhaust pipe from the overhead-valve engine passed. The engine featured wet-sump lubrication and a gear-driven magneto was installed. The
single-port cylinder head was fitted with a cast-aluminium casing designed
to enclose the rockers while leaving the valve springs exposed. The
pushrods were enclosed in chrome-plated tubes. The engine had a low
compression ratio and a camshaft that featured gradually curved lobes in
order to minimize wear and maximize engine longevity. The heavy flywheels ensured torque at low revs and a top speed of up to 75mph
(121kph). The crankcase incorporated a separate oil compartment, the
contents of which lubricated the engine via a hand-
metered gear-type oil pump.

The remainder of the Sloper was conventional for its
time. Typical were its sprung girder forks and a frame
devoid of rear suspension, as well as drum brakes front and
rear. The sprung saddle offered some comfort to
the rider, while curved steel mudguards
offered protection from weather and
road grime. The later Sloper models

Above: The Sloper was a fairly
conventional machine for its day with
sprung girder forks and drum brakes
back and front. The rear stand was
typical too.

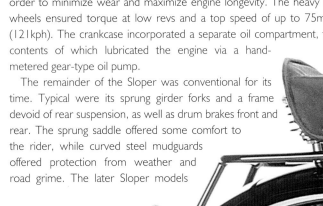

Right: In view of the lack of rear
suspension, both pillion pad and
saddle were sprung to give users
a degree of comfort on late
1920s roads.

had a redesigned frame that included an I-section forging as the top tube in order to strengthen the steering head. The later models were upgraded through the fitment of a 4-speed gearbox and a twin-port cylinder head. A side-valve model was later introduced but did not prove as popular as the overhead-valve model.

BSA's policy of sticking to reliable, utilitarian, thoroughly conventional motorcycles would stand them in good stead through the Depression. Working men might have nurtured dreams of exotic motorcycles and cars, but for most the reality of life was getting to work daily and on time without buses or trams. BSA were fully aware of this and built motorcy-

cles that served this need for basic transport and exploited the brackets of road taxation classes. In this way the company was able to consolidate its position as the major manufacturer in the British motorcycle industry. By 1930 the company was offering 18 different motorcycles ranging from a 174cc two-stroke to a number of variants of the Sloper. For example, the S30-13 was the standard Sloper, the S30-12 a lightweight version and yet another was a tuned version. To ensure it was recognized as a new sporting model, this machine carried a red star emblem. This marked the beginning of a line of BSA models which bore various "star" names, including both Empire Stars and Gold Stars.

Below: The Sloper featured a hand gearchange lever for its 3-speed gearbox. This lever can be seen on the side of the petrol tank where the shift gate arcs across the BSA emblem.

Below: The S27 Sloper employed a twin downtube frame between which tubes the exhaust pipe ran, before curving back and running along the offside of the motorcycle.

Below: The drum brake fitted in the front hub was operated by a cable that ran back to a hand lever on the handlebars via a point on the front of the girder forks.

Above: The overhead-valve engine had pushrods enclosed in chrome-plated tubes and they operated on gently profiled camshafts to ensure engine reliability.

BSA M20

SPECIFICATIONS
Year: 1940
Engine type: Side-valve single
Engine cycle: Four-stroke
Capacity: 496cc (30.26cu in)
Bore & stroke: 82 x 94mm
Horsepower: 13 @ 4200rpm
Top speed: 63mph (101kph)
Compression ratio: 4.9:1
Carburettor: Amal
Transmission: 4-speed
Brakes: F. & R. Drum
Ignition: Magneto
Frame: Tubular steel
Suspension: F. Girder forks.
R. None
Wheelbase: 54in (1372mm)
Weight: 369lb (167kg)
Fuel: 3 gallons (13.6lit)
Oil: 4 pints (2.27lit)
Tyres: 3.25 x 19in

BSA C15

SPECIFICATIONS
Year: 1959
Engine type: Ohv single
Engine cycle: Four-stroke
Capacity: 247cc (15cu in)
Bore & stroke: 67 x 70mm
Horsepower: 15bhp @
7000rpm
Top speed: 68mph (109kph)
Compression ratio: n/a
Carburettor: Amal
Transmission: 4-speed
Brakes: F & R. Drum
Ignition: Coil
Frame: Steel loop
Suspension: F. Telescopic forks.
R. Swingarm and shock absorbers
Wheelbase: 51.5in (1308mm)
Weight: 143lb (65kg)
Fuel: 2.5 gallons (11.4lit)
Oil: 3 pints (1.87lit)
Tyres: 3.25 x 17in

BSA M20 (1940)

During the 1920s and 1930s BSA submitted numerous motorcycles for test and evaluation by the War Office who favoured 350 and 500cc single-cylinder motorcycles for military mounts from the mid-1930s on. After failing to gain the necessary approval for certain of their motorcycles, BSA submitted their new 496cc side-valve single for testing in 1936. The officials considered that the engine showed excessive wear following the test and so BSA again failed to receive an order to supply military motorcycles. The company later submitted improved versions of the same motorcycle, which were subjected to a 10,000-mile (16,000km) reliability trial. These gained grudging approval – reliability was noted as only "fair" but the BSA M20 motorcycle as a whole was acknowledged as "suitable for WD (War Department) requirements". Following this, and the success of a BSA Gold Star-mounted Army team in the 1938 International Six Days Trial (ISDT) which was held in Wales, the first military orders were forthcoming in 1937 and 1938.

By the time war broke out in Europe, BSA was acknowledged as the largest motorcycle manufacturer in Britain. Because of its large production capacity, it is perhaps understandable that the M20 was the motorcycle produced in the largest numbers for the war effort. Production continued in batches which varied in minor details until 1942 when output was standardized. Minor upgrades continued to be made through the production run. Total production exceeded 126,000 motorcycles of this type. Some M20s were supplied to the allied armies of India, South Africa, Holland and that of neutral Ireland.

Above: BSA supplied many thousands of the tough and reliable 496cc M20 to the British Army and other allied forces during World War Two.

Below: The M20 was produced in vast numbers for the British Army and, like other military motorcycles of the time, was basically a militarized version of one of the company's prewar range.

Above: On the M20 the speedometer was mounted alongside the headlamp shell, while the ammeter was mounted within it along with the ignition switch.

Above: For military use the M20 was equipped with fittings especially specified by the War Department. These included the blackout headlamp shroud that covered most of the headlamp lens.

Left: The C15 was one of a new range of unit-construction motorcycles made by BSA during the late 1950s. Its 247cc engine was of a simple design.

Above: The C15 engine featured a plain big-end bearing, pressed crankshaft and 4-speed unit transmission.

Above: The BSA C15 featured styling typical of larger capacity machines of the time; a dual seat over a valanced mudguard, a headlamp nacelle and telescopic forks with a valanced front mudguard, for example.

Left: The BSA M20 in military trim usually carried a variety of unit markings, as well as the number of the contract under which it had been supplied on the tank.

Above: The BSA M20 was powered by a side-valve single-cylinder engine of 496cc displacement achieved through a bore and stroke of 82 x 94mm.

BSA C15 (1959)

In September 1958 BSA launched a new series of unit-construction singles which would remain in production until the demise of BSA manufacturing. The first of the series was the overhead-valve single-cylinder C15 of 247cc displacement which was based on the Triumph Tiger Cub. The C15 was a no-frills motorcycle designed as a basic commuter and it was manufactured as cheaply as possible. It used a plain big-end bearing with a pressed crankshaft, simple timing gear for the overhead valves and a skew gear drive to the points housing located behind the iron cylinder barrel. The cylinder head was cast in alloy and a chromed pushrod tube ran up to it from the crankcase.

An alternator was provided to power the ignition and electrics; it was mounted on the left-hand end of the crankshaft adjacent to the engine sprocket and primary chain. Transmission was 4-speed and the unit was fitted to a loop frame with conventional swingarm rear suspension and telescopic forks. Both front and rear brakes were drums in full-width hubs. The styling was reminiscent of some of the larger capacity bikes of the time; the headlamp was carried in a nacelle and a dual seat was fitted. The oil tank and toolbox were located above and behind the gearbox.

A year later there appeared trials and scrambles versions of the C15 identified by a suffix, C15T and C15S for the two respective models. They featured competition wheels and tyres and raised exhaust systems but were essentially similar to the roadgoing machine. The C15 later formed the basis of the B40, B44, B50 and was finally superseded by the B25 Barracuda.

BSA D1 BANTAM

SPECIFICATIONS
Year: 1949
Engine type: Single
Engine cycle: Two-stroke
Capacity: 123cc (7.5cu in)
Bore & stroke: 52 x 58mm
Horsepower: 4.5bhp @ 5000rpm
Top speed: 53mph (85kph)
Compression ratio: 6.5:1
Carburettor: Amal
Transmission: 3-speed
Brakes: F. & R. Drum
Ignition: Magneto
Frame: Tubular cradle
Suspension: F. Telescopic forks. R. None
Wheelbase: 50in (1270mm)
Weight: 170lb (77kg)
Fuel: 1.875 gallons (8.52lit)
Oil: Mixed with fuel
Tyres: 2.75 x 19in

Above: The Bantam was a tiny motorcycle and so used scaled-down versions of conventional components, such as a small diameter drum brake and telescopic forks.

Right: The BSA Bantam found favour with the GPO as a Telegram Bike. The Post Office operated fleets of Bantams in a distinctive red livery and fitted with leg shields. Other customers received their Bantams finished in green like this one.

BSA D1 BANTAM (1949)

How BSA came to produce the motorcycle they christened the Bantam in 1946 is a story that begins in the last months of World War Two. The German DKW motorcycle factory was part of the Auto-Union concern with headquarters in Chemnitz and one of its plants – the DKW factory – in Zschopau in what was to become East Germany. DKW had been amongst the pioneers of the two-stroke engine and had built large numbers of the RT-125 which had been designed in 1939. Following the Allied victory in 1945, like Germany itself, DKW's facilities were divided by the Iron Curtain. DKW restarted production of the RT-125 in the West while a new company on the other side of the divide known as IFA – later MZ – also produced the RT-125. However, this was not all. As part of war reparations, the design of the RT-125 was passed to the Allies. Harley-Davidson in the United States later produced the Hummer based on the RT-125, while BSA came up with the Bantam.

The Bantam was introduced by BSA in June 1946. It was designated the D1 although little mention was made of the motorcycle's German origins. To keep the cost of the Bantam to a minimum, most of the cycle parts were painted and chrome plate was kept to a minimum. Performance was not good with a top speed of less than 60mph (97kph) but fuel consumption was impressive at approximately 120 miles per gallon (42km/litre). Purchase price was also low, and combined with low running costs, it meant that the Bantam rapidly found favour as a commuter

bike. The British GPO (General Post Office) operated fleets of Bantams for telegram deliveries. GPO Bantams were equipped with leg shields and painted post office red.

The Bantam was a very basic machine with a rigid frame. The suspension was provided by a single-seat sprung saddle and telescopic forks. The frame was made from tubular steel onto which was fitted the two-stroke engine, very similar in design to the DKW version. The Bantam featured a 3-speed transmission and chain final drive. Wheels were 19 inches in diameter and covered by pressed-steel mudguards. Electrics were 6-volt

Right: The BSA Bantam was a most basic motorcycle with a two-stroke engine closely based on the prewar German DKW model.

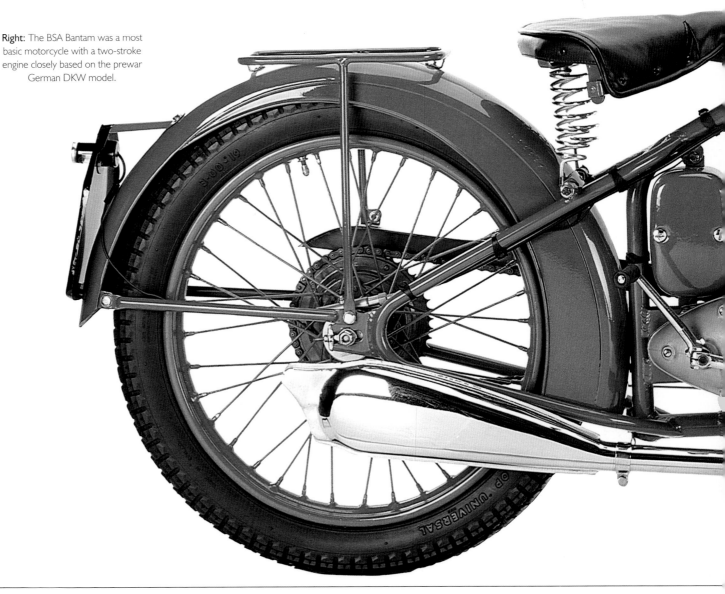

and limited to operating the front and rear lights. Petrol and two-stroke oil were carried and mixed in the curved petrol tank conventionally mounted on the top tube of the frame. The logo of the D1 – a bantam cock – was applied to the sides of the two-tone tank.

Later upgrades to the Bantam came in the form of 175cc displacement models, rear swinging-arm suspension and a 4-speed transmission before the model was finally discontinued by BSA in 1971. As well as commuter bikes, Bantams were used as novice machines, trials bikes and in small displacement classes for racing.

Left: The Bantam engine produced only 4.5bhp at 5000rpm, but the bike was popular as a cheap commuter motorcycle.

Below: The small capacity motorcycle was named after the diminutive Bantam cockerel. It was finished in green with cream panels on the tank on which a Bantam badge appeared alongside the maker's logo.

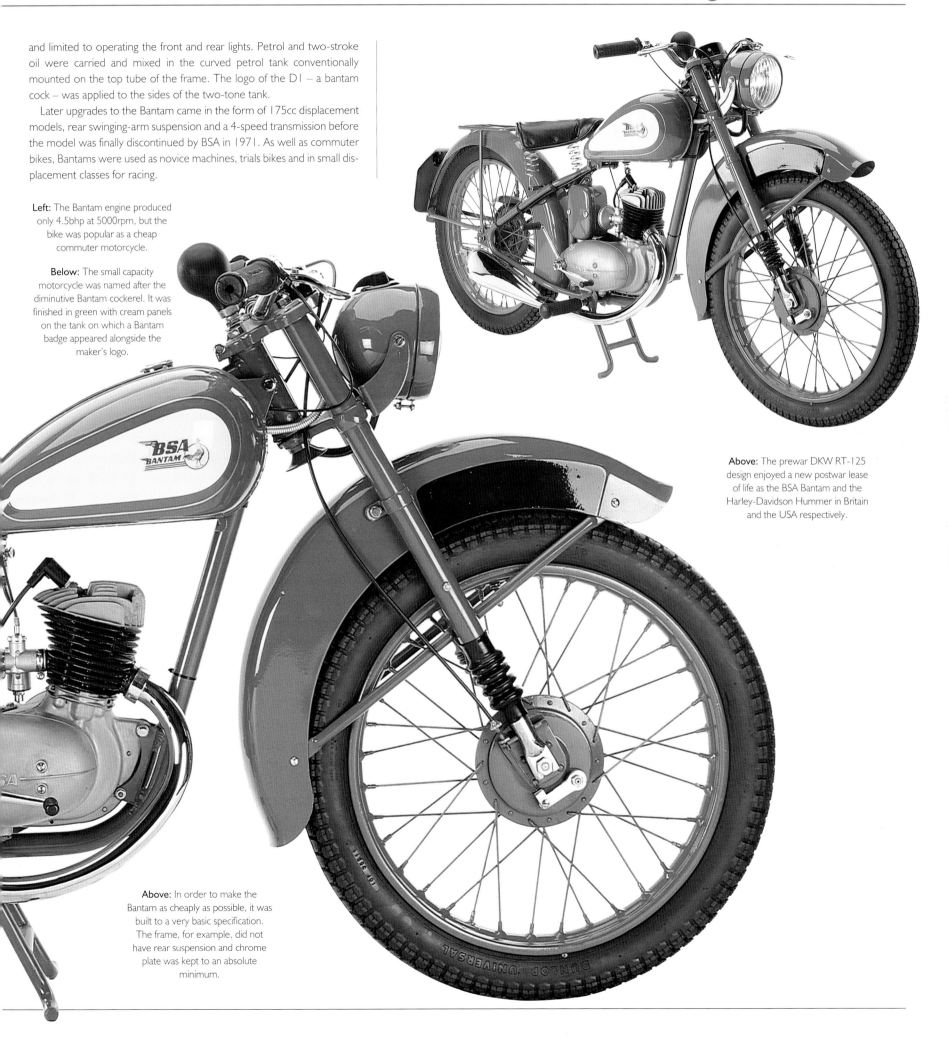

Above: The prewar DKW RT-125 design enjoyed a new postwar lease of life as the BSA Bantam and the Harley-Davidson Hummer in Britain and the USA respectively.

Above: In order to make the Bantam as cheaply as possible, it was built to a very basic specification. The frame, for example, did not have rear suspension and chrome plate was kept to an absolute minimum.

BSA B33

SPECIFICATIONS

Year: 1955
Engine type: Ohv single
Engine cycle: Four-stroke
Capacity: 499cc (30.5cu in)
Bore & stroke: 85 x 88mm
Horsepower: 23bhp @ 5500rpm
Top speed: 80mph (129kph)
Compression ratio: 6.8:1
Carburettor: Amal
Transmission: 4-speed
Brakes: F. & R. Drum
Ignition: Magneto
Frame: Tubular steel
Suspension: F. Telescopic forks.
R. Plunger
Wheelbase: 54in (1372mm)
Weight: 340lb (154kg)
Fuel: 3 gallons (13.6lit)
Oil: 4 pints (2.27lit)
Tyres: F. 3.25 x 19in.
R. 3.50 x 19in

Above: The three rifles in the BSA logo give a clear indication of Birmingham Small Arms origins as a co-operative of gunmakers.

BSA A10

SPECIFICATIONS

Year: 1962
Engine type: Vertical twin
Engine cycle: Four-stroke
Capacity: 646cc (39.4cu in)
Bore & stroke: 70 x 84mm
Horsepower: 34bhp @ 5750rpm
Top speed: 95mph (153kph)
Compression ratio: 6.5:1
Carburettor: Amal
Transmission: 4-speed
Brakes: F. & R. Drum
Ignition: Coil and points
Frame: Steel cradle
Suspension: F. Telescopic forks.
R. Swingarm and shock absorbers
Wheelbase: 56in (1422mm)
Weight: 430lb (195kg)
Fuel: 4 gallons (18.2lit)
Oil: 5.5 pints (3.13lit)
Tyres: F. 3.25 x 19in.
R. 3.50 x 19in

BSA B33 (1955)

As well as supplying rifles to the British Army during World War Two, the company produced over 120,000 units of the side-valve 500cc M20 motorcycle for the Allied forces. While these contracts were being fulfilled, BSA had an eye to postwar business. In order to expand production, during the war years it acquired Sunbeam, New Hudson and Ariel. Postwar the company first unveiled bikes such as the A7, a semi-unit parallel twin. By 1948 the company's range was comprehensive and ranged from utility sidecar machines, the M series, to sporting bikes and from 125cc lightweights to 650cc motorcycles. Through the 1950s it seemed as if BSA could do no wrong; their bikes were popular, sold well, and models like the Gold Star proved successful in competitive events, while their more utility machines, such as the M33 and B31/B33, established themselves as reliable commuter transport. Sales figures were good and supported such a diverse range.

The B33 was a 500cc version of the 350cc B31 which used a 71 x 88mm bore and stroke. The increase in capacity was achieved through enlarging the bore to 85mm but retaining the stroke. The B31 made its debut in 1945 and was followed by the B33 in 1947, and

the M33 in 1948. The M33 was intended for sidecar use and used both a prewar designation and some prewar parts. As times changed and the market for basic commuter machines declined, however, the workaday ohv singles were discontinued one by one; the M33 went in 1957, the B31 in 1959, and although the B33 did survive into the 1960s, it was only by one year.

Left: Equally conventional for the period were the telescopic forks, drum brake and valanced mudguard fitted at the front of the machine.

Below: The dual seat was mounted over the swingarm and shock absorber system of the rear suspension, which was conventional for its day.

Right: The single-cylinder B33 was a utility commuter bike built in the postwar years when the industry was shifting its emphasis to twin-cylinder engines.

Above: The B33 was the 500cc version of the single-cylinder motorcycle that was also available as a 350cc in the guise of the B31. Both had a common stroke of 88mm.

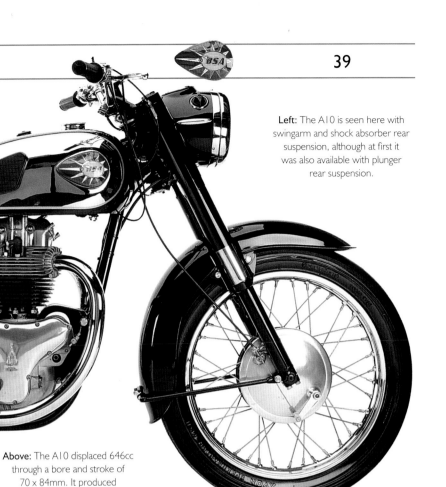

Above: The A10 displaced 646cc through a bore and stroke of 70 x 84mm. It produced 34bhp @ 5750rpm.

BSA A10 (1962)

The BSA A10 in its original guise was announced by BSA in October 1949 as a 1950 model. It was a 650cc twin available in both rigid- and plunger-framed versions. It was soon followed by a 500cc version known as the A7, which superseded an earlier model of similar capacity and the same designation. Both A7 and A10 cycle parts were common until the introduction of the swingarm rear suspension in 1954. The basic layout of the A10 engine was similar to the first BSA postwar twins although the cylinder head had been redesigned. It was, however, the colour of one of the new machines, golden beige, that was most noticeable and attracted most attention. The A10 Golden Flash was a plunger model and with a larger petrol tank it was primarily intended for export.

The plunger frame became standard across the range in 1951 when the rigid frame was dropped. The A10 proved popular for both solo and sidecar use. In the latter use it would exceed 70mph (113kph). Through a succession of minor upgrades to both engine and cycle parts the A10 remained in production until the introduction of the single top tube, duplex down tubes, swingarm frame in 1954. Slightly higher performance versions, namely

the Super Flash and Road Rocket, were introduced for export in 1953 and shown in the UK in 1954. The Super Flash used the plunger frame while the Road Rocket used the swingarm frame. With the use of the new frame, the engine and gearbox were made as two separate assemblies rather than being semi-unit in construction. Other improvements that coincided with the new frame were the fitment of an Amal Monobloc carburettor, a redesigned chrome-panelled petrol tank and a larger oil tank.

These "new" A10s were gradually upgraded in details as the production run continued, the full-width hub front brake appeared in 1955 and the swingarm frame was fitted as standard to all models, an anti-theft steering lock appeared in the same year. The rear hub was upgraded to full width in 1956 and a fully enclosed chaincase became available as an option that endured until 1962. The Golden Flash, Road Rocket and Shooting Star were three variants of the A10 available in the late 1950s, although the Road Rocket became the Super Rocket for 1958 and a scrambles variant, the Spitfire Twin, was made for the important American market. A number of engineering detail changes were made for 1960 including a redesign of the clutch, fitment of larger carburettors to the various A10 models and minor changes to the primary case, brake adjusters and choke lever. The Super Rocket was modified to a greater degree in 1961 when redesigned silencers that reduced noise but did not affect performance were installed. The brakes and gearbox were also slightly redesigned.

By now the A10 design was more than a decade old and plans were being made to introduce a new range of unit-construction twins, the A50 and A65. These two motorcycles were also of 500cc and 650cc displacement and for the first years of the 1960s they were offered alongside the A10 in dealers' showrooms. The last A10s in production were the Rocket Gold Star and the Super Rocket. The former was introduced in February 1962 and was a combination of the most tuned 650cc twin engine and the proven Gold Star frame and forks. Production of these machines was halted in the middle of 1963 by which time the A50 and A65 models were established.

BSA DBD GOLD STAR

SPECIFICATIONS
Year: 1961
Engine type: Ohv single
Engine cycle: Four-stroke
Capacity: 499cc (30.5cu in)
Bore & stroke: 85 x 88mm
Horsepower: 40bhp @ 7000rpm
Top speed: Dependent on gearing and tune
Compression ratio: 9:1
Carburettor: Amal
Transmission: 4-speed
Brakes: F. & R. Drum
Ignition: Magneto
Frame: Tubular duplex cradle
Suspension: F. Telescopic forks.
R. Swingarm and shock absorbers
Wheelbase: 56in (1422mm)
Weight: 295lb (134kg)
Fuel: 2 gallons (9.1lit)
Oil: 6 pints (3.4lit)
Tyres: F. 2.75 x 21in.
R. 4.00 x 19in

Above: On the Gold Star models BSA used a tank badge design that incorporated their winged B logo along with a gold-coloured star.

Right: The Gold Star was supplied in a variety of trims including road-racing and off-road competition specification. This is the scrambles – now known as Moto-X – version.

BSA DBD GOLD STAR (1961)

The origins of the Gold Star model name are interesting and are linked with the historic British race circuit at Brooklands. A gold star lapel badge was awarded to riders who completed a lap of the famous circuit at over 100mph (161kph). Walter Handley did this for BSA on a 500cc single running on alcohol in 1937 when he averaged 102.27mph (164.58kph). For the 1938 season the bike was not surprisingly renamed the Gold Star. The name reappeared after World War Two on another single-cylinder motorcycle.

The Gold Star appeared in 1948 as the B32GS, a 350cc single with a 71 x 88mm bore and stroke. This was a tuned version of the 350cc B31. The stroke was retained when the capacity of the Gold Star was enlarged to 500cc for the B34GS models. The first Gold Stars were supplied in a plunger frame and designated as ZB models. They became BB and CB models after the switch was made to swingarm frames in 1952, a move that anticipated a similar change to many of BSA's other motorcycles.

Ulsterman Bill Nicholson had considerable success in competition on a trials 350 during the 1950s. To make the machine suitable for the Clubman's TT it was necessary to alter the engine's characteristics; this was achieved through a change of camshafts, pistons, cylinder heads,

Below: The off-road versions of the Gold Star were supplied with minimal alloy mudguards and knobbly off-road pattern tyres.

valves and port sizes. A choice of five different camshafts were available to suit the engine's various guises and states of tune. From its introduction through the 1950s, the Gold Star came to be the stuff of legends mainly because of success in International Six Days Trials and Clubman's TT events at the Isle of Man. The 1949 ISDT saw 11 trophies go to BSA 500cc Gold Star-mounted riders while a rider on a 350cc Gold Star won that year's Isle of Man Clubman TT. The Gold Star was a versatile motorcycle and available in touring, trials, scrambles and racing versions.

For more than a decade the Gold Star was among the top sporting motorcycles in production. Its sequential upgrades were referred to by changes in the machine's designation – the CB models gave way to the DB models in 1955 and these were succeeded by the DBD models in 1957. It was this latter version that survived until the end of Gold Star production in 1963. The DBD prefix signified a larger inlet port and wider carburettor fixing stud spacing to allow fitment of the 1.5in (38mm) Amal GP carburettor. While the DB and DBD Gold Stars sold best when built to racer specification, because of their popularity in the Clubman TT events, they were also successful in off-road motorcycle sport. The

Above: The gearbox was a 4-speed item and gearing was altered through use of sprockets with differing numbers of teeth.

Clubman TT events were discontinued in the late 1950s, partially as a result of the dominance of the BSA Gold Star.

The scrambles version of the DBD Gold Star featured light alloy guards not dissimilar to the road-racing models, knobbly tyres, and larger diameter wheels to increase ground clearance. A smaller petrol tank was fitted while lights were not. Four-stroke scrambles motorcycles gave way to two-strokes in later years and the sport became known as Motocross, often abbreviated as Moto-X.

Below: For off-road models the ground clearance was enhanced through the use of 21- and 19-inch wheels front and back respectively.

Above: The famous Gold Star single-cylinder engine displaced 499cc through a bore and stroke of 85 x 88mm. Top speed was dependent on tune and gearing, especially sprocket sizes.

Left: The off-road competition Gold Star models were devoid of road equipment such as lights and number plates.

Above: Competition bikes did not have to conform to road traffic legislation especially with regard to noise levels, so the scrambles Gold Star had no silencers, but simply a straight-through pipe.

Left: The Gold Star name was coined by BSA after they had been awarded a Brooklands Gold Star for lapping the famous circuit at speeds in excess of 100mph.

BSA A65S SPITFIRE MKII

SPECIFICATIONS
Year: 1966
Engine type: Ohv vertical twin
Engine cycle: Four-stroke
Capacity: 654cc (39.9cu in)
Bore & stroke: 75 x 74mm
Horsepower: 55bhp @ 7000rpm
Top speed: 110mph (177kph)
Compression ratio: 10.5:1
Carburettor: Twin Amal
Transmission: 4-speed
Brakes: F. & R. Drum
Ignition: Coil
Frame: Steel cradle
Suspension: F. Telescopic forks. R. Swingarm and shock absorbers
Wheelbase: 54.12in (1375mm)
Weight: 382lb (173kg)
Fuel: 2 gallons/5 gallons option (9.09/22.7lit)
Oil: 5.5 pints (3.13lit)
Tyres: F. 3.25 x 19in. R. 4.00 x 18in

Above: Traditionally one of BSA's logos used a winged "B" and in this case it was incorporated into a winged design as well.

Right: Cigar-shaped silencers ran down each side of the motorcycle from each cylinder. Rear suspension was by swingarm and shock absorbers and final drive by a chain on the nearside.

BSA A65S SPITFIRE MK II (1966)

BSA's range of new motorcycles for 1962 was announced in January of that year. The twin cylinder machines were the 499cc A50 and the 654cc A65 based on a common stroke of 74mm. The difference in capacity was achieved by varying the bore. The motorcycles were based around tubular steel swingarm frames and telescopic forks. Contemporary road tests reveal that the machines were well received. The next development was the announcement of the 650cc Rocket A65R in October 1963, a sports A65. This motorcycle had a slightly tuned engine and a heavy duty clutch. This led to a variety of sports machines based on both 500cc and 650cc machines including the Cyclone, Cyclone Clubman, Lightning and Lightning Clubman, as well as the Wasp and Hornet for the US market. The 650cc Spitfire Hornet followed for the USA in 1964 and in 1965 it was added to the UK range of BSAs as the Spitfire Mk II. This was the top-of-the-range model in BSA's line-up of roadgoing twins.

Above: The Spitfire Mark II featured an overhead-valve parallel twin engine of 654cc displacement achieved through a bore and stroke of 75 x 74mm.

Below: The fuel tank was an optional five gallon item but was shaped to display lines that closely resembled racing bikes of the day, an appearance enhanced by the flat handlebars and bar-mounted speedo.

Right: The BSA Spitfire was equipped with a dual seat with a race-style shape and end piece typical of café racer styling of the period.

The Spitfire Mk II appeared sporting and sleek as a result of its straight handlebars and a sculpted petrol tank that flowed back into a race-style dual seat, similar to the previous year's Lightning Clubman models. The engine was in a slightly higher state of tune, however, with the compression ratio up at 10.5:1, and racing camshafts were fitted as were twin Amal Grand Prix carbs. A larger front drum brake was used to cope with the increased performance. In this form the Spitfire Mk II was made between 1965 and 1966. Later there were Mk III and Mk IV versions that featured modifications such as the use of a twin-leading-shoe (TLS) front brake and Amal Concentric carburettors. The model was eventually dropped in favour of the triple in 1969.

Above: By 1966 the BSA Spitfire Mk II was the top-of-the-range model in BSA's line-up of sporting parallel twins. Later it was superseded by the triple-cylinder-engined models.

Above: The 654cc twin produced 55bhp @ 7000rpm courtesy of a 10.5:1 compression ratio and a pair of Amal carburettors. As a result it was capable of around 110mph (177kph).

BSA A75 ROCKET 3

BSA A75 ROCKET 3

SPECIFICATIONS
Year: 1970
Engine type: Ohv triple
Engine cycle: Four-stroke
Capacity: 740cc (45.16cu in)
Bore & stroke: 67 x 70mm
Horsepower: 58bhp @ 7250rpm
Top speed: 120mph (193kph)
Compression ratio: 9.5:1
Carburettor: Triple Amals
Transmission: 5-speed
Brakes: F. TLS drum. R. Drum
Ignition: Coil
Frame: Duplex tube cradle
Suspension: F. Telescopic forks. R. Swingarm and shock absorbers
Wheelbase: 59in (1499mm)
Weight: 518lb (235kg)
Fuel: 4.8 gallons (21.8lit)
Oil: 6 pints (3.4lit)
Tyres: 4.10 x 19in

Above: The BSA Rocket 3 and the Triumph Trident shared the same basic three-cylinder engine, although it differed in details.

Right: The Rocket 3 was the result of Triumph/BSA's Bert Hopwood realizing that the company would need a new motorcycle engine in order to retain a significant percentage of the large capacity motorcycle market.

BSA A75 ROCKET 3 (1970)

In the 1960s the development of the superbike was in its infancy, but BSA/Triumph's chief designer, Bert Hopwood, knew that the company would need an engine that produced in the region of 60bhp to be competitive. Unfortunately there was insufficient time and money to design and develop a wholly new engine. Hopwood ruled out upping the capacity of an existing 650cc twin but realized that he could create a triple from Triumph's existing 493cc twin that was used in models such as the Daytona.

The resultant triples were badged as both Triumphs and BSAs. The BSA engine was inclined further forward than that of the Triumph and the new model, known as Rocket 3, was shipped to the USA where it met with high acclaim. The US importer wanted to prove the new machines in competition and in 1970 the American Motorcyclist Association waived the eligibility rule requiring overhead-valve engines to displace less than 500cc for US racing. This opened the way for a British team to race the new triples in the prestigious Daytona 200 mile race in 1970.

The company built a number of race-prepared triples, painting the BSAs red and the Triumphs blue. For BSA they recruited Dave Aldana, Jim Rice and Mike Hailwood, while Triumph signed up Gary Nixon, Gene Romero, Don Castro and Percy Tait. Honda brought a team of four riders to race works-prepared versions of the four-cylinder Honda 750. The pole position went to Romero. Hailwood and Nixon followed him with Dick Mann on his Honda next. Several riders dropped out with mechanical problems during the race, which was won by Dick Mann on the Honda with Gene Romero in second and Castro third.

The British factories were back for 1971 although Honda were absent this time. The engines were in a higher state of tune, and the frames had been built by Rob North which made the new machines faster but easier to ride. On BSAs were Hailwood, Mann, Aldana, Rice and Don Emde. On Triumphs were Paul Smart, Romero, Nixon, Castro and Tom Rockwood. Paul Smart qualified fastest with Harley riders Cal Rayborn and Mark Brelsford second and third. In the actual race, which was marred by a fatal accident in the early laps, both Smart and Hailwood went out with burned valves. Dick Mann finished first with Romero and Emde second and third. Dick Mann had set a new record average speed of 104.737mph (168.55kph) and the post-race American advertising for BSA screamed "BSA takes Daytona".

Closer to home, John Cooper on a Rocket 3 racer beat Giacomo

Agostini on an MV Agusta at the 1971 Mallory Park race of the year. The fortunes of BSA's racers in America took a downturn in 1972 as the struggling company could not afford the luxury of the expensive racing programme. Only Dick Mann and Gene Romero were retained. They finished 22nd and 25th at Daytona aboard the BSA and Triumph triples respectively.

The styling of the roadgoing Rocket 3 was radical for the time. It included exhaust pipes that are referred to as "raygun" pipes because of their three tubular ends to the silencers, evidence that the bike is a triple. Production of Rocket 3s stopped in 1971, the year after this machine was made, because of the collapse of the BSA operation. However, the Triumph Triple continued in production, albeit with an interruption caused by the workers' occupation of the Meriden Triumph plant.

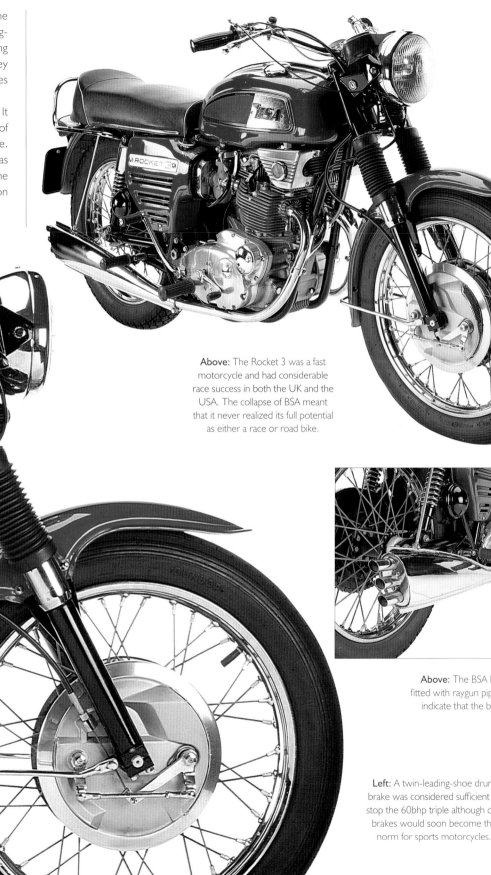

Above: The Rocket 3 was a fast motorcycle and had considerable race success in both the UK and the USA. The collapse of BSA meant that it never realized its full potential as either a race or road bike.

Above: The BSA Rocket 3 was fitted with raygun pipes which subtly indicate that the bike is a triple.

Left: A twin-leading-shoe drum brake was considered sufficient to stop the 60bhp triple although disc brakes would soon become the norm for sports motorcycles.

Above: The three-cylinder engine was initially made from one and a half 500cc unit-construction Triumph twin engines suitably refined by Bert Hopwood.

IVORY CALTHORPE

Year: 1930
Engine type: Ohv single
Engine cycle: Four-stroke
Capacity: 348cc (21.2cu in)
Bore & stroke: 74 x 81mm
Horsepower: n/a
Top speed: 70mph (113kph)
Compression ratio: n/a
Carburettor: Amal
Transmission: 3-speed
Brakes: F. & R. Drum
Ignition: Magneto
Frame: Duplex cradle
Suspension: F. Girder forks.
R. None
Wheelbase: n/a
Weight: 267lb (121kg)
Fuel: n/a
Oil: n/a
Tyres: F. 3.25 x 19in.
R. 4.00 x 19in

Above: The valves were operated by pushrods that ran in a single tube to the rocker box. The valve springs were exposed.

IVORY CALTHORPE II (1930)

Calthorpe started manufacturing motorcycles before World War One, but by the end of the 1920s it was best known for a single model, the Ivory Calthorpe. It was so named because of its distinctive ivory paint finish which distinguished it from the many black machines of the era. By 1930 it was known as the Ivory Calthorpe II. It featured a 348cc single-cylinder engine of Calthorpe's own design which was inclined forwards in the frame. The engine had the magneto positioned behind the cylinder and the dynamo positioned forward of it. Lubrication was dry-sump although the oil was carried in the forward section of the crankcase. The engine caught the motorcycling public's eye, as did the finish, and these factors undoubtedly helped sales. The remainder of the motorcycle was essentially conventional for its time. Transmission was by means of a proprietary 3-speed Burman box and the rigid frame was fitted with Webb girder forks.

Calthorpe upgraded the machine as the Ivory III for 1931 and the Ivory IV for 1932. These featured various modifications and options such as a choice of coil or magneto, while the larger Ivory IV was of 499cc dis-

Above: The Ivory Calthorpe was powered by a 348cc overhead-valve single-cylinder engine with a bore and stroke of 74 x 81mm.

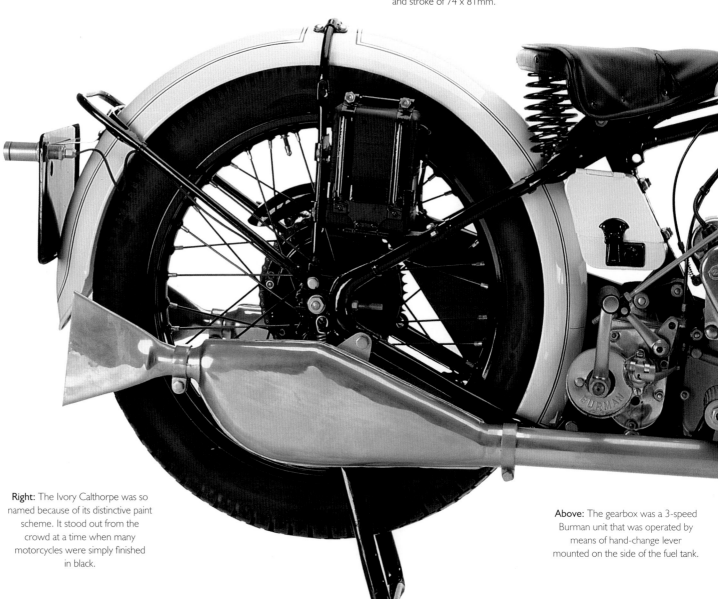

Right: The Ivory Calthorpe was so named because of its distinctive paint scheme. It stood out from the crowd at a time when many motorcycles were simply finished in black.

Above: The gearbox was a 3-speed Burman unit that was operated by means of hand-change lever mounted on the side of the fuel tank.

placement. In 1932 the firm introduced the Ivory Minor which was powered by a 247cc two-stroke engine. With changes, additions and subtractions to and from the range, the company continued motorcycle production through the years of the Depression. By 1937 their motorcycles were some of those sold exclusively through the prominent London motorcycle dealers, Pride & Clarke. However, in 1938 the company went into liquidation and little more was heard of their novel machines.

Right: The Ivory Calthorpe had quite a tall steering head. Front suspension was by girder forks.

Above: Girder forks, drum brakes, electric lights and valanced mudguards were the norm for British bikes by the early 1930s.

COTTON MODEL 7

SPECIFICATIONS
Year: 1928
Engine type: Single
Engine cycle: Four-stroke
Capacity: 348cc (21.2cu in)
Bore & stroke: 71 x 88mm
Horsepower: 2.75hp
Top speed: 75mph (121kph)
Compression ratio: 4.5:1
Carburettor: Amal
Transmission: 3-speed
Brakes: F. & R. Drum
Ignition: Magneto
Frame: Triangulated steel
Suspension: F. Side sprung girders. R. None
Wheelbase: 52.5in (1333mm)
Weight: 195lb (88.5kg)
Fuel: 2 gallons (9.1lit)
Oil: n/a
Tyres: 2.75 x 21in

Above: The logo visible on the magneto drive cover proclaims this to be an ohv Blackburne engine.

COTTON MODEL 7 (1928)

Cotton was a company based in Gloucester that began manufacturing motorcycles in 1920. It took its name from its founder, Francis Willoughby Cotton. The company was noted for its triangulated design of frame that had been patented by Cotton before motorcycle production began. The idea behind the design was that all the frame tubes should be straight, and therefore subject only to compression and tension forces, and triangulated so that stress was concentrated at the apex of any triangle. The steering head was supported by pairs of tubes running diagonally backwards to the rear axle. The wedge-shaped fuel tank was fitted between these tubes. This novel design of frame ensured good handling characteristics and persisted until 1939.

The marque had considerable Isle of Man TT success, the most notable of which was Stanley Woods' 1923 Junior TT victory. This victory helped to establish the name Cotton in the public's eye. The 1928 machine seen here was powered by an outside flywheel Blackburne engine while the

Above: The hand-operated gear lever of the Cotton was mounted on the frame adjacent to the right side of the fuel tank.

Model 7J used a side-valve JAP unit. The Depression brought hard times, and in order to stay in business Cotton offered motorcycles powered by proprietary engines from companies such as JAP and Blackburne. These were fitted to an extensive range of models. With the outbreak of war in 1939, however, the company temporarily closed its doors.

In the postwar years the company remained in Gloucester under the management of new directors, producing small-capacity two-strokes powered by Villiers proprietary engines. The machines were acceptable but little better than any of their rivals. During the 1960s and 1970s Cotton concentrated on the production of trials bikes with proprietary engines from companies such as Italian Minarelli. In 1980 the company was taken over by Armstrong.

Below: Cotton motorcycles were noted for their triangulated frame design that was patented before the company began motorcycle production.

Right: The Cotton Model 7 was powered by a Blackburne engine; the company's logo appears on the casting of the magneto drive.

Below: The Cotton used a slightly less common type of sprung girder forks. These were described as side sprung because of the position of the springs.

Above: The Model 7 used the ohv Blackburne engine, while the Model 7J used a side-valve JAP engine.

COVENTRY EAGLE N35 FLYING 350

SPECIFICATIONS
Year: 1937
Engine type: Ohv single
Engine cycle: Four-stroke
Capacity: 348cc (21.2cu in)
Bore & stroke: 69 x 93mm
Horsepower: n/a
Top speed: 60mph (97kph)
Compression ratio: n/a
Carburettor: Amal
Transmission: 4-speed
Brakes: F. & R. Drum
Ignition: Magneto
Frame: Tubular steel
Suspension: F. Sprung girder
forks. R. None
Wheelbase: n/a
Weight: n/a
Fuel: n/a
Oil: n/a
Tyres: 3.25 x 19in

Above: The Smiths
speedometer optimistically
read up to 85mph. Top speed
was actually nearer 60mph
(97kph).

COVENTRY EAGLE N35 FLYING 350 (1937)

The company was located in Coventry in the Midlands and its beginnings date from the Victorian era of bicycling. Coventry Eagle always used proprietary parts but through careful assembly and a high standard of finish they survived longer than many other of their competitors. During the late 1920s they offered the luxurious Flying 8 series alongside utterly utilitarian machines. The Flying 8 machines used V-twin JAP engines and sculptured tanks and were not dissimilar to Brough motorcycles in appearance, while the utility models were built with pressed-steel frames and small-displacement engines.

As the company advanced into the 1930s, they offered a comprehensive range of models to suit most pockets. Additions and subtractions were made to and from the line-up through the decade as the company struggled to cope with the economic hardships of the time. There were, for example, only three models listed for 1933, but for 1936 the company

announced its range of three Pullman Two Seaters. These were partially enclosed and had an unusual frame design consisting of a pressed-steel chassis bolted to an upper tubular section.

Brand new for 1937 were three machines powered by different sizes of overhead-valve Matchless engines. The motorcycles had displacements of 245cc, 348cc and 497cc and were known as the N25 Flying 250, N35 Flying 350 and N50 Flying 500 respectively. The middleweight N35 is typical of all three and featured the engine mounted vertically in the frame which was manufactured from tubular steel rather than the earlier pressed-steel construction. Webb girder forks were used at the front and the transmission was a 4-speed unit with a foot-change lever. The engine itself had the magneto mounted behind the cylinder and was lubricated by a dry-sump system. Production continued until the outbreak of war 1939 but was never resumed.

Below: An unusual feature is the
small tool box mounted in the vee
of the mudguard stays alongside
the rear wheel.

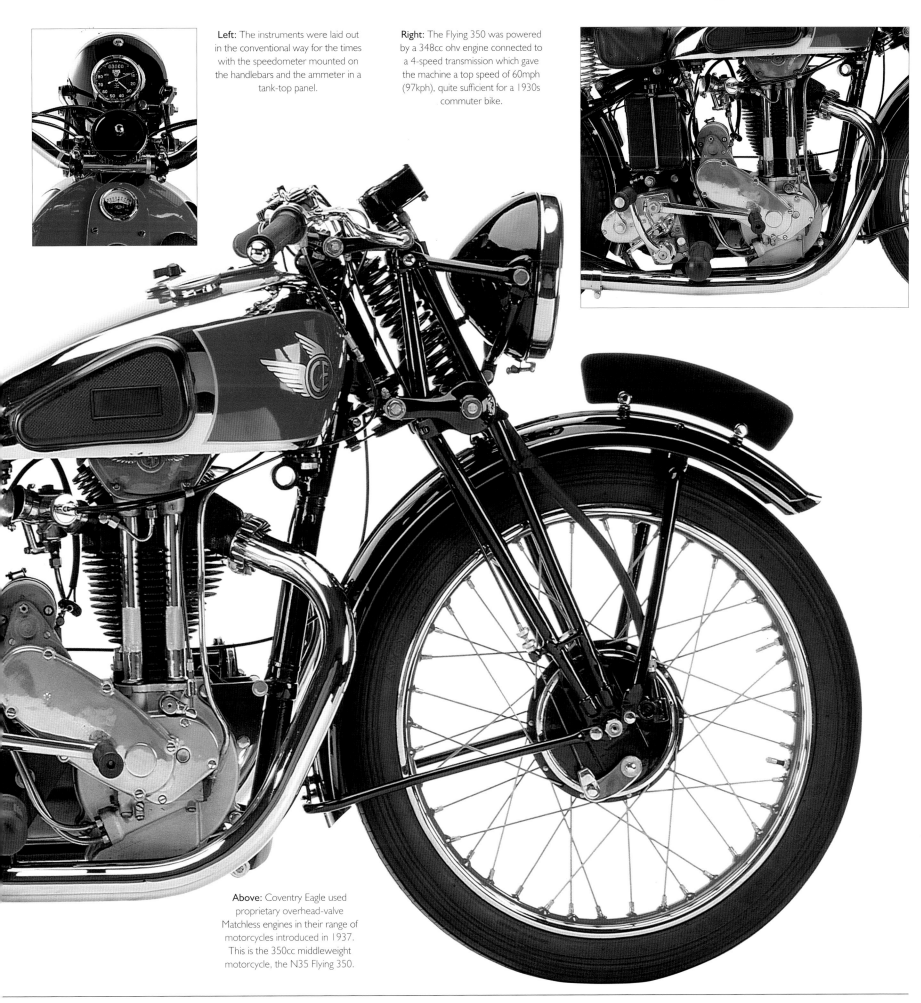

Left: The instruments were laid out in the conventional way for the times with the speedometer mounted on the handlebars and the ammeter in a tank-top panel.

Right: The Flying 350 was powered by a 348cc ohv engine connected to a 4-speed transmission which gave the machine a top speed of 60mph (97kph), quite sufficient for a 1930s commuter bike.

Above: Coventry Eagle used proprietary overhead-valve Matchless engines in their range of motorcycles introduced in 1937. This is the 350cc middleweight motorcycle, the N35 Flying 350.

DOUGLAS SIDE-VALVE TWIN

SPECIFICATIONS
Year: 1913
Engine type: Flat-twin
Engine cycle: Four-stroke
Capacity: 345cc
Bore & stroke: 60 x 61mm
Horsepower: 2.75hp
Top speed: n/a
Compression ratio: n/a
Carburettor: Amac
Transmission: 2-speed
Brakes: F. Stirrup. R. On belt-drive rim
Ignition: Magneto
Frame: Tubular steel
Suspension: F. Sprung girders. R. None
Wheelbase: n/a
Weight: n/a
Fuel: n/a
Oil: n/a
Tyres: 26 x 2.5in

Above: The acetylene carbide headlamp was made by the Birmingham company of Powell and Hanmer.

DOUGLAS SIDE-VALVE TWIN (1913)

Douglas was noted for producing flat-twin-engined motorcycles in England in the early part of the 20th century. The first Douglas motorcycle was designed by J.F. Barter who saw his ideas go into production with the assistance of the Douglas Brothers of Kingswood, Bristol who were involved in the foundry business. In 1912 a rider on a Douglas machine won the Junior TT at the Isle of Man. For many years the company produced only flat-twins although they manufactured machines in a variety of capacities, including 350cc, 500cc and 600cc displacements.

The machine seen here is one of Douglas' smaller capacity flat-twins from 1913 with a 2-speed transmission and belt final drive. During World War One Douglas received contracts to supply the British Army with motorcycles; in fact all their production between 1916 and 1918 went to the British Army. After the war their designs were built under licence in

Above: The hand pump installed on the top of the petrol tank was to allow the rider to pump lubrication oil to the engine while on the move.

Germany by Bosch. In the late 1920s the firm built special speedway bikes, but in the main concentrated on flat-twins.

The Douglas family relinquished control of the company in 1932 and after a reorganization the company attempted to offer cheaper motorcycles which it built in larger quantities. The new range was faithful to longitudinally mounted flat-twin engines with the exception of the Endeavour which featured a transversely mounted flat-twin engine of 498cc. After World War Two Douglas concentrated on 348cc flat-twins with transversely mounted overhead-valve flat-twin engines including the Dragonfly. In the postwar years the company, which by then was part of Westinghouse in Bristol, diversified into the distribution of Vespa Scooters in the UK. Production of Douglas motorcycles stopped in 1956 although the distribution of Vespas continued for some time longer.

Right: The cylinders were positioned in a fore-and-aft configuration and the carburettor was an Amac unit. Douglas enjoyed competition success at the Isle of Man during this period.

Left: Prior to the development of adequate electric lighting systems, acetylene carbide was used as a light source for front and rear illumination on motorcycles.

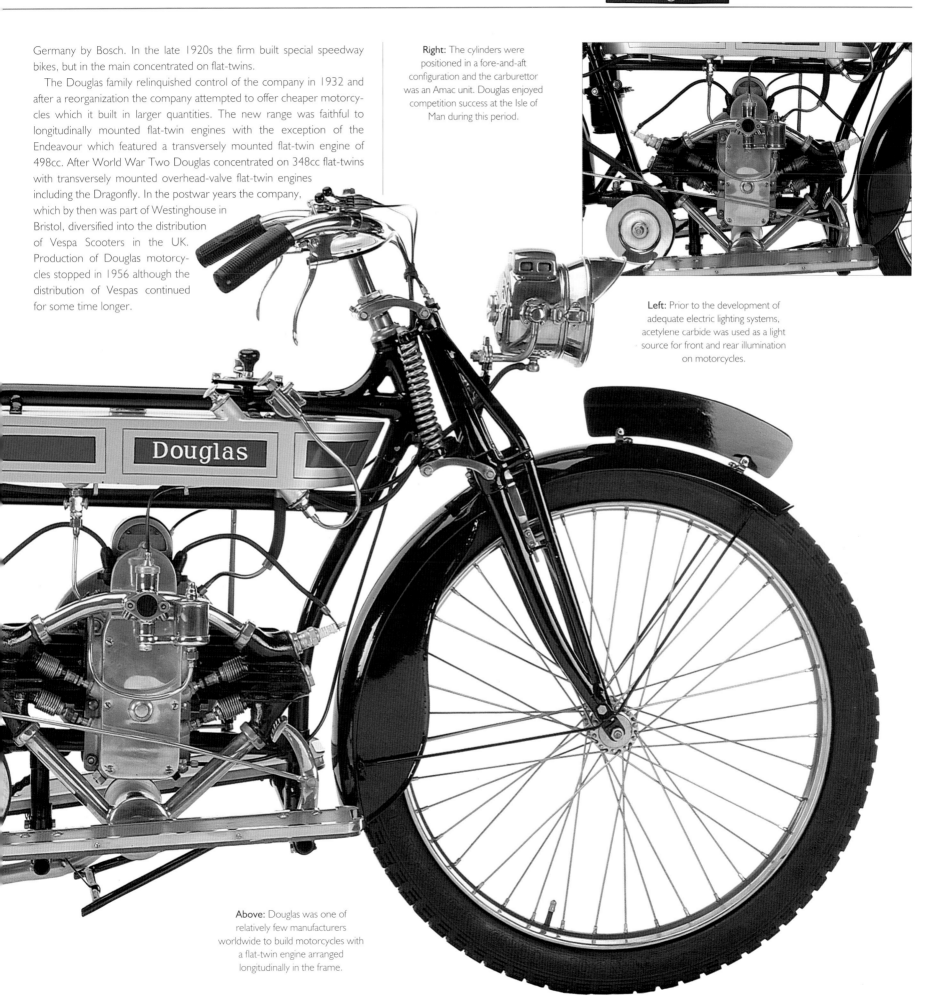

Above: Douglas was one of relatively few manufacturers worldwide to build motorcycles with a flat-twin engine arranged longitudinally in the frame.

EXCELSIOR MECHANICAL MARVEL (1933)

EXCELSIOR MECHANICAL MARVEL

SPECIFICATIONS
Year: 1933
Engine type: Ohv single
Engine cycle: Four-stroke
Capacity: 246cc (15cu in)
Bore & stroke: 63 x 79mm
Horsepower: 25bhp
Top speed: n/a
Compression ratio: n/a
Carburettor: n/a
Transmission: 4-speed
Brakes: F. & R. Drum
Ignition: Magneto
Frame: Tubular steel
Suspension: F. Sprung girder forks. R. None
Wheelbase: n/a
Weight: n/a
Fuel: n/a
Oil: n/a
Tyres: n/a

Above: The four valves in the cylinder head were operated by a pair of camshafts positioned fore and aft of the single cylinder.

Right: The Excelsior Mechanical Marvel was the result of a Lightweight Isle of Man TT win in 1929. The company usually made more utility-type machines.

In 1874 a company known as Bayliss, Thomas and Company was formed in Coventry in order to manufacture penny-farthing bicycles. Its involvement with motorcycles began in 1896 when it offered for sale bicycles fitted with Minerva engines. The company quickly developed their ideas and by 1902 were offering a belt-drive machine with a 2.75hp single-cylinder engine which was inclined forward under the front downtube of the frame. The fuel and oil tanks were located within the central part of the diamond-shaped frame.

The company was taken over by R. Walker & Son in 1919 and moved to Tyseley in Birmingham. Like many other manufacturers, it produced motorcycles with proprietary engines from companies such as Blackburne and JAP. The majority of machines built by Excelsior were utility models, but such was the nature of the motorcycle business in the 1920s that Excelsior was prepared to build anything it thought it could sell. They produced race bikes and campaigned them at Brooklands and in the Isle of Man TT races. After the debut of the 350 Sports, Excelsior went on to a Lightweight TT victory in 1929 with a 250cc race bike.

For the 1930s the Excelsior company produced a range of bikes with Villiers engines fitted, including numerically designated models of 147cc, 196cc and 247cc displacement. Larger-capacity models had 245cc and 300cc ohv JAP engines. The company introduced a new machine in June 1933 at the annual TT races. This Isle of Man bike became known as the Mechanical Marvel. Its single-cylinder engine was the most distinctive feature of the motorcycle and was made for Excelsior by Blackburne. The single cylinder was positioned vertically, its piston displaced 246cc and featured four radial valves in the cylinder head. The valve operation was complex but controlled by a pair of camshafts arranged fore and aft of the cylinder. Each camshaft moved a single pushrod in a tube angled outwards from the barrel and this moved a piston in the rocker box. The pistons each moved two rockers in order to open and close the four valves. The Mechanical Marvel had twin carburettors, a skew drive to the magneto and dry-sump lubrication. In this form the motorcycle was fast enough to win the TT race but it was a notoriously difficult machine to tune. It was less successful in 1934, although still listed in Excelsior's range as the D14.

The Excelsior range was gradually upgraded during the 1930s and the models given names such as Manxman (see overleaf) that capitalized on the Mechanical Marvel's TT win. Essentially the company saw out the decade manufacturing a conventional range of two- and four-stroke motorcycles. An example of these was the Model JO powered by a 122cc Villiers engine, while an exception was the unusual Viking E9 which was a fully enclosed machine with a water-cooled engine. The company's post-war production was confined to lightweight motorcycles.

Above: The race-style filler cap used on the top of the fuel tank was designed for easy topping up of the tank during the race.

Above: The Mechanical Marvel was powered by an overhead-valve single-cylinder engine that had two exhaust ports – hence the exhaust pipe on either side of the machine.

Left: Sprung girder forks, flat handlebars, a drum brake and minimal mudguard were state of the art for the front end of an early 1930s race bike.

Above: The engine displaced 246cc through a bore and stroke of 63 x 79mm and produced 25bhp as a result of the four-valve cylinder head.

Left: The Mechanical Marvel had both racing lines and a number of racing features, such as the rear-set footpegs and controls to allow the rider to crouch over the tank.

EXCELSIOR G12 MANXMAN (1937)

The Manxman was an attempt by Excelsior to lift its name above all the other companies who offered proprietary-engined motorcycles. It was launched in 1935 in two versions with differing displacements – 246cc and 349cc. The two engines had the same stroke; the different displacement was achieved by varying the diameter of the cylinder bore. The engines were single cylinder with a shaft-driven single overhead camshaft and the mag-dyno behind the cylinder was gear-driven. The bevel box cover had the Legs of Man – the famous symbol of the Isle of Man – cast into its alloy top. Lubrication was dry-sump.

The motorcycle was clearly designed for racing and featured a 4-speed foot-change gearbox, cradle frame and capacious petrol tank. In Excelsior's catalogue the Manxman was listed in both sports and racing form and the latter model also featured rear-set footrests, different tanks and mudguards, as well as a slightly modified engine that incorporated different internal components and an oil drain from the cam box. Despite the machine's name, it never actually won an Isle of Man TT race.

Above: The three-legged symbol of the Isle of Man was cast into the alloy top of the bevel gear housing.

Right: The Excelsior Manxman of 1937 was a late 1930s sports 350 motorcycle intended for club racing. Despite its name, associating it with the island famous for motorcycle racing, the machine never claimed a TT victory, although it was widely respected in its day.

In 1936 a 496cc version of the Manxman, the F14, appeared and the race models were listed as FR11 and FR12. These featured megaphone exhausts and wraparound oil tanks rather than a conventional tank with a tool and battery box on the other side. By 1937, the year this machine was made, the Manxman range included the short-stroke 249cc G12 and GR12 models that were similar in design to the works race models of the previous year, although without the radial four-valve cylinder head of the works bikes. The 349cc G12, GR12 and the 496cc G14 models were upgraded in a similar way and the G15 was added to the range. This latter motorcycle was a 496cc sports special with a bronze cylinder head, increased compression ratio, racing-type mag-dyno and close ratio gears. The Manxman range ran on slightly upgraded for the next three years, with H, J and then K prefixes signifying the year of production, until the outbreak of war called a halt to production.

Below: The wraparound oil tank seen immediately below the front of the saddle was introduced in 1936. It fitted around the rear mudguard.

Right: The Manxman was assembled with components typical of sports machines of the 1930s. It used conventional girder forks and a mudguard typical of British bikes but it featured competition-inspired touches too.

Below: Production of the Manxman was halted on the outbreak of war in 1939 and the company later turned its attention to lightweight Villiers-powered machines for military purposes.

Above: The 349cc short-stroke engine fitted to the Manxman featured a shaft-driven single overhead camshaft which operated both inlet and exhaust valves.

EXCELSIOR WELBIKE

SPECIFICATIONS
Year: 1943
Engine type: Single
Engine cycle: Two-stroke
Capacity: 98cc (6cu in)
Bore & stroke: 50 x 50mm
Horsepower: 1.5bhp
Top speed: 31mph (50kph)
Compression ratio: 6:1
Carburettor: Villiers
Transmission: Single-speed
Brakes: F. None. R. Drum
Ignition: Magneto
Frame: Welded tubular steel
Suspension: None
Wheelbase: 39.5in (1003mm)
Weight: 70.5lb (32kg)
Fuel: 0.8 gallons (3.64lit)
Oil: Mixed with fuel
Tyres: 2.25 x 12.5in

EXCELSIOR WELBIKE (1943)

Excelsior's production capability was put to other uses than the production of motorcycles to assist the war effort. However, when the need for lightweight motorcycles for British airborne paratroopers was realized, Excelsior became involved in their production and supply. The prototype Welbike, so called because it was made in Welwyn, Hertfordshire at the Military Research Establishment, was designed to fold up so as to fit into an airdrop container. Trials, testing and evaluation were carried out before production was handed over to Excelsior who, prior to the war, had manufactured the Autobyke, a lightweight two-stroke.

Three batches of Welbikes – referred to as Motor Cycle, Solo 98cc (Make and type Excelsior, Welbike, Folding) in military jargon – were manufactured, each a slight improvement on the one before. The basic design included a 98cc Villiers two-stroke engine mounted horizontally in the frame and had a clutch mounted on a countershaft from where drive was taken to the rear wheel. The small fuel tank was partially divided and mounted across the front of the frame. The seat and handlebars folded in order to enable the Welbike to be fitted into an air-drop canister. It took around 11 seconds to extract one from the canister and make it ready to ride. Welbikes were used in European Allied airborne operations including the ill-fated Operation Market Garden drop at Arnhem in Holland in 1944.

Postwar, Brockhouse Engineering manufactured the Brockhouse Corgi, which was based on the Welbike design and engine. Subsequently the concept of the mini-bike was proven and numerous machines were sold around the world by companies as diverse as Harley-Davidson and Honda.

Above: The engine plate included lubrication details for the small 98cc Villiers Junior engine.

Below: The Excelsior Welbike was intended for use by British paratroops and designed to be parachuted into combat with them. It was packed, folded, into an air-drop canister. When it landed, the soldiers uncased it, folded up the seat and handlebars and rode away.

Above: The Welbike folded virtually flat inside its air-drop canister. Once on the ground, it could be quickly readied for action.

Below: The Welbike was a war baby devised for a specific military purpose. It was also the forerunner of many of the diminutive mopeds later manufactured around the world.

Above: This view of the Welbike's protective canister shows the internal padding that was used to cushion the motorcycle from the effects of it being dropped from an aircraft.

FRANCIS-BARNETT MODEL 10 PULLMAN (1928)

FRANCIS-BARNETT MODEL 10 PULLMAN

SPECIFICATIONS
Year: 1928
Engine type: In-line twin
Engine cycle: Two-stroke
Capacity: 343cc (21 cu in)
Bore & stroke: 79 x 70mm
Horsepower: n/a
Top speed: 60 mph (97kph)
Compression ratio: n/a
Carburettor: Villiers
Transmission: 3-speed
Brakes: F. & R. Drum
Ignition: Magneto
Frame: Bolted tubular steel
Suspension: F. Sprung girder forks. R. None
Wheelbase: n/a
Weight: n/a
Fuel: 1.75 gallons (7.96lit)
Oil: Mixed with fuel
Tyres: 3.25 x 19in

This company was founded in 1919 through the collaboration of Arthur Barnett and Gordon Francis. Barnett was at the time already producing motorcycles in Coventry. These were sold under the Invicta name and were assembled using Villiers and JAP engines. The first machine produced by the new company was introduced in 1920 with a bolted tubular frame and a JAP engine. The Francis-Barnett company manufactured machines with triangulated steel frames from 1923 onwards and became noted for the production of lightweight motorcycles. They were powered by a variety of Villiers engines, including those of 147cc, 172cc and 196cc displacement.

The Model 10 Pullman was Francis-Barnett's attempt to market a luxury motorcycle. It was not a huge success because its increased cost far outweighed the benefits of its luxury features and only average performance. The Pullman was powered by a Villiers two-stroke engine that was mounted lengthways into the frame. This was of unusual appearance in order to accommodate the engine which was constructed as a unit with the gearbox. This meant that the front and rear downtubes were considerably splayed to pass either side of the engine while the external flywheel protruded between them. Also of unusual appearance was the fuel tank which was a triangular item that was fitted between the frame tubes.

The frame was of a simple design; six pairs of straight tubes, one bent pair and a steering head were bolted together to complete it. While the

Pullman was discontinued in 1929 after only two seasons' sales, certain of the features of its construction survived in other Francis-Barnett products. The engine remained to power the Model 16 Dominion of 1930. The bolted-up frame system was retained and the company claimed to have experienced no breakages with it, other than in accidents. This unorthodox frame, claimed the manufacturers, could be dismantled and stowed in a golf bag. Reassembly was aided by the fact that the pairs of tubes which differed in length were identified by stamped-in numbers.

The Model 19 was introduced by Francis-Barnett in 1931 as a 147cc motorcycle. It was not supplied with lights whereas the otherwise identical Model 20 was. For the following year the bikes were renamed the 23 Merlin and 24 Kestrel as Francis-Barnett started a policy of both numbering their bikes and naming them after birds. The Plover for example was a 1936 Model; there were also Lapwings and Seagulls. The Cruiser was a new model from Francis-Barnett that broke with this tradition in 1933. It remained in the range for several years and was fitted with a Villiers 249cc two-stroke engine with a bore and stroke of 63 x 80mm. It was intended to offer safe, reliable transport to ordinary people and featured a certain amount of weatherproofing. The Cruiser, a popular motorcycle in this guise, survived until the outbreak of World War Two and was one of the machines on which Francis-Barnett established its good reputation.

Right: The Pullman is by any standard an unorthodox motorcycle. Its construction differed from most other marques of the time in most respects, despite the fact motorcycle manufacturers were still generally experimenting with different methods of manufacture.

Above: Francis-Barnett made the unusual claim that their Pullman frame could be dismantled and stowed in a golf bag. However, they made no suggestion as to the stowage of the remainder of the components.

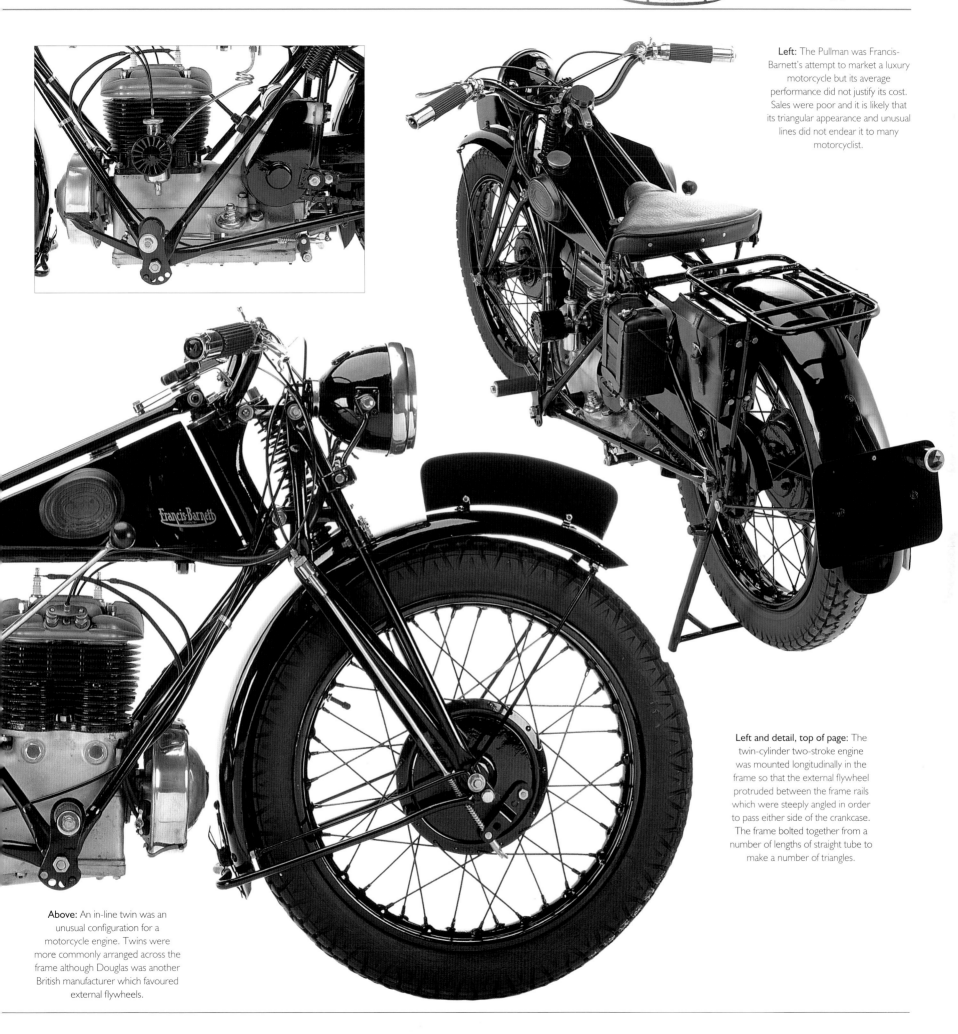

Left: The Pullman was Francis-Barnett's attempt to market a luxury motorcycle but its average performance did not justify its cost. Sales were poor and it is likely that its triangular appearance and unusual lines did not endear it to many motorcyclist.

Left and detail, top of page: The twin-cylinder two-stroke engine was mounted longitudinally in the frame so that the external flywheel protruded between the frame rails which were steeply angled in order to pass either side of the crankcase. The frame bolted together from a number of lengths of straight tube to make a number of triangles.

Above: An in-line twin was an unusual configuration for a motorcycle engine. Twins were more commonly arranged across the frame although Douglas was another British manufacturer which favoured external flywheels.

SPECIFICATIONS

Year: 1958
Engine type: Single
Engine cycle: Two-stroke
Capacity: 197cc (12 cu in)
Bore & stroke: 59 x 72mm
Horsepower: 8bhp @ 4000rpm
Top speed: 55mph (88kph)
Compression ratio: n/a
Carburettor: Villiers
Transmission: 4-speed
Brakes: F. & R. Drum
Ignition: Magneto
Frame: Tubular steel
Suspension: F. Telescopic forks. R. Swingarm and shock absorbers
Wheelbase: 49.75in (1264mm)
Weight: 245lb (111kg)
Fuel: 2 gallons (9.1lit)
Oil: Mixed with fuel
Tyres: 3.00 x 19in

Above: The small fuel tank held 2 gallons (9.1lit) of petrol mixed with oil.

FRANCIS-BARNETT FALCON 81 (1958)

After World War Two the Francis Barnett company returned to the motorcycle market with an autocycle – the Powerbike 50 – and a light-weight motorcycle – the Model 51 Merlin. As in prewar days the latter machine was a Villiers-engined motorcycle. In 1947 the company became part of the AMC group which also produced Matchless and AJS machines. Francis-Barnett products were again based around two-stroke engines of their own and Villiers designs and for a while little changed.

The two postwar models remined in production with minor upgrades; for 1948 the Powerbike was fitted with tubular girder forks in place of the blade ones for example. For 1949 the original Merlin was superseded by two new models based around the Villiers 10D engine, still called Merlins, and the Falcon in two forms using the 6E engine. These new models used the same rigid frame and were equipped with telescopic forks. In this form

the utility models remained in production for several years with only a colour option available for variety; for example, Azure Blue was offered in 1951.

The range was enlarged for 1952 when two motorcycles were offered with swingarm rear suspension. The Villiers 10D-engined version was the Merlin 57 and with the 6E it was known as the Falcon 58. Trials versions were also offered. All the rigid models and Merlins were discontinued for 1954. The Falcon 58 became the 67, although it was produced in almost the same form as before, and some models known as Kestrels were added to the range. So production continued with additions and subtractions to the range until 1958. In this year the Falcon fitted with the 197cc Villiers 10E engine became known as the 81. It was simply a utility commuter two-stroke and, in combination with off-road machines, such products remained in the Francis-Barnett inventory until the company's eventual demise in 1966.

Below: The Falcon 81 was an unremarkable two-stroke commuter bike which remained in production after Francis-Barnett became part of the AMC group.

Right: The 1958 Francis-Barnett Falcon was fitted with a 197cc Villiers 10E engine and simply described as the Falcon 81.

Right: A headlamp nacelle, telescopic forks, valanced mudguard and blade-like number plate are all typical of 1950s' British bikes.

Above: The Villiers 10E engine was unit construction and incorporated a 4-speed gearbox. Final drive was by means of a chain.

FRANCIS-BARNETT TRIALS 85

SPECIFICATIONS
Year: 1962
Engine type: Single
Engine cycle: Two-stroke
Capacity: 249cc (15.2cu in)
Bore & stroke: 66 x 73mm
Horsepower: n/a
Top speed: Dependent on sprocket/gearing
Compression ratio: 9.25:1
Carburettor: Amal
Transmission: 4-speed
Brakes: F. & R. Drum
Ignition: Magneto
Frame: Tubular steel
Suspension: F. Telescopic forks. R. Swingarm and shock absorbers
Wheelbase: n/a
Weight: 271lb (123kg)
Fuel: n/a
Oil: Mixed with fuel
Tyres: F. 3.00 x 21in. R. 4.00 x 19in

Above: Francis-Barnett used Villiers two-stroke engines for their motorcycles but put their own brand name on the primary cover.

FRANCIS-BARNETT TRIALS 85 (1962)

The Francis-Barnett company, which enjoyed a reputation for producing some of the best utility motorcycles around, became part of the Associated Motor Cycles (AMC) Group in 1947. From then on, its products were based around two-stroke engines of AMC and Villiers designs. The Trials 83 entered the company's range in 1959 powered by a 250cc AMC two-stroke engine. It was derived from the Scrambler 82 which was based around the 250cc AMC engine in a high state of tune, a swingarm frame, Girling shock absorbers and a set of Norton forks. The trials version featured the same frame and forks but differed in details.

The Trials 85 made its first appearance in 1960 and it survived in various guises with the AMC engine until 1966. By 1962 Francis-Barnett had long been part of AMC, producers of both the AJS and Matchless marques which had considerable trials and scrambles pedigree. They persevered with this unpopular two-stroke AMC engine into the 1960s until the collapse of AMC and the end of motorcycle production in 1966. The reason for the unpopularity of the AMC engine was because it featured an unusual design of piston, cylinder barrel and cylinder head that proved unreliable for a number of reasons, including poor piston-ring sealing. The Wipac energy transfer ignition system also gained the engine a reputation for poor electrics.

Since its inception, the International Six Days Trial (ISDT) was regarded as a highly prestigious event and manufacturers prepared motorcycles especially for their national teams. For the 1962 event held in Bavaria, Germany, Francis-Barnett machines were chosen as the mount for the English team, possibly as an attempt to prove them.

Despite this success the company had only four more years remaining in the motorcycle manufacturing industry as the market for commuter bikes was contracting. Cheap cars were becoming available and more widely affordable, not to mention the popularity of the Italian-made motor scooter which offered purchasers a mount with more style than a traditional two-stroke motorcycle.

Below: The Francis-Barnett Trials 85 was an unusual machine to be manufactured by AMC whose other marques – AJS and Matchless – already enjoyed considerable off-road competition success.

Left: The front suspension used Norton forks; there were Girling shock absorbers at the rear.

Above: The two-stroke AMC engine was not popular with buyers. Reliability was a perennial problem, and the electrical system proved unsatisfactory.

Above: The Trials 85 used a 249cc two-stroke engine made by AMC themselves, rather than one bought in from Villiers as was normal practice.

SPECIFICATIONS
Year: 1955
Engine type: Single
Engine cycle: Two-stroke
Capacity: 197cc (12cu in)
Bore & stroke: 59 x 72mm
Horsepower: 8.4bhp @ 4000rpm
Top speed: Dependent on gearing
Compression ratio: 7.25:1
Carburettor: Villiers
Transmission: 4-speed
Brakes: F. & R. Drum
Ignition: Magneto
Frame: Cast alloy beam
Suspension: F. & R. Metalastic rubber in torsion elements.
Wheelbase: 52in (1321mm)
Weight: 225lb (102kg)
Fuel: n/a
Oil: Mixed with fuel
Tyres: F. 2.75 x 21in.
R. 4.00 x 18in

Above: Many British manufacturers bought their two-stroke engines from Villiers, and Greeves were no exception as this primary cover logo shows.

Right: Greeves motorcycles were characterized by unusual components, such as the front suspension arrangement using metalastic bushes.

GREEVES TRIALS 20T (1955)

The Greeves company was named after Bert Greeves who came into the motorcycle industry by an indirect route, because he had a disabled cousin, Derry Preston Cobb. Greeves fitted an engine to his invalid cousin's wheelchair and the pair started the commercial manufacture of invalid carriages. The Invacar company flourished after World War Two and the duo decided to begin to manufacture motorcycles. To do this they embarked on a development plan which included entering a prototype in competitive off-road events. As a result the machine became known to the general public and competition allowed both spectators and competitors to see its advanced – albeit unusual – design features. The Greeves used rubber bushes as its suspension medium in a similar way to the invalid carriages. As a consequence Greeves motorcycles had a somewhat unusual appearance through the use of this rubber torsion suspension system. The early motorcycles featured this set-up both front and rear, but the rear suspension was changed to a more conventional hydraulically damped system in the mid-1950s.

The first engine used was a 197cc Villiers two-stroke which was fitted into a duplex loop frame. Drum brakes and a dual seat completed the unorthodox motorcycle. In 1953 the first production machines were assembled using a unique frame that included a cast alloy beam. There were two roadgoing models, the 3-speed 20R and the deluxe 4-speed 20D and two off-road models. These were the 20T and 20S, the suffixes indicating trials and scrambles respectively.

The Trials model 20T had a 21-inch front wheel to increase ground clearance and both the off-road models had wheel hubs unusually fitted with plain bearings which had proved successful during the development of the machines. The four machines had a common frame while many of the cycle parts were fitted to suit the use to which the machine was to be put. As a result the Trials 20T had minimal alloy mudguards and a small fuel tank. The frame was based around the cast alloy I-section beam that ran up from the engine mounts and incorporated the headstock. The casting provided the mounting places for the swingarm pivot although the swingarm itself was tubular steel. The tubular steel section of the frame that carried the fuel-tank mounts and the rear suspension mounts was joined to the cast alloy section during the casting process meaning that the join was permanent.

Above: Greeves motorcycles were constructed around an unusual cast-alloy-beam frame into which the other tubes were permanently cast.

In 1957 the company built a machine known as the Fleetmaster that utilized a British Anzani two-stroke twin engine. At the end of that decade the company marketed models named after famous trials and scrambles, namely the Scottish and the Hawkstone, which reflected the success of the Greeves marque off-road. In the 1960s the company also produced 250cc road-racing motorcycles and its own design of engine. For the off-road machines Greeves continued to use a cast alloy beam in place of front downtubes and fitted a 246cc Villiers engine. With this design of motorcycle their riders, including Dave Bickers and Brian Stonebridge, dominated the 250cc class in motocross for several years. In 1963 Greeves machines were chosen as the mount for the ISDT team that included Triss Sharp. The ISDT bikes were powered by the Mk 36a Villiers two-stroke engine of 246cc displacement and incorporated leading-link forks. Production of Greeves machines stopped during the 1970s, mainly as a result of increasing competition from imported makes and Bert Greeves' retirement.

Above: The Greeves Trials 20T was designed for optimum ground clearance and lightness, hence the alloy mudguards and 21-inch diameter front wheel.

Left: The rear suspension on the 20T used similar metalastic bushes to the front so as to control the movement of the swingarm on rough terrain.

Above: In typical trials bike manner, the exhaust pipe is kept as high as possible and upturned to avoid it coming into contact with the ground.

HESKETH V1000

SPECIFICATIONS
Year: 1982
Engine type: V-twin
Engine cycle: Four-stroke
Capacity: 992cc (60.5cu in)
Bore & stroke: 95 x 70mm
Horsepower: 86bhp @
6500rpm
Top speed: 130.5mph
(210kph)
Compression ratio: 10.5:1
Carburettor: Twin Dell'Orto
Transmission: 5-speed
Brakes: F. Twin discs. R. Disc
Ignition: RITA Electronic
Frame: Duplex tubular cradle
Suspension: F. Telescopic
forks. R. Swingarm and shock
absorbers
Wheelbase: 59.5in (1510mm)
Weight: 498lb (226kg)
Fuel: 5 gallons (22.7lit)
Oil: 6 pints (3.4lit)
Tyres: F. 100/90V19.
R. 130/90V17

Above: For its logo the Hesketh used the coat of arms of Lord Hesketh, the man behind this ill-fated and short-lived attempt to revitalize the British motorcycle industry.

Right: Styling of the Hesketh V1000 was typical of the late 1970s and early 1980s when components such as angular fairings and tanks were globally fashionable.

HESKETH V1000 (1982)

This motorcycle was the fruit of an ambitious but remarkably short-lived attempt to relaunch the much lamented British bike industry by the English peer Lord Hesketh. The motorcycle was launched in 1980 but production did not get underway properly until 1982. This was a consequence of numerous engineering defects that had to be rectified in order to make the machine function properly. Particular attention had to be given to the gearshift mechanism, to reducing the amount of noise made by the engine, and to making the lubrication system leak-proof.

The complex 90-degree V-twin engine was developed by Weslake and featured four valves and two camshafts per cylinder. The engine itself weighed in excess of 220lb (100kg) and looked clumsy partially because of the large covers on the cylinder heads required to enclose the cam chains. The exhausts exited from the front of each cylinder barrel, the front exhaust leading into a silencer on the left side of the bike and the rear into a silencer on the right. Starting was by means of an electric starter. The 5-speed transmission was of a constant mesh design. The remainder of the bike used components and materials that were state-of-the-art at the time of its construction. The front forks were proprietary items from the Italian Marzocchi company, while the 280mm brake discs and calipers were also Italian. These components came from Brembo.

The composite wheels, 17-inch rear and 19-inch front, were made from alloy by Astralite. The duplex cradle frame was of a tubular design that utilized the engine as a stressed member, the frame downtubes ran down to either side of the front cylinder barrel and bolted to the casting. The frame, immediately forward of the swingarm pivot point, bolted to the base of the rear cylinder casting. The swingarm was damped by a pair of adjustable three-position shock absorbers. Final drive was via a wet multiplate clutch by chain to the rear wheel sprocket. The clutch, like the brakes, was hydraulically operated from the handlebar lever.

The V1000 featured a mini-fairing, sometimes referred to as a bikini fairing, while the Vampire models were fully faired versions of the V1000. The styling of both the Vampire and the V1000 now looks dated but it was typical of the era in which it was designed and built. Angular styling of items such as the mini-fairing and fuel tank was not unlike that of early 1980s Japanese bikes with which the Hesketh was intended to compete. Criticisms were made of the tall seat height of 33 inches (812mm).

The manufacturer, Hesketh Motorcycles Ltd, went into receivership after fewer than 150 motorcycles had been built. Other companies, including Hesleydon Ltd, Mocheck Ltd and Mick Broom Engineering, sought to continue production, but despite their efforts, it is believed that a total of fewer than 250 Heskeths were built up to 1988.

Above: The clocks; speedometer, tachometer, chronometer, mileometer and trip meter were contained in an instrument binnacle positioned behind the windscreen of the bikini fairing.

Below: The lines of the dual seat flowed out of those of the fuel tank. A criticism of the machine voiced after its launch was that the tall seat height made it difficult to ride for many riders.

Left: The styling of the Hesketh was acceptable for its time of manufacture and compared favourably with Japanese sports machines of the period. Indeed a Hesketh on the road is still an imposing sight.

Left: The components used in the construction of the machine were of the highest quality. The telescopic forks were Italian, made by Marzocchi, while the duplex cradle frame used the engine as a stressed member.

Above: The engine, a 90-degree V-twin, was developed by Weslake for Hesketh. It was a heavy dohc unit and certain aspects of its styling, such as the camshaft covers, did little to enhance its appearance.

Right: The wheels were made from alloy by Astralite. The front one was 19 inches in diameter and fitted with a pair of Italian Brembo brake discs and calipers for which the hydraulic fluid master cylinder was located on the handlebars, as is normal practice.

HRD 350 RACER

SPECIFICATIONS
Year: 1925
Engine type: Ohv single
Engine cycle: Four-stroke
Capacity: 344cc (21cu in)
Bore & stroke: 74 x 80mm
Horsepower: 20bhp
Top speed: 85mph (137kph)
Compression ratio: n/a
Carburettor: Amal
Transmission: 3-speed
Brakes: F. & R. Drum
Ignition: Magneto
Frame: Steel tube
Suspension: F. Spring forks.
R. None
Wheelbase: n/a
Weight: 300lb (136kg)
Fuel: n/a
Oil: n/a
Tyres: 3.00 x 19in

Above: The 3-speed Burman gearbox was controlled by a hand-change lever on the right side of the fuel tank.

Right: HRD stands for Howard R. Davies, the initials of the man who designed and built these machines using JAP overhead-valve single-cylinder engines.

HRD 350 (1925)

The initials HRD were those of Howard R. Davies, whose involvement with motorcycles started when he was an apprentice at AJS. He became an ardent enthusiast and raced a Sunbeam motorcycle prior to World War One, and went on to race a 350cc AJS after it. On the AJS he won the 1921 Isle of Man Senior TT. This was particularly noteworthy because he had beaten 500cc machines on his 350. Three years later, in 1924, he founded his own motorcycle manufacturing company.

HRD machines were designed by E. J. Massey and generally used JAP engines and Burman gearboxes in their own frames. They were fitted with Druid sprung girder forks, drum brakes and a shapely, slim, flat fuel tank. The machines were finished in black although the tank was pin-striped in gold and carried the manufacturer's initials picked out in the same colour. The bikes had sporting lines with a low saddle and dropped handlebars. Notice on this 1925 machine, for example, how the line of the saddle continues that of the fuel tank into the rear seat pad. Such aesthetic considerations were not always taken into account by motorcycle manufacturers in the 1920s.

Aboard one of his eponymous motorcycles Howard Davies won the 1925 Senior TT at the Isle of Man. He also placed second in the 1921 and 1925 Junior TTs. Some HRD machines were powered by JAP side-valve engines of 490cc displacement, but it was the overhead-valve machines

that had racing success. The overhead-valve JAP engine used in the race-bikes had twin exhaust ports and was coupled to a hand-change 3-speed Burman gearbox. Both primary and final drive were by chains. The oil tank was located behind the seat post under the saddle.

Two years after Davies' TT victory Freddy Dixon won the Junior TT on an HRD motorcycle. This was in 1927, ironically the same year as HRD closed for financial reasons. This was a familiar story for companies who viewed racing success as the chief priority. The business had failed but Davies was still held in high regard because his motorcycles were of such high quality. This explains why, in 1928, OK Supreme bought the rights to the company and hired Davies' designer, E. J. Massey. OK Supreme later sold the HRD name to Philip Vincent who manufactured Vincent-HRD motorcycles. One of the reasons Vincent wanted to use the HRD brand name was because his philosophy about the design and marketing of motorcycles was similar to Davies'. He too wanted to build small numbers of high quality sports machines. The original HRD designs were a success to the extent that a German company, Hako, copied them. This manufacturer, named after its founder, Hans Korn, also based its machines on the 348 and 490cc displacement JAP engines between 1924 and 1925. Hako subsequently changed its name to HKR – Hans Korn of Rothenburg – and made similar machines between 1925 and 1926, when it ceased trading.

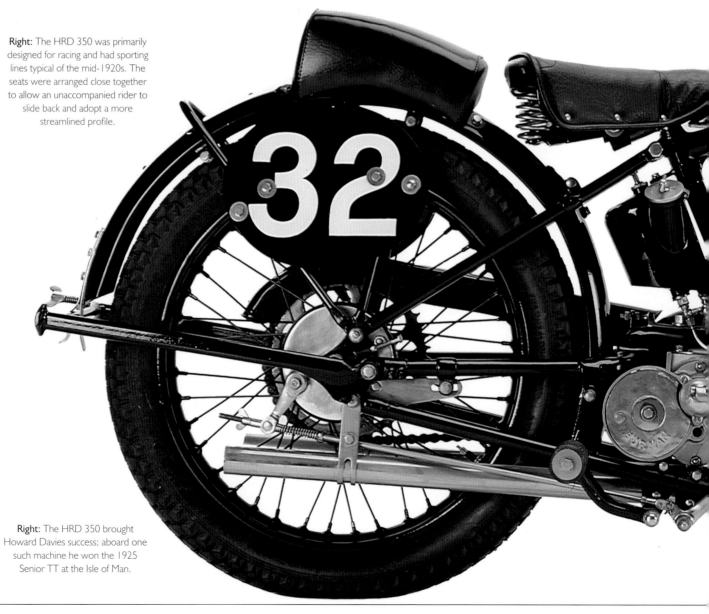

Right: The HRD 350 was primarily designed for racing and had sporting lines typical of the mid-1920s. The seats were arranged close together to allow an unaccompanied rider to slide back and adopt a more streamlined profile.

Right: The HRD 350 brought Howard Davies success; aboard one such machine he won the 1925 Senior TT at the Isle of Man.

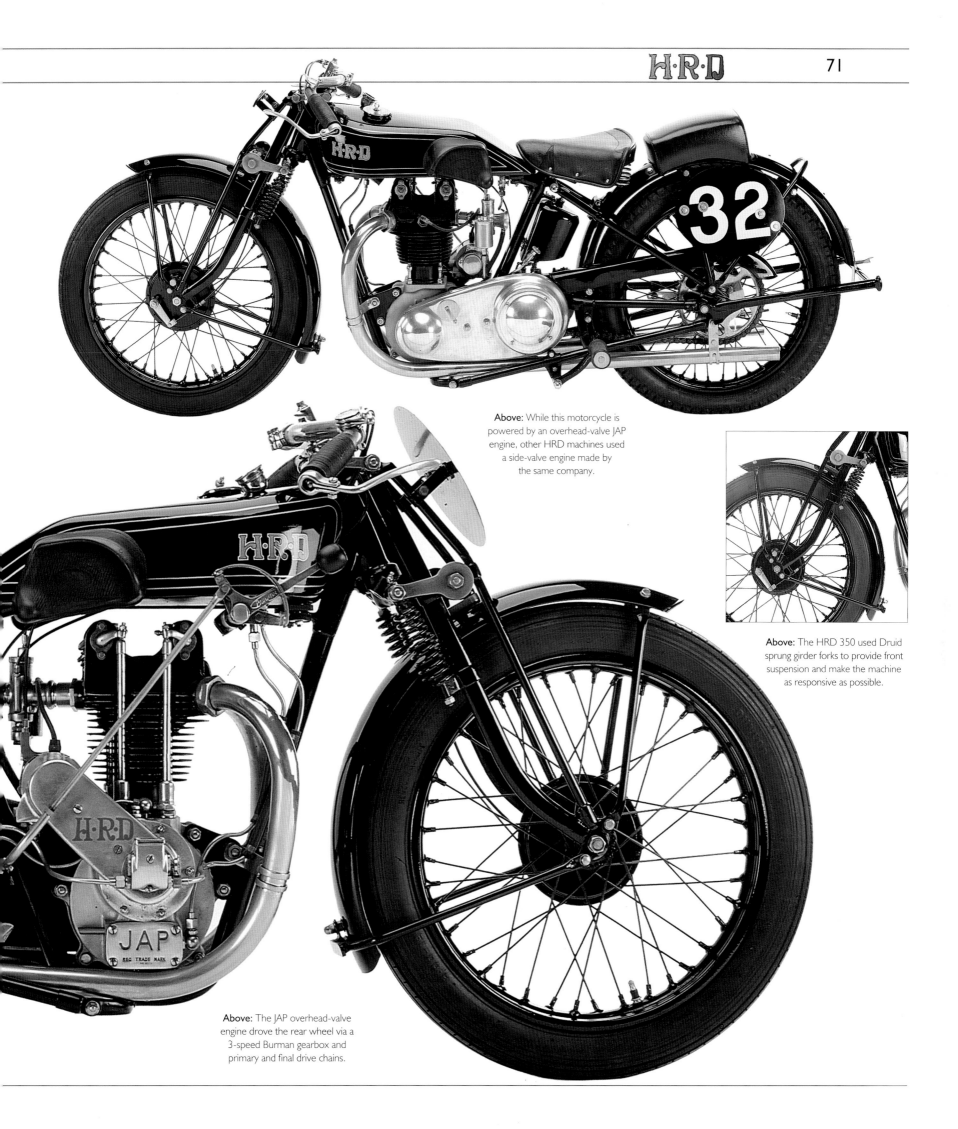

Above: While this motorcycle is powered by an overhead-valve JAP engine, other HRD machines used a side-valve engine made by the same company.

Above: The HRD 350 used Druid sprung girder forks to provide front suspension and make the machine as responsive as possible.

Above: The JAP overhead-valve engine drove the rear wheel via a 3-speed Burman gearbox and primary and final drive chains.

JAMES D1 FLYING ACE

SPECIFICATIONS
Year: 1932
Engine type: Ohv V-twin
Engine cycle: Four-stroke
Capacity: 499cc (30.5cu in)
Bore & stroke: 64 x 77.5mm
Horsepower: n/a
Top speed: n/a
Compression ratio: n/a
Carburettor: Amal
Transmission: 3-speed
Brakes: F. & R. Drum
Ignition: Magneto
Frame: Bolted steel tubular
Suspension: F. Sprung girders.
R. None
Wheelbase: n/a
Weight: n/a
Fuel: n/a
Oil: n/a
Tyres: F. 3.25 x 19in.
R. 3.50 x 19in

Above: The makers of the Flying Ace included nice details such as the brand name cast into the face of this foot pedal.

Right: The D1 Flying Ace was one of the last V-twin-engined motorcycles made by James as the Depression era market was moving towards lightweight machines. The two exhaust pipes were designed so that one pipe was on either side of the machine for a symmetrical appearance.

JAMES D1 FLYING ACE (1932)

James traced its roots back to Harry James' Birmingham-based pedal-cycle manufacturing company which was founded in the closing decades of the nineteenth century. It produced its first motorcycle in 1902. The company had an innovative style and used engines from FN as well as those of their own design. One unorthodox machine made in 1908 featured one-sided wheel fixings, hub-centre steering and drum brakes and was powered by James' own engine. Hub-centre steering and single-sided wheel attachments have been in vogue much more recently: the former in a 1990s Yamaha and the latter in a 1980s BMW, for example.

The factory burned down in 1920 which was a considerable setback and as a result production was badly affected for two years. Following this interruption the company produced singles and V-twins in relatively small numbers. For the 1930s their range included both James- and Villiers-powered motorcycles of small displacement because the company had identified which way their market was moving. These bikes were conventional with rigid frames and girder forks, and were typical of utility machines of the period. A 499cc Rudge-engined machine, the C3, was offered briefly in 1931. The company concentrated their range solely on utility bikes from then on.

The Flying Ace of 1932 was a model that derived from a range of V-twins from 1930. In that year the machines were called the Models B1, B2 and B3. Only the B1 had an overhead-valve engine although all dis-

placed 499cc and had the same bore and stroke of 64 x 77.5mm. These motorcycles featured 3-speed transmissions although a 4-speed unit was available as an extra-cost option. The range of V-twins was trimmed to two for 1931 – the C1 and C2 being overhead-valve and side-valve offerings respectively. They were also given names: the ohv machine became the Flying Ace, while the side-valve was tagged the Grey Ghost. Both continued for 1932 as the D1 and D2 and were improved by the fitment

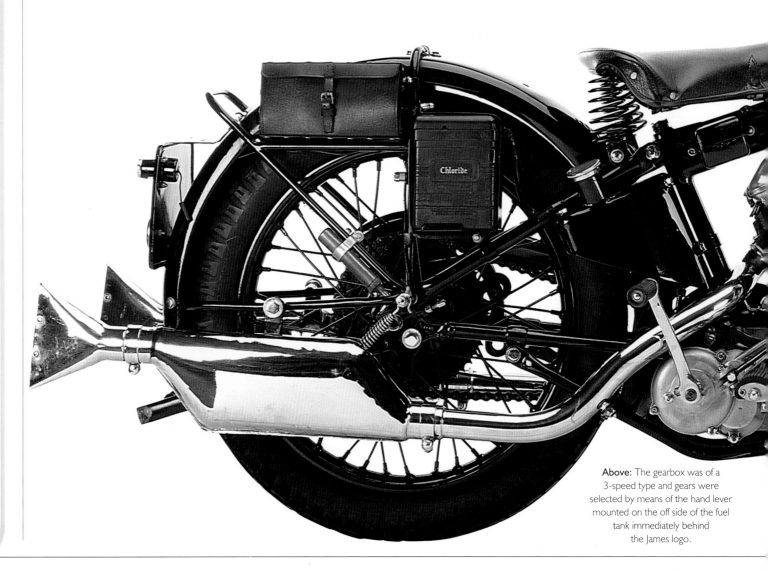

Above: The gearbox was of a 3-speed type and gears were selected by means of the hand lever mounted on the off side of the fuel tank immediately behind the James logo.

Left: The inlet valves of both cylinders of the V-twin engine were supplied with fuel by a single carburettor mounted on a manifold between the cylinder barrels.

of oil-bath chain cases. The overhead-valve V-twin was dropped for 1933 as the company concentrated more on small-capacity machines, but the side-valve model became the E2 Flying Ghost. It ran on for a couple more years unchanged. This, the final James V-twin-engined bike, was finally dropped in 1936. By 1937 all the engines were bought in from Villiers.

World War Two saw James' factory once again almost destroyed in the Blitz. Despite this, by 1943 the James ML – Military Lightweight – was rolling off the production line. It was intended for airborne soldiers. The ML, of which 6,000 were manufactured, had a 122cc engine and became the basis of a civilian model postwar. Later a new range of machines was introduced that included the Captain, Commodore, Comet, Colonel and Cadet. In the mid-1950s AMC acquired the company and a number of AMC engines appeared in the James range. Towards the end of the 1950s James fitted an AMC engine into the model called the Flying Cadet. It was a mixture of Cadet cycle parts mated to the AMC two-stroke engine. Production stopped in 1964.

Right: The magneto for the ignition was positioned in front of the forward cylinder. The drive to it is contained within the distinctively shaped cover that connects to the crankcase.

Below: The D1 did not have rear suspension other than that provided in the springing of the solo saddle. Provision of rear suspension as a matter of course came postwar.

Left: Equipment required to make the Flying Ace legal for road use included the horn and headlamp mounted on the girder forks as well as the number plate fitted on the front mudguard, and the rear light and number plate mounted on the rear mudguard.

Above: The oil pump to provide engine lubrication was gear-driven and affixed to the crankcase in order to facilitate this. The lubrication oil flowed to and from it through metal tubes.

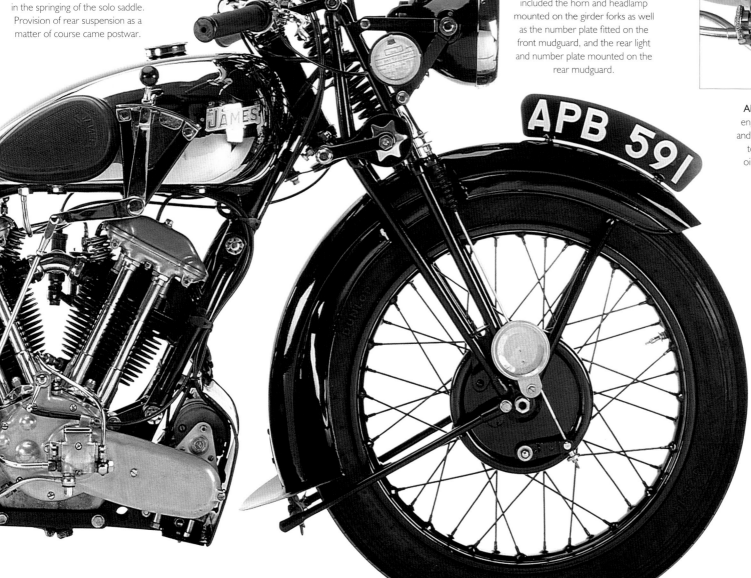

APB 591

JAP SPEEDWAY MOTORCYCLE

JAP SPEEDWAY MOTORCYCLE

SPECIFICATIONS
Year: n/a
Engine type: Single
Engine cycle: n/a
Capacity: 500cc (30.5cu in)
Bore & stroke: n/a
Horsepower: n/a
Top speed: Dependent on sprocket
Compression ratio: n/a
Carburettor: Amal
Transmission: Single-speed
Brakes: None
Ignition: n/a
Frame: Tubular cradle
Suspension: None
Wheelbase: n/a
Weight: 180lb (82kg)
Fuel: 4 pints (2.27lit)
Oil: n/a
Tyres: F. 21in. R. 19in

Above: JAP was noted for the manufacture of engines which it sold to other firms, but the company also made speedway motorcycles in its own right.

Right: Speedway motorcycles are a particularly specialized form of racing machine, being designed solely for use in cinder-track competition.

The initials JAP stand for J.A. Prestwich which was the name of a company based in Tottenham, London that was chiefly famous for supplying engines to other manufacturers. The company was founded in 1903 and did build complete motorcycles until 1908 when a decision was made only to build engines for supply to others. In the postwar years the engine factory was taken over by Villiers who also supplied their engines to other manufacturers. During the 1930s the JAP company produced its own frames designed especially for speedway use.

Speedway was one area of motorcycle competition where JAP-engined machines were particularly successful. Speedway is a fast spectacular form of motorcycle sport that takes place on quarter-mile oval cinder tracks. It originated in the America in the early years of the twentieth century and was imported to Britain during the 1920s. Speedway bikes are devoid of brakes and riders slow down by sliding the machines sideways into the turns while travelling anti-clockwise around the track. Unusually speedway is a team sport; the racing is divided into a series of four races with two riders from each team participating in each race. The placings are awarded points and the team with the highest number of points wins the meeting. Speedway is popular in the UK, USA and Scandinavia.

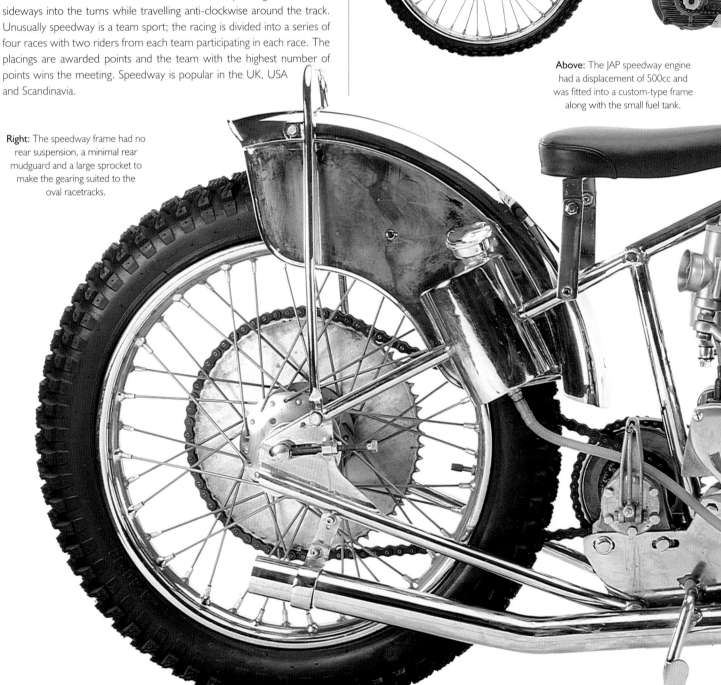

Above: The JAP speedway engine had a displacement of 500cc and was fitted into a custom-type frame along with the small fuel tank.

Right: The speedway frame had no rear suspension, a minimal rear mudguard and a large sprocket to make the gearing suited to the oval racetracks.

Below: The JAP speedway bike was totally devoid of suspension having both a rigid frame and forks.

Below: Speedway bikes such as this JAP have no brakes and rely on the rider sliding them into the turns to slow down during races.

When speedway racing first attracted the crowds, Douglas machines were pre-eminent, but as the sport evolved, the tracks changed and riding styles changed to suit them. Rudge machines with a shorter wheelbase were then particularly successful until the advent of the JAP speedway engine in 1931. This machine's dominance of the sport lasted until ESO machines made in Czechoslovakia began to be used outside their country of origin in the late 1950s. ESO became part of Jawa in 1966 and the Czechoslovakian dominance of speedway continued until the mid-1970s. In 1974 a British firm, Weslake Ltd from Rye in Sussex, announced their four-valve speedway engine. The four-valve engine was not necessarily faster in terms of top speed but it developed its power more quickly, which is what gave it the edge in speedway competition. The Weslake was dominant through the remainder of the 1970s and the early 1980s.

A speedway motorcycle such as this is an example of a completely specialized machine, even more so than trials and scrambles bikes. The basic shape of speedway bikes has not altered since the 1940s. The motorcycles are designed only to turn left by sliding into the turns so they have steeply angled forks to give fast steering and improved control while sliding. Speedway bikes do not have brakes in accordance with the rules and carry only enough fuel and oil for four laps at a time. Because of the cornering technique the design of footpegs is asymmetric. The rider puts his right foot on a peg in the normal fashion but has the left peg designed to enable him to put his foot down quickly and frequently. American Bruce Penhall and New Zealander Ivan Mauger are two of speedway racing's legends who have both been world champion on more than one occasion.

Left: To keep weight to a minimum, the small tank only held enough fuel for one short race.

Right: The knobbly tyres used in speedway are similar to those used in off-road competition and are intended to give traction in the loose surface of the cinder track.

MATCHLESS G3L

Above: The G3L used an overhead camshaft 350cc single-cylinder engine for its motive power. The engine had been in use by AMC long before the outbreak of war.

Right: The Matchless G3L was produced in great numbers for the British Army during World War Two. In this form with telescopic front forks it was probably the wartime despatch rider's – Don R in military parlance – favourite military machine because of its ease of riding.

MATCHLESS G3L (1941)

Founded in 1899, Matchless had acquired AJS in 1931 and by 1935 it had introduced a model style common to both marques. This was the G3 Clubman. In 1937 the company acquired Sunbeam and became AMC – Associated Motor Cycles – Ltd. The AMC identity was retained when in 1943 the Sunbeam name was sold to BSA. In 1938 World War Two was looming and during the war years the company was to build 80,000 Matchless 350cc motorcycles. These were the G3 and G3L models.

The prewar G3 Clubman used an overhead-valve single-cylinder engine that was positioned vertically in the frame. Prior to this Matchless engines had been inclined forwards. The new engine featured hairpin valve springs and dry-sump lubrication. The magneto and dynamo were located behind the cylinder where they were chain-driven from the crankshaft. A Burman 4-speed gearbox was fitted with the engine into a tubular steel duplex cradle frame. The frame lacked suspension at the rear but was equipped with girder forks at the front. In this basic form the motorcycle lasted until 1940 when the frame was redesigned to incorporate a single downtube.

The wartime requirement for military motorcycles meant that the G3 (in a slightly revised form) became AMC's military motorcycle. At first AMC offered the War Department the G3WO (the WO suffix indicated War Office) which, with a number of modifications, became the G3. Approximately 18,500 G3WO motorcycles were supplied to the British Army. The G3WO was based on the new single downtube frame – still with girder forks but with the addition of a coat of khaki paint. In this form it was supplied to the Army, although minor upgrades were made between batches progressively supplied to fulfil different contracts.

The girder forks of the G3WO were superseded in 1941 by the telescopic forks of the G3L, although it was not until 1942 that the G3L reached despatch riders in any numbers. The L suffix indicated lightweight – the new model was lighter than its predecessor. The telescopic forks enhanced the handling characteristics of the Matchless and soon established it as a favourite with military riders. It had a reputation for a decent level of on- and off-road performance. The teledraulic forks, for example, offered twice the suspension travel of the girder forks still used by other British motorcycle manufacturers at the time. Like its predecessor the G3L was upgraded during its production run. Some of the, admittedly minor,

Above: Army despatch riders were expected to be able to carry out numerous repairs and checks to their machines and to this end a selection of tools were carried in the asymmetric tool box fitted to the frame behind the gearbox and oil tank.

changes were made to simplify production, while others were intended to improve the machine. Standardized components, such as pannier frames, were also fitted.

In its final form the Matchless G3L can almost be considered the first "modern" motorcycle: in postwar years telescopic forks quickly became the norm. Matchless introduced civilian variants of the G3L in 1946. They manufactured both 348cc and 497cc displacement machines as did AJS. The AJS machines were almost identical to the Matchless models except for the position of the magneto. Both companies went on to produce competition versions of these motorcycles. The differences between roadgoing and competition models were minimal and were basically confined to wheels, tyres and mudguards.

Above: Military motorcycles were painted in drab colours to camouflage them. The British Army used a flat green for European combat areas and a sand yellow for vehicles deployed in North Africa. This G3L is finished as one used in North Africa in the campaigns against Erwin Rommel's Afrika Korps.

Left: Although most of the motorcycles used by the British Army were military versions of civilian bikes, a number of specifically military fittings were installed. These included the blackout cover over the headlamp and the military panniers and rack on the rear mudguard.

Right: The telescopic forks were termed teledraulic by AMC, manufacturer of the Matchless G3L. They were considered an innovation at the time simply because all the other machines in use by the British forces were fitted with the conventional sprung-girder forks.

MATCHLESS G9

MATCHLESS G45

Right: The Matchless G9 was introduced as a new model in 1949. It used a twin-cylinder engine but shared many of its other parts with the Matchless singles.

MATCHLESS G9 (1953)

The Matchless company was founded in 1899 by the Collier brothers and for its first years it used a wide variety of proprietary engines from the likes of JAP and De Dion. Harry and Charlie Collier had considerable Isle of Man TT successes on Matchless machines in the earliest years of the event. By the start of the 1930s Matchless produced a range of singles of varying capacities and a V-twin intended for sidecar duties. The company experimented with a couple of vee configuration engines: a V-twin and a V-four that was essentially two V-twins joined together.

The G3 Clubman was introduced in 1935 and it set the style for the Matchless range from then on. During the postwar years Matchless and AJS models were identical (AJS had been acquired in 1931) although the parent company persevered with marketing both brands, even going so far as to advertise them separately. AMC later took over Francis-Barnett, James, Norton and the US manufacturer Indian of Springfield, Massachusetts. The company went into decline soon after and later became part of a group owned by Dennis Poore. He transferred production to Andover in Hampshire and continued production of Norton and AJS machines. Matchless then gradually faded into history.

After World War Two, the company produced a range of both singles and twins. Both were used extensively for competitive motorcycling; the singles in off-road events, and both singles and twins for road- and circuit-racing. The G9 was introduced as a new model in 1949. It was a typically British parallel twin, although it had three main bearings. The camshafts ran fore and aft and both dynamo and magneto were gear-driven. Its cycle parts were common to the sprung single. The G9 was manufactured until 1959 with only minor changes made to it through its ten-year production run.

Right: The cycle parts used on the G9, such as the forks and fuel tank, were used across the Matchless range. The production run of the G9 lasted a decade.

Above: The parallel-twin engine displaced 498cc, the camshafts ran fore and aft and the dynamo and magneto were gear-driven.

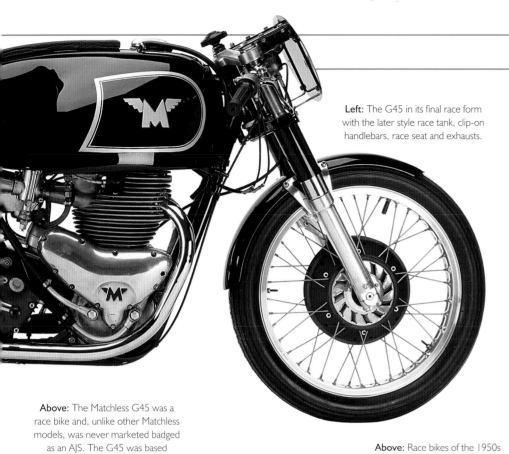

Left: The G45 in its final race form with the later style race tank, clip-on handlebars, race seat and exhausts.

Above: The Matchless G45 was a race bike and, unlike other Matchless models, was never marketed badged as an AJS. The G45 was based around the 498cc parallel-twin engine of the G9 but in a higher state of tune.

Below: Matchless had pioneered swinging arm rear suspension during the war years on the G3L and so used it on their postwar models.

Above: Race bikes of the 1950s have a grace and thoroughbred style not found in the majority of roadgoing machines of the same era with a few notable exceptions, such as Vincent.

MATCHLESS G45 (1957)

As both AJS and Matchless were part of AMC, and their machines were almost identical except for the badges, it was perhaps a surprise that the 7R was only ever built as an AJS racer. This imbalance was redressed in 1953 when the Matchless G45 was announced. This twin was also a racer and it was only ever assembled as a Matchless. The G45 was closely based on the 498cc twin engine which had powered racers in the 1951 Clubman's TT. A hybrid, the twin engine mounted in an AJS 7R frame, had been entered in the Manx Grand Prix of 1952. Derek Farrant brought it home first to what became a somewhat controversial win because the event was not officially open to prototype machines.

The announcement that a batch of similar machines would be built in 1953 went some way to resolving the issue. The G45 engine followed the G9 design closely, but the camshafts and pistons were changed for racing parts and alloy cylinder barrels were fitted. Triple valve springs were installed along with a racing magneto and the various covers were cast in magnesium alloy. A pair of twin Amal GP carburettors supplied as much fuel and air mixture as was required for racing and a rev counter enabled the rider to keep an eye on the engine's performance. This engine was fitted to a frame that was essentially the 7R unit modified to accommodate the twin-cylinder engine with its two exhaust pipes.

In this form the G45 continued until 1956 when the cycle parts were refined slightly, and a new-style tank, clip-on bars and different exhausts were instituted. The motorcycle was unchanged for the following year. This was 1957 and it proved to be the last production year for the G45 as it was becoming less competitive on race circuits.

Right: The clip-on bars are so described because they are fitted to the fork tubes and allow the rider to lean forward over the tank to create a streamlined shape.

Above: The rear seat is long and features a raised tail section to allow the rider to slide back on the seat to lower his profile and so enhance streamlining.

Right: The Matchless was a British parallel twin in the style of early 1960s café racers. It had minimal, race-inspired lines and could exceed 100mph (161kph).

MATCHLESS G12CSR (1960)

The CSR suffix first appeared in 1958 on a slightly tuned version of the Matchless 593cc twin that had been introduced in 1956 by AMC as the G11. The new models for 1958 were the G11CS and G11CSR. The former was a street scrambler with siamesed exhaust pipes, wide section tyres, a small fuel tank, alloy guards and removable lights. The latter was a sports-styled machine based around the CS engine, frame, exhaust and fuel tank but fitted with a competition dual seat and removable lights. The real racer was the new 496cc G50, the prototype of which competed in the Isle of Man TT of the same year. Production continued with much of the Matchless range unaltered for 1959, although the twins were offered with larger displacement. Displacement of the twin was now 646cc and it was offered as the G12 in four models, namely the G12, G12dl, G12CS and G12CSR. These were the standard, de luxe, CS and CSR models. The differences were minor, the standard G12 had alternator and coil ignition while the others retained their magneto. The standard model had a slightly different finish to the de luxe models, while the CS and CSR were as they had been in 1958.

AMC owned both AJS and Matchless and the company produced almost identical motorcycles with AJS and Matchless badges on. The AJS models comparable to the Matchless G11CSR and G12CSR machines were the AJS 30 CSR and AJS 31 CSR. The race bikes were an exception to this rule: the G50 and AJS 7R models were more distinct from another. Later the Matchless variant of the CSR twin was given the name Monarch and the Apache for export sales to the USA. The 650 was the basis of the motorcycle that won the 500-mile race at Thruxton, Hampshire in 1960. One of the last improvements to the CSR was the provision of a duplex cradle frame from 1961 onwards. The CSR tag was used on a smaller capacity range of single-cylinder 250cc machines from 1962.

The company, if not British motorcycling, was in decline by 1962 and the famous competition workshop at the Woolwich factory was closed. This ended a long chapter of works competition successes, particularly in off-road motorcycle sport such as trials and scrambles. Norton had been

Right: The flat dual seat over a small rear mudguard and vertical rear shock absorber looks almost austere, but the rakish angle of the silencer suggests speed.

Below: Matchless were noted for the manufacture of single-cylinder-engined motorcycles but felt obliged to follow the postwar trend within the British industry towards twins.

Above: The engine was an overhead-valve vertical parallel twin fitted with a single Amal carb. In this 1960 form it was capable of over "the ton".

acquired by Associated Motor Cycles Ltd in 1956, but by 1966 sales of AMC machines had dropped to such an extent that liquidation was inevitable. Manganese Bronze bought the assets of the company and developed the Norton-Villiers group as a going concern. This group later absorbed BSA/Triumph. In the course of these various amalgamations the AJS and Matchless names soon disappeared permanently with the exception of a two-stroke scrambler that was badged as an AJS for a short period. This was the AJS FB Ajay powered by a 247cc single-cylinder engine with a 4-speed gearbox. The FB Ajay was a curious mixture of old and new elements, such as an alloy tank and plastic mudguards. The name Matchless, however, was a thing of the past.

Above: The G12CSR soon gained the nickname of coffee shop racer as a result of its suffix. The nickname may have been slightly derogatory, suggestive of sporting pretensions rather than actual prowess.

Left: The Matchless featured a chromed petrol tank at a time when painted ones were more the norm. The winged M on the tank was Matchless's famous logo and it continued to be used despite AMC's ownership of the firm.

Right: A full hub-width drum brake was used to stop the G12CSR and laced to a 19-inch diameter front wheel as was normal practice.

Norton

NORTON MODEL 18

SPECIFICATIONS
Year: 1927
Engine type: Single
Engine cycle: Four-stroke
Capacity: 490cc (29.9cu in)
Bore & stroke: 79 x 100mm
Horsepower: 18bhp
Top speed: 80mph (129kph)
Compression ratio: n/a
Carburettor: Amal
Transmission: 3-speed
Brakes: F. & R. Drum
Ignition: Magneto
Frame: Steel diamond
Suspension: F. Sprung girder forks. R. None
Wheelbase: n/a
Weight: 336lb (152kg)
Fuel: 2.75 gallons (12.5lit)
Oil: 4 pints (2.27lit)
Tyres: 3.25 x 19in

Right: The Model 18 used what is known as a steel "diamond" frame so-called because of its diamond-like profile.

NORTON MODEL 18 (1927)

Norton is one of the legendary names of the British motorcycle industry; it was founded as the Norton Manufacturing Company by James Lansdowne Norton in 1901. His first motorcycles used Swiss Moto-Rêve and French Peugeot engines and were built in England under licence. Aboard a V-twin Norton, Rembrandt H. "Rem" Fowler won the twin-cylinder class of the 1907 Isle of Man TT, the first running of the event. A single of 633cc was marketed in 1908 and another model of 490cc in 1911. By 1913 the company was known as Norton Motors Ltd. Norton produced its first overhead-valve single in 1922. It was the Model 18, an example of which is illustrated here. During this period the company was expanding and moved to new premises in Bracebridge Street, Aston, Birmingham. Production was running at about 4,500 motorcycles per year. In 1924 Nortons won both the Sidecar TT and the Senior TT on the Isle of Man, the victorious riders and passenger being George Tucker and Walter Moore, and Alec Bennett respectively.

Above: The Norton Model 18 used a newly designed overhead-valve engine Its antecedent, the Model 16, was a side-valve.

Below: The fishtail exhaust pipe was positioned on the left side of the bike. There was no rear suspension.

Above: The gearbox was a 3-speed assembly mounted into the frame in the conventional position behind the engine with the oil tank attached to the frame above it.

In 1925 J. L. Norton passed away but the company continued in business. The racing department saw the arrival of Joe Craig as boss and he oversaw the firm's win at the 1926 Isle of Man TT with a 348cc overhead-valve single. Walter Moore, the racing sidecar passenger, designed the first overhead-camshaft Norton before leaving to work for NSU in Germany. With the new ohc engine Alec Bennet and Stanley Woods were able to dominate the 1927 TT. Participation in racing was encouraged because it was seen to demonstrate both the speed and reliability of the Norton and thereby to promote sales. Some felt that Norton's roadgoing bikes looked dated by the end of the 1920s but a revamp was not long in coming. Arthur Carroll replaced Moore in the design department and redesigned Norton's engine into a unit that would endure until 1963.

Below: the Model 18 had a long slim fuel tank located between the parallel top tubes of the bicycle-like frame. Rubber knee grips were affixed to the tank.

Above: The Norton Model 18 featured an unusually shaped headlamp. Lights were powered by electricity, which was superseding carbide by this time.

Above: The magneto was located forward of the engine and its drive was sited in the horizontal alloy cover connecting it to the crankcase. The valves and rockers were exposed atop the engine.

NORTON 16H

SPECIFICATIONS
Year: 1942
Engine type: Side-valve single
Engine cycle: Four-stroke
Capacity: 490cc (29.9cu in)
Bore & stroke: 79 x 100mm
Horsepower: 12bhp @ 4800rpm
Top speed: 60mph (97kph)
Compression ratio: 4.9:1
Carburettor: Amal
Transmission: 4-speed
Brakes: F. & R. Drum
Ignition: Magneto
Frame: Tubular steel
Suspension: F. Girder forks.
R. None
Wheelbase: 54in (1372mm)
Weight: 388lb (176kg)
Fuel: 3.25 gallons (14.8lit)
Oil: 3 pints (1.7lit)
Tyres: F. 3.0 x 19in.
R. 3.50 x 19in

Above: The carefully gilded logo looks somewhat incongruous on the military drab paintwork.

NORTON MODEL 16H (1942)

Prewar Norton models were generally given numerical/alphabetical designations and in the early 1930s their range consisted of machines such as the 348cc JE and CJ, the 490cc 16H and the 588cc Model 19, amongst others. The line-up was gradually updated through the 1930s; for example, Norton introduced a 4-speed gearbox in 1933. The last years before World War Two saw the introduction of the Racing International models, which were also referred to as the Manx Grand Prix bikes and were the foundations on which the postwar Manx Norton was based.

The Norton 16H was a side-valve single-cylinder machine that went into production long before the outbreak of World War Two. Its history stretched back to 1911. During the 1920s it had been a sporting motorcycle and it had been modernized for the 1930s. The 490cc single was initially fitted with a 3-speed gearbox but this had been upgraded to a 4-speed in 1935. The 16H was considered the most suitable machine for

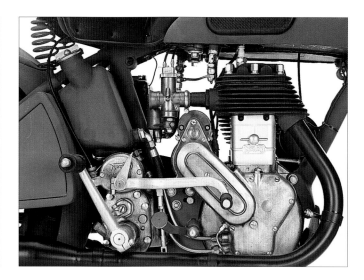

Below: The large panniers are typical of the equipment fitted to the 16H for military duties.

Above: The 16H Norton was manufactured in large numbers for the British Army during World War Two. It was closely based on a prewar design.

military purposes during the months prior to the outbreak of war and it remained in production as Norton's military motorcycle based on the 1937 civilian model. Through the war years Norton's Bracebridge Street works supplied 100,000 of their 16H models to the British Army. In much smaller numbers they supplied the Big 4 sidecar outfit with a driven sidecar wheel to make it suitable for cross-country use. The 16H was reintroduced after the war in a slightly updated frame but it was essentially the same machine in civilian colours.

Right: Front suspension was by means of girder forks. The speedometer was mounted on a bracket fixed to the handlebars.

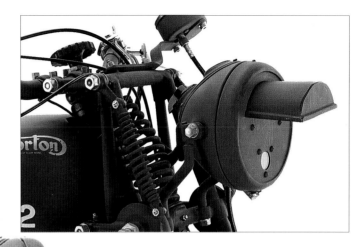

Left: The 490cc side-valve engine was built by Norton for many years. Here it is seen with enclosed valve gear and the 4-speed gearbox that was first fitted in 1935.

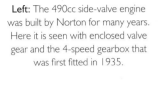

Left: The British War Department specified a number of military fittings including the blackout headlamp cover designed to minimize light "scatter" from the lamp.

NORTON 30M MANX (1954)

NORTON MANX

SPECIFICATIONS
Year: 1954
Engine type: Ohc single
Engine cycle: Four-stroke
Capacity: 498cc (30.39cu in)
Bore & stroke: 86 x 85.8mm
Horsepower: 47bhp @ 6500rpm.
Top speed: (est) 120mph (193kph)
Compression ratio: 9.53:1
Carburettor: Amal
Transmission: 4-speed
Brakes: F. TLS drum. R. Drum
Ignition: Magneto
Frame: Duplex cradle
Suspension: F. Telescopic forks. R. Swingarm and shock absorbers
Wheelbase: 54.5in (1384mm)
Weight: 309lb (140kg)
Fuel: 3.5 gallons (15.9lit)
Oil: 6 pints (3.4lit)
Tyres: F. 3.00 x 19in. R. 3.50 x 19in

As Norton returned to civilian motorcycle production after World War Two, they updated their wartime 16H single as a ride-to-work and side-car machine. During 1946 they also produced a number of road-racing machines in time for the Manx Grand Prix of that year. These were the first postwar racers and closely based on the prewar Norton racers; listed as the 348cc 40M and 498cc 30M, they were also the first to be known as Manx Nortons. Both were built around Carroll-type overhead-camshaft singles with a shaft and bevel drive to the camshaft. The engine resembled the prewar designs and used a magneto and Amal carburettor. The frame was of the cradle type with plunger rear suspension and the forks were the Norton Roadholders, and in this form the motorcycles became referred to as "garden gate" Nortons.

By 1950 the much vaunted swingarm "Featherbed" frame was in use and racers including Geoff Duke and Artie Bell brought competition success to Norton. By 1951, production Manx Nortons were assembled with the Featherbed frame, a new gearbox and 19-inch diameter wheels. The famous Featherbed frame had been developed by Rex McCandless over an eight-year period and was so-called because works Norton rider Harold Daniell likened it to lying on a feather bed in terms of comfort. It was made commercially available in the early 1950s. This was after Norton's 1-2-3 wins in both the Junior and Senior TTs at the Isle of Man in 1950. Geoff Duke followed these with a Junior TT win in 1951. In this

form the frame was a great success and production continued almost unaltered until 1954.

Through the production run there were to be regular updates and improvements to the Manx models of different capacities, such as the short-stroke design engine introduced for both 350cc and 500cc displacement engines. In 1954 the Manx Nortons were fitted with a larger twin-leading-shoe front drum brake while the engine was partially redesigned. The stroke of the engine was shortened and the way in which the frame was assembled was altered in that the rear subframe was now welded, rather than bolted, on. Other upgrades during the 1950s included a switch to full-width hubs, use of the AMC gearbox, redesigned cylinder heads with integral pushrod tunnels and a revision to the bevel drive for the camshaft.

These changes brought the Carroll-type engine to its final form and by 1960 the Manx Norton was approaching its peak of development as a race bike. It featured the Featherbed frame, an AMC gearbox (a result of Norton's acquisition by AMC), Roadholder telescopic forks and the short-stroke engine which all made it a formidable machine. Mike Hailwood rode one to an Isle of Man TT win in 1961. The last Manx Norton was made in 1962 and was the swansong for Norton's Bracebridge Street works. Shortly after the works – AMC owned since 1956 – was closed and production moved south to AMC's London factory. There were to be more fine Norton motorcycles, notably the Commando, but none quite so evocative of the glory days of TT racing as the Manx Norton.

Above: The Norton Manx used a large diameter twin-leading-shoe front brake assembly to optimize braking, especially on tight twisty road circuits such as the famous Isle of Man course.

Right: The Manx is equipped with rear-set foot controls which allow the rider to crouch forward over the handlebars but still change gear and operate the rear brake pedal.

Right: The large capacity fuel tank had sculpted curves in its rear corners to allow room for the rider's knees while maximizing fuel capacity.

Above: The Rex McCandless-designed "Featherbed" frame was the basis of the Manx Norton, although there were slimline and wideline versions of this frame.

Right: The Manx Norton's reputation as a successful racing motorcycle was assured after the 1-2-3 victories in the Junior and Senior TTs of 1950.

Left: Race bikes do not need a headlamp, so the rider's number was displayed in place of it.

Left: The lines of the racing 30M Manx are basic and brutal. There is nothing fitted to the motorcycle that is not connected with making it go, stop and handle well.

Below: The 498cc single-cylinder engine used in the 30M was referred to as the "short stroke" Manx to differentiate it from earlier models. The stroke was shorter than the bore diameter meaning the machine would rev highly.

NORTON MODEL 88

SPECIFICATIONS
Year: 1955
Engine type: Vertical twin
Engine cycle: Four-stroke
Bore & stroke: 66 x 72.6mm (30.33cu in)
Horsepower: 29bhp @ 6000rpm
Top speed: 88mph (142kph)
Compression ratio: 6.8:1
Carburettor: Amal
Transmission: 4-speed
Brakes: F. & R. Drum
Ignition: Magneto
Frame: Steel tubular
Suspension: F. Telescopic forks. R. Swingarm and shock absorbers
Wheelbase: 55.5in (1410mm)
Weight: 380lb (172kg)
Fuel: 3.5 gallons (15.9lit)
Oil: 4.5 pints (2.56lit)
Tyres: F. 3.00 x 19in. R. 3.50 x 19in

Above: Smiths are a well-known British automotive instrument maker. They supplied their components to many British car and motorcycle firms including Norton.

NORTON MODEL 50

SPECIFICATIONS
Year: 1959
Engine type: Ohv single
Engine cycle: Four-stroke
Capacity: 348cc (21.24cu in)
Bore & stroke: 71 x 88mm
Horsepower: 20bhp
Top speed: 75mph (121kph)
Compression ratio: n/a
Carburettor: Amal
Transmission: 4-speed
Brakes: F. & R. Drum
Ignition: Magneto
Frame: Steel tubular
Suspension: F. Telescopic forks. R. Swingarm and shock absorbers
Wheelbase: 55.5in (1410mm)
Weight: 360lb (163kg)
Fuel: 3 gallons (13.6lit)
Oil: 4 pints (2.27lit)
Tyres: 3.25 x 19in

NORTON MODEL 88 (1955)

The vertical twin-cylinder engine made by Norton Motors Ltd was first shown to the motorcycling public at the Earl's Court, London Show of 1948 as part of the 1949 Norton range. It powered the Model 7 Dominator. The engine, a 360-degree parallel twin had been designed by Herbert "Bert" Hopwood and was to be the basis of Norton's twins for approximately 30 years. The Model 7 used a plunger-type frame and remained in production until 1956. By then it had been overshadowed and superseded by the Model 88, a twin-cylinder-engined motorcycle with the Featherbed frame which had been introduced in 1951.

The mass-produced Featherbed frame for road use was fabricated from mild steel tube but closely followed the design of the racing frame albeit with a braced headstock. The front forks were of a design similar to the racing ones, and valanced mudguards were fitted front and rear. The engine was standard Dominator, as was the gearbox, and these two components were fitted to steel plates which bolted into the frame. The fuel tank fitted to the frame top tubes while the instruments and switches were mounted to the top of the forks. The Model 88 was initially made only for export markets as a result of the economic constraints of the times, but when it was sold in its home market it proved immediately popular with customers. The new frame set the benchmark for handling and was the one by which other machines would in future be judged.

By 1955 the Model 88 had been slightly upgraded more than once; a new finish for 1952, new mudguards for 1953 and a bigger front brake for 1954, for example. However, the major changes were made in 1955 when the engine was fitted with the same alloy cylinder head as the Model 7 and an Amal Monobloc carburettor. The frame was made stronger and for the first time included a welded-on, rather than bolted, rear subframe. In this redesigned form the machine stayed in production until 1963, although minor improvements continued to be made, notably to the clutch and gearbox.

Above: The overhead-valve twin-cylinder engine in the Model 88 was fitted with an alloy cylinder head and an Amal Monobloc carburettor.

Above: Norton's attention to engineering detail shows in this close-up of the throttle and brake on the right handlebar.

Below: The Model 88's production run lasted until 1963, albeit in an upgraded form and with a redesigned version of the frame.

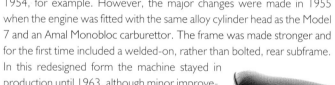

Above: A 4-speed gearbox and swingarm frame afforded a degree of comfort to the Model 88 that made it a popular machine in its day.

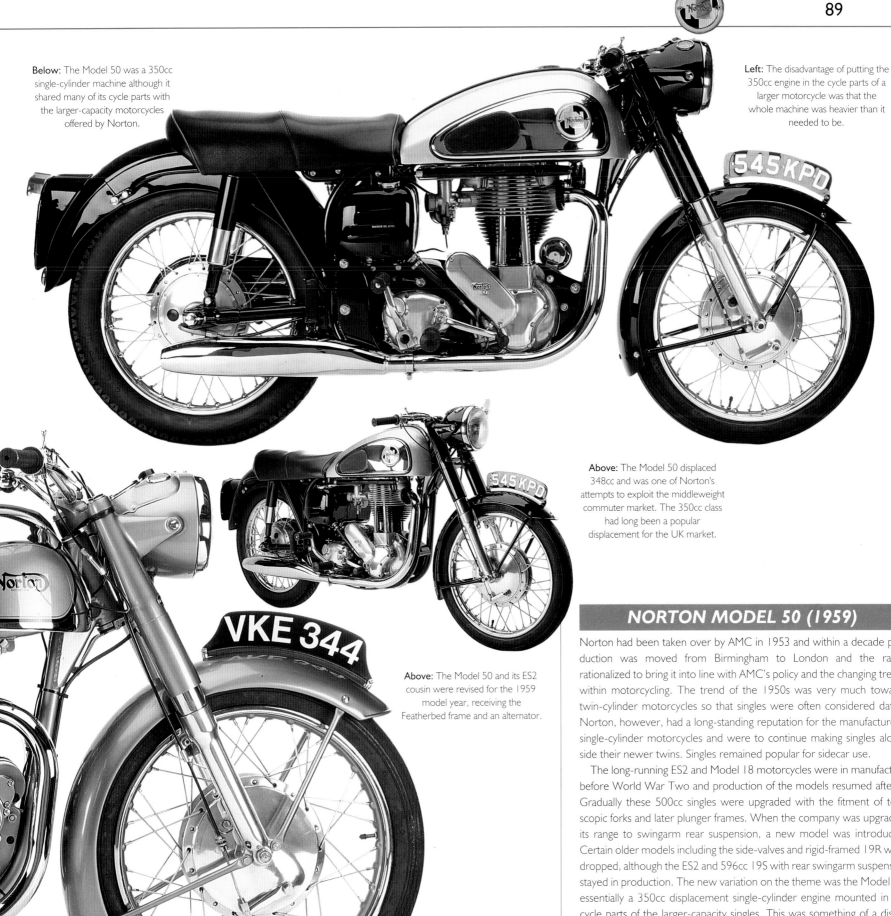

Below: The Model 50 was a 350cc single-cylinder machine although it shared many of its cycle parts with the larger-capacity motorcycles offered by Norton.

Left: The disadvantage of putting the 350cc engine in the cycle parts of a larger motorcycle was that the whole machine was heavier than it needed to be.

Above: The Model 50 displaced 348cc and was one of Norton's attempts to exploit the middleweight commuter market. The 350cc class had long been a popular displacement for the UK market.

Above: The Model 50 and its ES2 cousin were revised for the 1959 model year, receiving the Featherbed frame and an alternator.

NORTON MODEL 50 (1959)

Norton had been taken over by AMC in 1953 and within a decade production was moved from Birmingham to London and the range rationalized to bring it into line with AMC's policy and the changing trends within motorcycling. The trend of the 1950s was very much towards twin-cylinder motorcycles so that singles were often considered dated. Norton, however, had a long-standing reputation for the manufacture of single-cylinder motorcycles and were to continue making singles alongside their newer twins. Singles remained popular for sidecar use.

The long-running ES2 and Model 18 motorcycles were in manufacture before World War Two and production of the models resumed after it. Gradually these 500cc singles were upgraded with the fitment of telescopic forks and later plunger frames. When the company was upgrading its range to swingarm rear suspension, a new model was introduced. Certain older models including the side-valves and rigid-framed 19R were dropped, although the ES2 and 596cc 19S with rear swingarm suspension stayed in production. The new variation on the theme was the Model 50, essentially a 350cc displacement single-cylinder engine mounted in the cycle parts of the larger-capacity singles. This was something of a disadvantage because the weight of these parts was greater than it needed to be for a 350. Some of the large-capacity singles were dropped as the decade moved on, the 19S was discontinued in 1958 for example, but the smaller-capacity Model 50 remained in production until the 1960s. The smaller-capacity twins, such as the Norton Jubilee, overshadowed the last years of the Model 50.

NORTON 650SS

Right: The 650SS was a sports road bike developed from a series of parallel-twin-engined Nortons with rear suspension provided by swingarm frames.

NORTON 650SS (1961)

As a result of the racing successes of the early 1950s, Norton Motors Ltd were, in many people's minds, associated with the best-handling motorcycles in the world. It was no secret that this reputation had been gained through use of the Rex McCandless-designed Featherbed frame. The equally famous Roadholder forks had been introduced in 1948 and the combination of these forks with the Featherbed frame in 1950 was sensational. The trend towards the parallel-twin engine, led by Triumph, caused Norton to consider installing a twin-cylinder engine in the famous frame. The first machine to combine these components was the Model 88 Dominator. It was announced, for export only, in November 1951. Twin-cylinder Nortons with rear suspension were soon manufactured for the British domestic market in the guise of the Model 88 and later the 77, 99 and 650. The Featherbed frame was partially redesigned in 1960, and in September 1961 the 650SS made its appearance.

Above: The parallel-twin engine displaced 646cc and achieved this through a bore and stroke of 68 x 89mm. In the 650SS guise it produced 49bhp @ 6800rpm.

Right: The 650SS was a well-balanced motorcycle. Acceleration was good, top speed impressive and the machine was happily free from vibration at higher revs.

The 650SS engine was fitted with the race-proven downdraught cylinder head as had been used on the company's TT race bikes that year. It also featured solid skirt pistons and a flywheel and big end journals (the part of the shaft in contact with the bearing) larger than those used on the 500cc and 600cc models. Road tests of the time found the 650SS capable of speeds between 110 and 120mph (177 to 193kph) dependent on conditions and that 50 miles per gallon (18km/lit) was achievable. The road testers noted that acceleration was impressive, brakes were good and handling remained as precise as ever. The Norton twin was soon to be increased in capacity to 745cc by increasing the cylinder bore but retaining the 89mm stroke. As before the machine, the Atlas, was initially made for export only. The 650SS though remained in production in an extended run that lasted until 1970.

Right: The stylised headlamp shell mounted to the front fork tubes also contained the ignition switch and the instruments.

Left: The Featherbed frame was "slimmed down" in 1960 by employing waisted top rails.

Above: The 650SS was conventionally constructed with the 4-speed gearbox mounted into the tubular steel cradle frame behind the engine and under the oil tank.

NORTON COMMANDO FASTBACK (1969)

NORTON COMMANDO FASTBACK

SPECIFICATIONS

Year: 1969
Engine type: Parallel twin
Engine cycle: Four-stroke
Capacity: 745cc (45.46cu in)
Bore & stroke: 73 x 89mm
Horsepower: 56bhp @ 6500rpm
Top speed: 115mph (185kph)
Compression ratio: n/a
Carburettor: Amal
Transmission: 4-speed
Brakes: F. TLS drum. R. Drum
Ignition: Coil
Frame: Steel cradle
Suspension: F. Telescopic forks. R. Swingarm and shock absorbers
Wheelbase: 56.75in (1441mm)
Weight: 398lb (180kg)
Fuel: 5.5 gallons (25lit)
Oil: 5 pints (2.84lit)
Tyres: 4.10 x 19in.

Above: The Commando's full-width twin-leading-shoe drum brake featured an air vent covered with a mesh grille to cool the braking components.

Norton was acquired by Associated Motor Cycles Ltd – AMC – in 1956. This change of ownership led to the firm's experimenting during the 1960s with partially enclosed motorcycles, most notably the 250cc Norton Jubilee. The company moved its production facility from Birmingham to London in 1963 and in subsequent years Norton motorcycles became a combination of Norton, AJS and Matchless parts. In 1966 AMC went into liquidation; Dennis Poore of Manganese Bronze bought the company and moved its motorcycle production to the former Villiers factory in Wolverhampton. He was interested in continuing production of the 647 and 745cc twins, especially the Commando, for the important and lucrative US market.

The Fastback was a café-race-styled version of the Commando launched in 1969 – the Commando itself had been launched in 1967.

This styling incorporated both a race-style tailpiece and a dual seat over the rear wheel, while further forward were flat race-type handlebars and a long sleek petrol tank. The Fastback featured what was termed "Isolastic" rubber mounts for the engine, gearbox, swingarm, exhaust system and rear wheel. These components were all bolted together as a single unit and then attached to the frame by the three Isolastic mounts. The purpose of the Isolastic system was to reduce the vibrations transmitted to the rider from the engine through the frame and handlebars. The proven Norton 745cc Atlas engine was used to power the Commando along with the 4-speed AMC gearbox – the two units were connected by a triplex primary chain. The famous Roadholder forks were retained at the front and fitted with a hub that featured a large twin-leading-shoe brake.

Below: The Fastback Commando of 1969 combined café racer styling with the proven twin-cylinder Norton engine. It had a long sleek fuel tank that flowed into a dual seat and then into the tailpiece.

Above: The Commando engine had what Norton described as Isolastic rubber mounts for the engine and gearbox aimed at minimizing vibration.

Left: The Atlas engine was tilted forward slightly in the frame. Its Isolastic mounting meant that it could be revved hard without undue vibration marring handling.

Above: The tailpiece of the seat unit clearly owed its styling to the race bikes of the day, albeit encumbered by the addition of a rear light and number plate bracket.

NORTON COMMANDO MARK II (1975)

NORTON COMMANDO MARK II

SPECIFICATIONS
Year: 1975
Engine type: Parallel twin
Engine cycle: Four-stroke
Capacity: 829cc (50.6cu in)
Bore & stroke: 77 x 89mm
Horsepower: 60bhp @ 6200rpm
Top speed: 115mph (185kph)
Compression ratio: 8.5:1
Carburettor: Twin Amals
Transmission: 4-speed
Brakes: F. Single disc. R. Drum
Ignition: Coil
Frame: Duplex tubular
Suspension: F. Telescopic forks.
R. Swingarm and shock absorbers
Wheelbase: 57in (1448mm)
Weight: 430lb (195kg)
Fuel: 5.2 gallons (23.6lit)
Oil: 5 pints (2.84lit)
Tyres: 4.10 x 19in

Above: The tank held just over five gallons of petrol. The black and gold livery is a hallmark of the Roadster; Interstate models were silver and black.

Right: The Norton Commando in its Mark III form was a more refined version of the Mark II (seen here) intended to increase sales in America. Electric starting and disc brakes were two of the improvements.

The Commando was introduced in the late 1960s as a fast and refined version of the traditional British parallel twin. The early models were of 750cc displacement and capable of reaching almost 120mph (193kph) and the machine in its later forms had considerable potential especially for export sales. However, the British motorcycle industry was contracting. In 1970 Dennis Poore had become Chairman of Norton-Villiers Ltd. What followed throughout that decade marked the death throes of the British motorcycle industry as a whole. After consultation with Manganese Bronze Holdings, Norton-Villiers Ltd and the Department of Trade and Industry, Norton-Villiers Ltd absorbed BSA and Triumph to become Norton-Villiers-Triumph and subsequently NVT Motorcycles Ltd.

While these political wranglings were ongoing, the Commando was redesigned and the range streamlined. In 1973 the larger capacity 829cc models were introduced with a number of refinements aimed at making them more reliable. The larger displacement Commandos featured a rubber-mounted engine and transmission designed to reduce the vibration felt by the rider. This new Commando handled well and was smooth at high speed. The Fastback was dropped in the same year but the other 750cc Commando variants, Roadster, Interstate and Hi Rider, continued until later in the year.

The new Commando displaced 828.9cc although it was described by Norton as an 850. The increase in capacity had been achieved by increasing the bore of the earlier model's cylinders while retaining the stroke. The manufacturers claimed 60bhp @ 6200 rpm although a maximum of 5800rpm was recommended for continuous riding which equated to 100mph (161kph). The engine had a redesigned cylinder barrel bolted to the crankcases. The flywheel was redesigned to suit the heavier pistons. These Commandos were known as Mark Is while the Mark II, a slightly redesigned Mark I, appeared in 1974. The political situation involving Norton production appeared to be resolved by 1975. Both Norton and

Below: The rear suspension, gearbox and clutch were all strengthened when the Commando's engine was bored out to 829cc.

Above: Although the last Norton Commandos had electric starters, they also retained the kickstart pedal located in the normal position on the gearbox as a back-up starting device.

Triumph motorcycles, a twin and a triple respectively, were to be produced by the group and the Mark III Commando was soon to follow. Gradually the American market had begun to insist on further changes, including a quieter exhaust note, in order to appeal to a wider market. The Mark III was introduced in the autumn of 1975 with electric start and disc brakes. The change to a left-foot gearshift was also made at this time and required a number of detail engineering changes that were both costly and complex.

The assumption that the company's future was assured had been premature, and numerous changes to the structure of the company and the NVT group continued to be made. A seemingly bewildering array of small companies existed within the space of a few years; one to make and distribute spares, another for the motorcycles themselves, a racing workshop, and a

Above: By the time the Norton Commando Mark IIs and IIIs were in production, Norton motorcycles was in danger of going out of business as a result of political wrangling and industrial uncertainty.

fourth to develop new machines, all working at separate factories around the country from Hampshire to Staffordshire. While the Mark III Commando appealed to the important US market and could compete with the Japanese imports in terms of refinement, the financial problems facing the manufacturers in England would force its early demise. The last Triumph Trident was made in 1975 and the final Commando Mark III machines were completed in the Wolverhampton factory in early 1977 when the factory was in the hands of the Official Receiver.

The last days of production for the Commando were paralleled by continuing development of the Wankel Rotary project, evaluation of an air-cooled two-stroke twin and experimentation with an amalgam of Triumph and Norton parts. This latter motorcycle consisted of an Isolastic frame fitted with a Triumph Triple engine which had been overbored to 900cc. It was known as the Trisolastic, is reputed to have performed well and, given the trend towards Japanese multis of the time, may have had a future had circumstances been different.

Above: Like the Triumph twin-cylinder engines, the larger displacement of later Norton parallel twins was achieved by enlarging the engine's bore rather than stroke.

NORTON INTERPOL II

SPECIFICATIONS
Year: 1983
Engine type: Twin chamber rotary
Engine cycle: Wankel rotary
Capacity: 588cc (35.9cu in)
Bore & stroke: Rotary
Horsepower: 85bhp @ 9000rpm
Top speed: 124mph (200kph)
Compression ratio: 9.0:1
Carburettor: Twin SU
Transmission: 5-speed
Brakes: F. Twin discs. R. Disc
Ignition: CDI Electronic
Frame: Pressed steel monocoque
Suspension: F. Telescopic forks. R. Swingarm and shock absorbers
Wheelbase: 58.5in (1486mm)
Weight: 518lb (235kg)
Fuel: 5 gallons (22.7lit)
Oil: 7 pints (4lit)
Tyres: F. 100/90 V 18. R. 110/90 V 18

Above: The Interpol II used state-of-the-art components including the front brakes which comprised twin discs and hydraulic calipers.

Right: The Interpol II was the culmination of many years of experimentation work by NVT, Norton and various subsidiaries who attempted to find a viable way of using the Wankel rotary engine for a motorcycle.

NORTON INTERPOL II (1983)

The rotary engine principle was developed extensively by a German, Felix Wankel, in the course of the 1930s, 1940s and 1950s. Wankel was employed at BMW during the Nazi regime, and later with NSU. It was at the latter company that the engine, by now known as the Wankel rotary, became sufficiently developed to be a practical means of propulsion. The Wankel rotary engine features a triangular rotary piston that turns on an eccentric shaft inside a specific "figure-of-eight"-shaped housing. The rotor turns within the housing with its three apices following and always in contact with the peritrochoid curve of the inner surface of the cylinder. Three separate working chambers are formed in this way and for each turn of the rotor the Otto-cycle is completed in turn in each chamber. The Otto-cycle is the familiar induction, compression, ignition, exhaust sequence of the four-stroke engine.

NSU offered patent licences to numerous car and motorcycle manufacturers, of which DKW (subsequently Hercules) and Suzuki later marketed rotary-engined motorcycles. The DKW machine was powered by a fan-cooled rotary engine made by Fichtel and Sachs AG who had bought a NSU-Wankel licence in 1960. The British connection developed when BSA became interested in the Fichtel and Sachs rotary engine in the DKW/Hercules machine. David Garside, a development engineer, was employed by the BSA group and began work on air-cooled rotary-powered motorcycles at the Umberslade Hall research centre.

One of the major difficulties with the manufacture of a successful rotary engine for a motorcycle lies in cooling it adequately. Drive is taken from one end of the eccentric shaft by a hydraulically damped duplex primary chain. The engine flywheel and generator are positioned on the other end. The CDI ignition is triggered by a pickup mounted adjacent to the flywheel. The three tips of the rotor form a seal against the inner surface of the housing by being spring-loaded while the surfaces are coated with tungsten carbide to increase wear-resistance.

This development work continued against a background of financial difficulties at BSA. The company subsequently became part of the NVT group where Chairman Dennis Poore showed interest in the potential of the Wankel engine. When NVT went into liquidation the rotary project,

Below: The rotary engine was partially concealed by the bodywork, including the fairing and the conventional seat, tank and sidepanels which were of an integrated design.

Right: The police bike came equipped with rear-mounted panniers, police lights front and rear and a fairing suitable for carrying police markings. The engine was designed to maximize the time between maintenance intervals while remaining reliable.

Right: For such an innovative machine the view from the riding position is surprisingly conventional; handlebars, clocks, fairing, tank and, special to police bikes, the various patrol extras.

Right: Because the Interpol II was designed for police use, it came equipped with a large fairing and windshield aimed at providing as much weather protection as possible.

Above: Early rotary engines suffered from problems with cooling because of their unique design. Another problem arose when attempting to seal the tips of the triangular rotor within each combustion chamber.

including the twin-rotor engine, survived because of Poore's interest and work continued on what was to become the Interpol II.

The successful development of a twin-rotor air-cooled rotary engine meant that next a complete motorcycle could be designed. The machine was conceived especially for police and service use and so had some features incorporated specifically for these users. By the end of 1979 the team, which by now included Doug Hele, had completed 25 Mark I machines, but the motorcycle did not enter production. The reason for this was because of reservations expressed by the Department of Trade and Industry (DTI) who had a controlling interest in NVT at this time. The DTI did not think that the machine would sell in sufficient numbers to justify the risk of manufacture.

However, production of Mark II prototypes began in early 1981. In order to test these machines realistically and evaluate them over several months, Norton offered motorcycles to the traffic departments of police forces around the country. More than 20 forces took up the offer and evaluated the machines through 1981 and 1982. On the whole they returned favourable reports although certain recurrent problems needed resolving. Approximately 140 slightly refined motorcycles were delivered to police forces during 1983 as well as batches to the Ministry of Defence and the RAC. Total deliveries of the Interpol II amounted to 350 machines to police, MoD and RAC. Experience with this machine led to the production of a limited run of air-cooled rotary-engined Classics, and subsequently to the liquid-cooled Commander and F1 models, but sales remained tiny.

NORTON NRS588

SPECIFICATIONS
Year: 1992
Engine type: Twin chamber rotary
Engine cycle: Wankel rotary
Capacity: 588cc (35.9cu in)
Bore & stroke: Rotary
Horsepower: 95bhp @ 9500rpm
Top speed: 180mph (290kph)
Compression ratio: 9.2:1
Carburettor: Twin Keihin
Transmission: 6-speed
Brakes: F. Twin disc. R. Disc
Ignition: CDI electronic
Frame: Twin-spar alloy beam
Suspension: F. Telescopic forks. R. Swingarm and monoshock
Wheelbase: 55.1in (1400mm)
Weight: 298lb (135kg)
Fuel: 5 gallons (22.7lit)
Oil: 7 pints (4lit)
Tyres: F. 12/60-17. R. 18/67-17

Above: The front suspension and brakes are equally important in terms of handling and the NRS588 relies on twin discs and calipers, as well as WP suspension components.

NORTON NRS588 (1992)

Norton had last won the Isle of Man TT win in June 1973 when mono-coque-framed machines developed by Peter Williams and powered by Norton Commando twin-cylinder engines held off a strong Japanese chal-lenge. That was all set to change in 1992 when Steve Hislop was entered in the Senior TT riding a Norton rotary-powered racebike.

The story of Norton's rotary engine-powered racers goes back to 1987 when Brian Crighton approached the company with a view to build-ing a racer based around the Interpol II engine. The Norton company had changed hands in January of 1987 when Philippe Le Roux had taken con-trol, and he sanctioned the construction of a prototype racer based on an Interpol II. Testing at MIRA showed the machine to be capable of more than 170mph (274kph). This was promising and Le Roux authorized fur-ther funding for the racing project.

The frame was found to be too flexible to cope with the racer's power and so a Spondon alloy frame was used for the next prototype along with Kayaba forks. This racer placed well in its first outings and the company planned a major racing campaign for 1988. Nortons appeared on the grid at numerous events including the TT, but problems were experienced with the machines' handling rather than the engine. Some of the unpre-dictable handling characteristics were caused by the unusual way in which the rotary engine delivered the power. White Power suspension compo-nents were especially engineered for the bike. This brought a third place finish for Trevor Nation at the British Championship F1 race at the British Grand Prix at Donington Park.

John Player brand sponsorship from Imperial Tobacco gave the team a boost for 1989, 1990 and 1991. Successes were balanced by reliability and personnel problems within the team, but development work contin-ued unabated, including experiments with water-cooling and new fairings. A major problem centred on the fact that the FIM had difficulty in classify-ing the rotary racers, which cast doubts for a time over their eligibility for Grands Prix. Successes in 1990 included Robert Dunlop's popular win in the Superbike race at Ulster's North West 200 Road Race and Trevor

Below: Racebikes tend to use state-of-the-art technology. The NRS588 was no exception and was up to the minute in the early 1990s. The Harris twin-spar alloy frame is of a type that has since become the norm for sports bikes.

Above: The fairing is adorned with sponsors' decals including those of brake component manufacturer EBC, exhaust maker Micron, Regina chains, NGK spark plugs, Goodridge hoses and Renthal handlebars.

Left: The alloy box-section swingarm and monoshock rear suspension unit is fitted with a three-spoke magnesium alloy wheel and designed to minimize unsprung weight while enhancing handling.

Above: As the rotary engine is almost completely concealed behind the race fairing, there is little, at a glance, to distinguish the NRS588 from other Grands Prix motorcycles of the time, with the exception of the Norton logo.

Left: Before Steve Hislop won the Isle of Man TT aboard this rotary powered racer, there had been considerable development work into the viability of a racing rotary engine, and a prolonged dispute with the FIM about its displacement and therefore its eligibility for racing.

Nation's second place in the Senior TT at the Isle of Man. For 1990 the Norton team contested the International F1 Cup series and also the Shell/Motor Cycle News F1 Supercup and the MCN TT Superbike series.

"Rocket" Ron Haslam joined the team for 1991 to ride alongside Trevor Nation. Norton were to contest the Supercup British Championship series, the MCN TT Superbike races and the British Grand Prix at Donington Park. The next generation of Norton racer, the NRS588 (the NRS indicates Norton Racing Services while 588 is the machine's displacement in cubic centimetres), was first wheeled out in 1991 with performance parts including a Harris frame, WP suspension components and 17in diameter PVM magnesium wheels. This chassis was fitted with a liquid-cooled Norton rotary engine and a 6-speed gearbox connected by a Kevlar-reinforced primary drive. Final drive was by means of a chain driven through an 18-plate wet clutch. In almost this form the NRS588 took Norton and Steve Hislop to their much-sought-after Isle of Man TT win in 1992. Despite this, however, the future was far from assured for Norton, and the company has changed hands several times since then.

Left: This rotary racer used a liquid-cooled version of the twin chamber rotary engine which was connected to a 6-speed transmission.

NUT SPORTS

SPECIFICATIONS
Year: 1914
Engine type: V-twin
Engine cycle: Four-stroke
Capacity: 678cc (41.4cu in)
Bore & stroke: n/a
Horsepower: 5hp
Top speed: 60mph (97kph)
Compression ratio: n/a
Carburettor: Amac
Transmission: 3-speed
Brakes: F. None. R. Drum
Ignition: Magneto
Frame: Steel diamond
Suspension: F. Sprung girder forks. R. None
Wheelbase: 56in (1422mm)
Weight: 275lb (125kg)
Fuel: n/a
Oil: n/a
Tyres: 3.00 x 26in

Above: The diamond-shaped NUT logo – NUT stands for Newcastle Upon Tyne. In front of it is the oil pump for the engine.

NUT SPORTS (1914)

NUT is an acronym that stands for Newcastle Upon Tyne; it was the name given to motorcycles produced in that city in the first decades of the twentieth century. Motorcycle production started as a result of a motorcycle commissioned by Hugh Mason. Mason was a wealthy man and he requested cycle dealer Jack Hall to build him a motorcycle based around an MMC engine. This was a success and over the next few years several more were built and sold under the name Bercleys. In 1912 Jack Hall began working with a company named after its proprietor, Sir William Angus Sanderson. With the help of Sanderson, and using JAP engines specified by Mason, the NUT brand was a serious proposition. In the same year Mason designed a TT model which he rode to victory in the Junior TT in the Isle of Man in 1913. The surge in demand for NUT motorcycles immediately afterwards caught the company unawares and

they struggled to cope. This quality machine was one of those made in that boom period and is powered by a 50-degree JAP V-twin engine.

The company were involved in war work for much of World War One. A luxury JAP-engined V-twin was announced in 1919, but then the Sanderson company withdrew its backing in order to move into car production. Another backer was found and production continued until the company was forced into liquidation. In 1923 NUT was resurrected and a new range of machines was produced. The company enjoyed a brief period of profitability. Recurring financial problems, however, ensured that NUT motorcycle production was not continuous. Another range of models was introduced in 1931 using JAP V-twins in 500cc and 700cc overhead-valve configuration as well as a 750cc side-valve. The machines were conventional in design and manufactured to a high standard. The range was continued and extended for 1932 and 1933, but production was minimal and finally ceased permanently in the latter year.

Below: The V-twin NUT was a stylish sports machine for its day and it boasted novel features, such as the cylindrical fuel tank held in place by metal straps.

Right: The NUT Sports used a belt drive system to provide final drive from the gearbox to the dummy rim on the rear wheel, which doubled as the braking surface.

Left: The 3-speed gearbox was a Sturmey Archer unit. Gear changes were made by means of the lever visible below the fuel tank.

Below: The NUT had an unusual design of girder forks to provide front suspension, but was reliant on rear-wheel braking only.

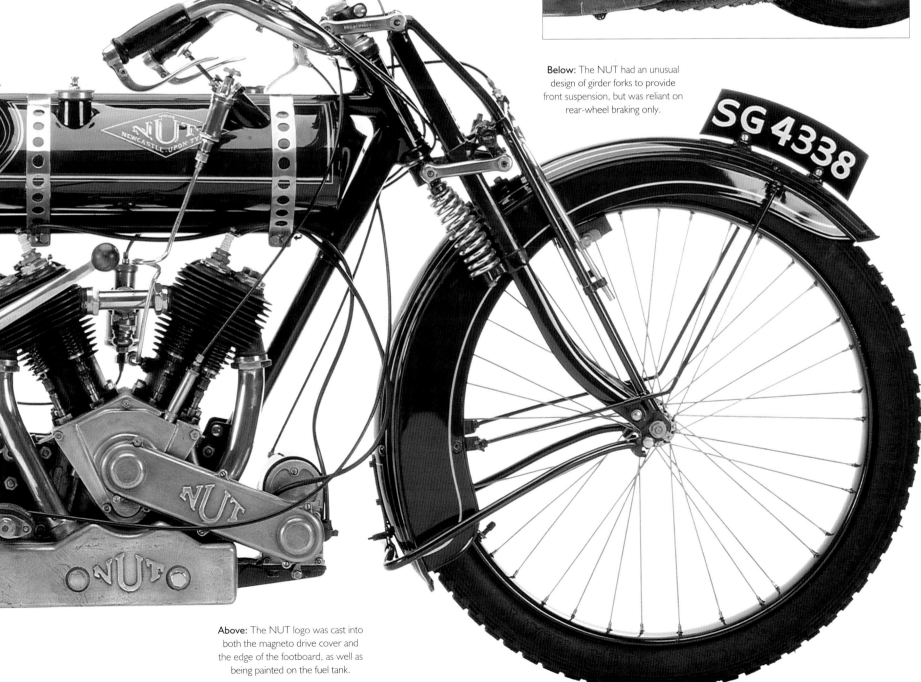

Above: The NUT logo was cast into both the magneto drive cover and the edge of the footboard, as well as being painted on the fuel tank.

SPECIFICATIONS
Year: 1932
Engine type: Ohc single
Engine cycle: Four-stroke
Capacity: 248cc (15.1cu in)
Bore & stroke: 70 x 64.5mm
Horsepower: 10bhp
Top speed: 60mph (97kph)
Compression ratio: n/a
Carburettor: n/a
Transmission: 3-speed
Brakes: F. & R. Drum.
Ignition: Magneto
Frame: Tubular cradle
Suspension: F. Girder forks.
R. None
Wheelbase: n/a
Weight: 270lb (122kg)
Fuel: n/a
Oil: n/a
Tyres: n/a

OK-SUPREME LIGHTHOUSE (1932)

OK was founded in 1899; its early motorcycles used De Dion, Minerva, Precision and Green engines. In the interwar years the company manufactured motorcycles with proprietary engines from Blackburne, Bradshaw and JAP. In 1928 a rider on an OK machine won an Isle of Man TT race. The partners who had formed the company had split up in 1926 and one of them, Ernest Humphries, decided to append Supreme to the marque's name and continue producing motorcycles. During the 1930s the company only manufactured four-strokes with proprietary engines.

In 1932 the company catalogued eight different models that ranged in displacement from 148cc upwards. One of these was the Lighthouse. Lighthouse was more of a nickname than an official manufacturer's designation, but it stuck. The name derived from the fact that the inclined engine, a single, had a vertical camshaft drive with a sight glass set in the top of the camshaft housing which allowed the rider to inspect the camshaft. The machine was an innovative way of producing an overhead-camshaft engine and was designed by George Jones and Ray Mason.

The firm produced a range of models until the outbreak of World War Two – something for everyone was their intention. Each year the range of both side-valve and overhead-valve models underwent slight modifications. By 1938 there were 14 models in the OK-Supreme line-up. The war saw OK-Supreme's factory switch to military production to help the war effort and full-scale motorcycle production regrettably did not resume after the cessation of hostilities in 1945.

Above: The Lighthouse was so known because of the sight glass positioned at the top of the engine where it is clearly visible in this photograph.

PANTHER 120S (1964)

This company was originally known as P&M after its founders, Jonah Phelon and Richard Moore. The factory was based in Cleckheaton, West Yorkshire. In 1900 the company fitted engines designed by Jonah Phelon to frames made by the Beeston Humber Company. Later Humber went on to build these machines under licence. The partnership with Moore was formally entered into in 1905, and it enabled commercial production to commence. All P&M machines had chain drive and the engine was positioned so as to take the place of the front frame downtube. Typical engines used were single-cylinder side-valve and overhead-valve units.

Granville Bradshaw redesigned the motorcycle in 1923 and the Panther brand name was adopted, although the image suggested by this new identity was not wholly appropriate. The company introduced a lightweight single in 1932 as an economy bike and called it the Red Panther. An earlier line of lightweights were Villiers two-stroke-engined

motorcycles referred to as Panthettes. The engine used in the Panther of 1923 was a 500cc unit. It was gradually increased in displacement, to 594cc in 1929 and 650cc in 1959. The Panther 100 of 1935 was this big single with a BTH magneto. Production of it had continued through the years of the Depression while the smaller capacity machines had also been produced as an economy measure at this time.

During World War Two the company built aircraft parts, but it resumed motorcycle production after the cessation of hostilities. Panther stuck to its tried and tested forward-inclined engine formula and produced a range of overhead-valve models with displacements of 249cc, 348cc and 594cc. Telescopic forks appeared in 1947. Production of singles continued until the 1960s. The 120S of 1964 shown here was one of the last Panthers made. It had been introduced in 1959 and, like many of the large-displacement Panthers before it, was primarily intended for sidecar use. The firm also experimented with scooters and mopeds in the 1950s and 1960s but finally closed in receivership in 1967.

Below: The Panther 120S was a solid, dependable, workaday motorcycle popular for sidecar use. There was little distinctive about it beyond the engine, and by 1964 it had almost reached the end of the road.

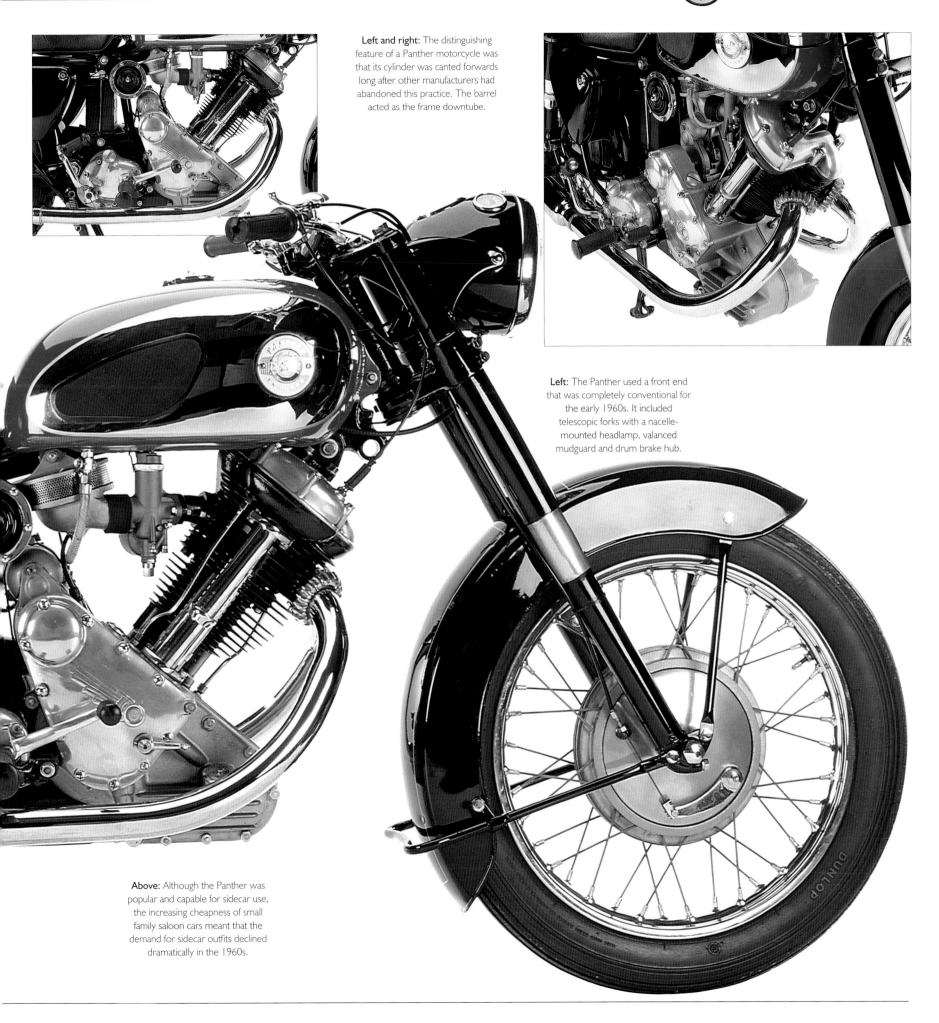

Left and right: The distinguishing feature of a Panther motorcycle was that its cylinder was canted forwards long after other manufacturers had abandoned this practice. The barrel acted as the frame downtube.

Left: The Panther used a front end that was completely conventional for the early 1960s. It included telescopic forks with a nacelle-mounted headlamp, valanced mudguard and drum brake hub.

Above: Although the Panther was popular and capable for sidecar use, the increasing cheapness of small family saloon cars meant that the demand for sidecar outfits declined dramatically in the 1960s.

RADCO 250

Above: The intertwined R and C of the Radco logo derived from the name Radnall & Co.

RADCO 250 (1922)

Radco was a small English company that flourished in Birmingham between the wars after having been founded by E.A. Radnall in 1913. It manufactured medium-capacity machines which it termed "the king of lightweights". The range includud 211cc and 247cc two-strokes that featured external flywheels, such as this 250. This machine was typical of lightweights of the day, although it did feature an unusual design of footboards and the primary chain was not enclosed.

Later the company went on to produce 247cc overhead-valve models with an engine of their own design. Like many other British manufacturers, Radco often bought in two-stroke engines from Villiers, in this case 145cc and 198cc units. The largest capacity machines from Radco were the 490cc JAP-engined singles which were produced in three forms: Touring, Sport and Supersport.

Motorcycle production ceased in 1932, from which time the company concentrated on the manufacture of components such as handlebars and control levers. In 1954 Radco returned briefly to two-wheeler production and manufactured a lightweight machine called the Ace which featured a 99cc 4F Villiers two-stroke engine. This was fitted to a simple loop rigid frame equipped with leading-link forks. It failed to catch on and little more was heard of the company until the mid-1960s. A new machine – a mini bike – was offered in 1966 but this also failed to attract many customers.

Right: In the 1920s many motorcycles were still clearly derived from bicycles, as the lines of the 1922 Radco frame show. It uses what is described as a diamond frame.

Left: The Radco featured 3-speed transmission; gear changes were made by means of the sturdy lever on the right-hand side of the engine. Note that the primary drive chain below it is exposed.

Right: This hand pump was provided for the rider to lubricate the engine with oil while he was riding the machine.

Above: The Radco was powered by a lightweight two-stroke engine and the fuel tank was located between the frame tubes.

RALEIGH MH31

RALEIGH MH31

SPECIFICATIONS
Year: 1931
Engine type: Ohv single
Engine cycle: Four-stroke
Capacity: 495cc (30.3cu in)
Bore & stroke: 79 x 101mm
Horsepower: n/a
Top speed: 75mph (121kph)
Compression ratio: n/a
Carburettor: Amal
Transmission: 3-speed
Brakes: F. & R. Drum
Ignition: Magneto
Frame: Steel tube
Suspension: F. Sprung girder forks. R. None
Wheelbase: n/a
Weight: 295lb (134kg)
Fuel: 2.5 gallons (11.4lit)
Oil: n/a
Tyres: F. 3.00 x 19in. R. 3.25 x 18in

Above: Raleigh is probably best known as a manufacturer of bicycles, but it did diversify into motorcycles in the early years of the 20th century and again between 1919 and 1933.

RALEIGH MH31 (1931)

This English company is better known as a bicycle manufacturer, but motorcycles were made for more than one period in the company's history. The first were produced in the early 1900s after the company's founding in 1899. Production halted in 1905, but after 1919 motorcycles were again produced in the Nottingham factory. Raleigh also manufactured engines and gearboxes which they sold to other companies under the Sturmey Archer name.

The 1930 range of Raleigh motorcycles included a number of vertical side-valves and some overhead-valve models. The subsequent 1931 range was similar with models listed as the MO, MA, MT and MH. They had engines with cylinders inclined forwards, a rear-mounted magneto, redesigned frames and forks. Engine displacement varied; it ranged from 225cc to 598cc. The MH31 seen here was a 1931 model, as indicated by the 31 suffix in the machine's designation. The MH prefix implied that it was one of the overhead-valve models with displacement of 495cc.

Below: Girder forks, drum brakes, no rear suspension and a sprung saddle was the arrangement typical of British motorcycles before and immediately after World War Two.

Like the smaller 348cc MT31, it featured a forward-inclined single-cylinder two-port engine with a rear-mounted Lucas magdyno. The tank had been redesigned for 1931 to give the machine more modern lines, although the gear change was still a hand-change mechanism. Provision was made for the rider to carry out repairs and maintenance by the addition of a leather tool pouch within a metal frame.

In 1933 the company stopped two-wheeler production preferring to concentrate on the manufacture of three-wheeler cars and vans. Production of these had also stopped by 1935 when Raleigh returned solely to bicycle manufacture.

Below: The diamond frame and girder forks were manufactured by Raleigh in Nottingham. The valve springs on top of the single cylinder were left exposed.

Left: The 3-speed Sturmey Archer gearbox was made by Raleigh itself. The company also supplied gearboxes to other manufacturers, such as Norton and Brough.

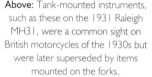

Above: Tank-mounted instruments, such as these on the 1931 Raleigh MH31, were a common sight on British motorcycles of the 1930s but were later superseded by items mounted on the forks.

Above: The MH31 was a single-cylinder motorcycle typical of the early 1930s with its forward-inclined cylinder barrel.

THE LIGHT REX

SPECIFICATIONS
Year: 1907
Engine type: Side-valve single
Engine cycle: Four-stroke
Capacity: 453cc (27.6cu in)
Bore & stroke: 81 x 88mm
Horsepower: 3.5hp
Top speed: n/a
Compression ratio: n/a
Carburettor: Longuemare
Transmission: Single-speed
Brakes: F. None. R. Expanding
band and rubber block
Ignition: Magneto
Frame: Steel diamond
Suspension: F. Sprung tube
forks. R. None
Wheelbase: n/a
Weight: 135lb (61kg)
Fuel: n/a
Oil: n/a
Tyres: 26 x 2in

LIGHT REX 3.5HP (1907)

This English company was founded in Earlsdon, Coventry in 1900 and it flourished until 1933. It produced both singles and V-twins, and after halting manufacture of its own engines went on to use proprietary Blackburne engines. Early models featured a variety of innovative techniques in their manufacture. One 372cc machine incorporated a silencer cast in one piece with the cylinder barrel.

The Light Rex, as the 1907 3.5 horsepower model was known, featured a belt-drive transmission, and a total-loss lubrication system dependent on the rider pumping oil from the tank into the engine. Both brakes operated on the rear wheel – the foot pedal operated the brake on the inside of the belt-drive rim while the hand lever operated the internal expanding band brake. The company's motorcycles offered a degree of comfort that was considered noteworthy for the time. The Rex cantilever saddle and footrests, as well as the pedals on this 1907 model, were considered an improvement on the 1906 model.

The first Rex manufactured after World War One was a 550cc side-valve single, but this was also dropped in favour of models with Blackburne engines. Rex offered their machines in two wheelbases, the choice depending on whether or not a sidecar was to be attached. In 1922 Rex amalgamated with Acme, who were also based in Coventry, to form Rex-Acme. The new company's products soon notched up racing success with Walter Handley in the saddle. He ultimately became a director and then later left to race on other marques. The Depression was not kind to the company which survived by manufacturing machines completely from bought-in parts. The factory was taken over by a sidecar manufacturer, Mills-Fulford, in 1932 who halted motorcycle production in the following year.

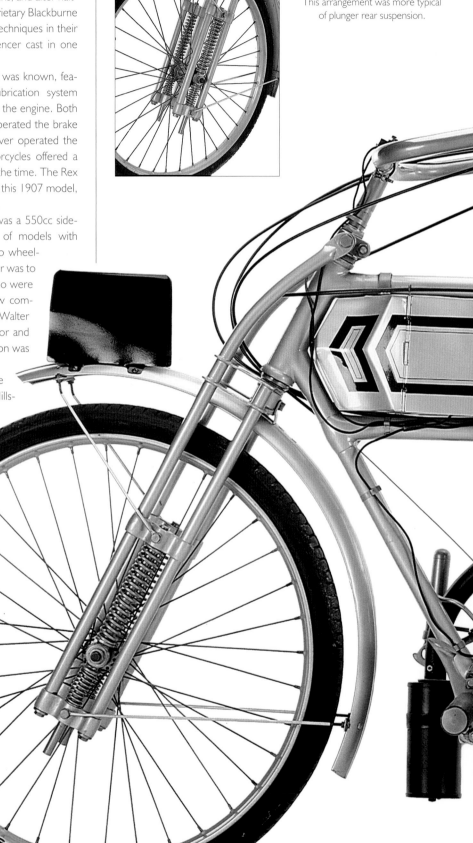

Left: The Light Rex had front suspension of an unusual design. Springs above and below the axle allowed movement up and down. This arrangement was more typical of plunger rear suspension.

Right: The front end of the Light Rex was evidence of its bicycle ancestry. Front suspension was fitted, but a front brake was absent.

Right: The Rex combined a dummy rim as both the drive sprocket for the belt drive and the braking surface for the rubber block-type rear brake.

Above: The foot brake pedal operated a brake block that was squeezed against the inner surface of the belt-drive rim.

Below: The Rex of 1907 was clearly bicycle-derived with a diamond-type frame and a single-cylinder engine installed into the frame. Drive was direct as there was no gearbox.

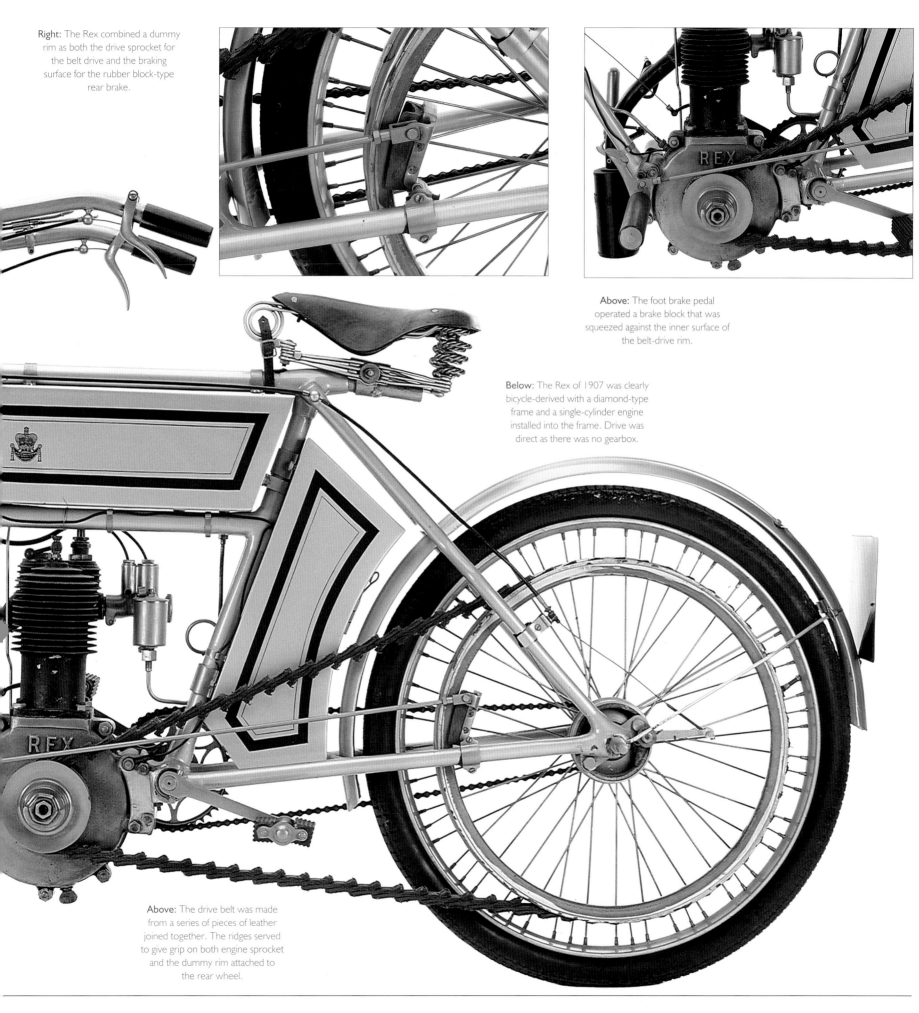

Above: The drive belt was made from a series of pieces of leather joined together. The ridges served to give grip on both engine sprocket and the dummy rim attached to the rear wheel.

ROYAL ENFIELD

ROYAL ENFIELD V-TWIN (1922)

The New Enfield Cycle Company was formed in Worcestershire in the closing years of the nineteenth century to embrace the bicycle portion of Eadie Manufacturing and the Enfield Manufacturing Company. Until this point in 1896, the companies, which had the same owners and origins in light engineering, had been separate entities. Eadie Manufacturing made bicycles which were sold by the Enfield Manufacturing Company. The Enfield name had been adopted when the company won contracts to supply the Royal Small Arms factory at Enfield in Middlesex. The Royal prefix was added in 1893 when their bicycles were displayed in Birmingham. By 1897 the company had dropped the "New" prefix and was simply known as Enfield Cycle Company.

Enfield diversified into powered vehicles when it began work on three- and four-wheelers fitted with proprietary engines from companies such as

De Dion. They manufactured their first motorcycle in 1900; it featured a 211cc Minerva engine mounted over the front wheel. The company continued with production of more conventional motorcycles until 1905 and then it concentrated on making car components for a five-year period. A new factory was constructed in the town of Redditch in 1907. Motorcycle production resumed when a MAG V-twin engined motorcycle was made. This was soon followed by a 770cc JAP-engined V-twin. From then on Enfield produced motorcycles with engines of its own design.

In the years after World War One the company concentrated on production of a large displacement V-twin of 976cc specifically intended for sidecar use. A medium-weight four-stroke was introduced in 1924 with a JAP engine although the company later installed an engine of their own design and manufacture. Later in the 1920s a 996cc V-twin sidecar outfit ridden by E. Magner, a Swede, broke the One Mile World Record.

ROYAL ENFIELD V-TWIN

SPECIFICATIONS
Year: 1922
Engine type: V-twin
Engine cycle: Four-stroke
Capacity: 976cc (59.6cu in)
Bore & stroke: 85.5 x 85mm
Horsepower: 6-8hp
Top speed: n/a
Compression ratio: n/a
Carburettor: Amal
Transmission: 2-speed
Brakes: F. & R. Dummy rim
Ignition: Magneto
Frame: Steel tube
Suspension: F. Sprung girder forks. R. None
Wheelbase: n/a
Weight: 320lb (145kg)
Fuel: n/a
Oil: n/a
Tyres: 26 x 3in

Above: Front suspension was by sprung girder forks; lighting remained fairly rudimentary in the early 1920s.

Below: The V-twin still retained many bicycle-type features including the rigid diamond frame, dummy rim brakes front and back, and a sprung saddle.

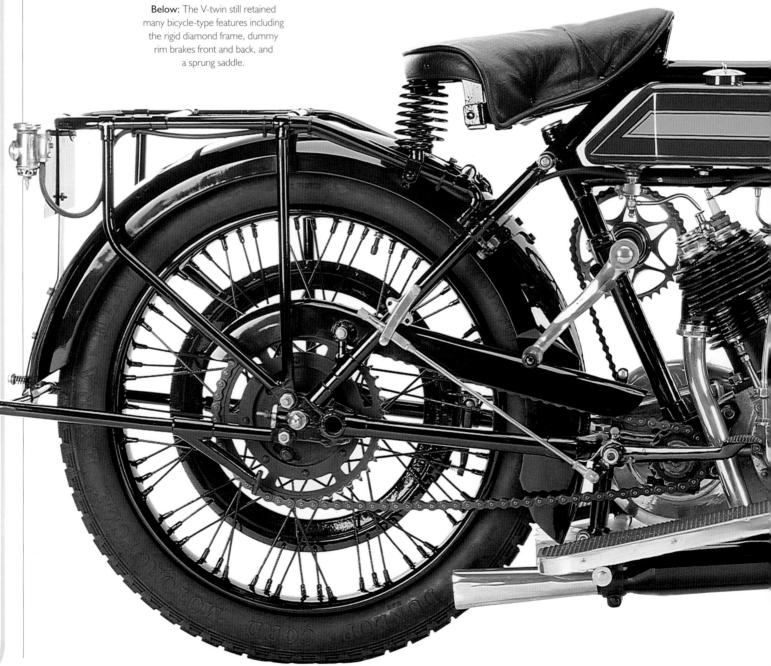

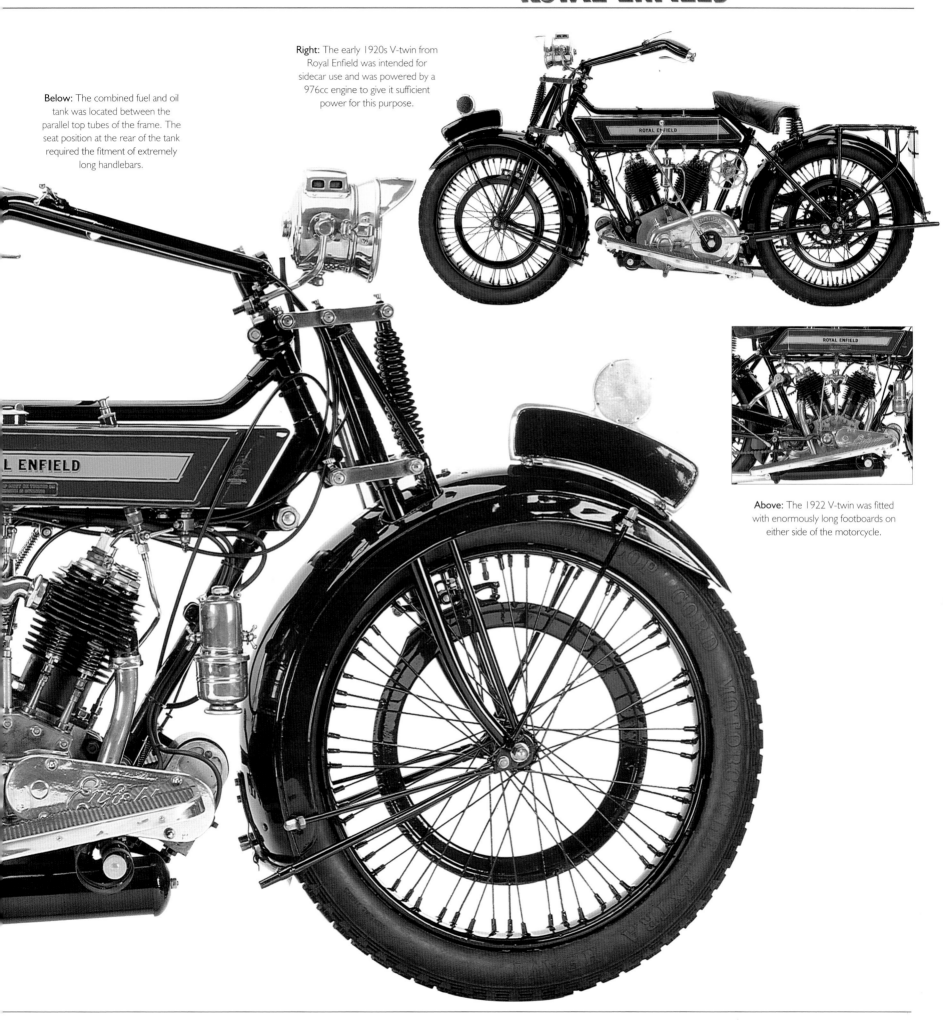

Below: The combined fuel and oil tank was located between the parallel top tubes of the frame. The seat position at the rear of the tank required the fitment of extremely long handlebars.

Right: The early 1920s V-twin from Royal Enfield was intended for sidecar use and was powered by a 976cc engine to give it sufficient power for this purpose.

Above: The 1922 V-twin was fitted with enormously long footboards on either side of the motorcycle.

ROYAL ENFIELD JF BULLET

SPECIFICATIONS
Year: 1937
Engine type: Ohv single
Engine cycle: Four-stroke
Capacity: 499cc (30.5cu in)
Bore & stroke: 84 x 90mm
Horsepower: 19bhp @ 5000rpm
Top speed: 80mph (129kph)
Compression ratio: n/a
Carburettor: Amal
Transmission: 4-speed
Brakes: F. & R. Drum
Ignition: Magneto
Frame: Steel cradle
Suspension: F. Sprung girder forks. R. None
Wheelbase: 54in (1372mm)
Weight: 364lb (165kg)
Fuel: 2.75 gallons (12.5lit)
Oil: n/a
Tyres: F. 3.25 x 19in. R. 3.50 x 19in

ROYAL ENFIELD JF BULLET (1937)

In 1928 the Royal Enfield firm adopted saddle tanks and centre-spring girder forks for its range of motorcycles. Later, after World War Two, they would be one of the first motorcycle manufacturers to adopt swinging-arm rear suspension. From 1930 onwards Royal Enfield motorcycles were given alphabetical designations. The Model A, for example, was a 225cc two-stroke while the Model Z Cycar was an unusual enclosed 148cc machine made in 1934. The range developed through the 1930s and vertical singles appeared in 1936.

The Model JF was one of these singles and it was given the Bullet name which had already been used for other models by the company. It was a 499cc single with a four-valve cylinder head. The speedometer was mounted in front of the handlebars while the ammeter and ignition switch were mounted in a panel on top of the petrol tank which was finished in chrome with painted panels. The machine was fitted with a new style of silencer. The Royal Enfield range was altered for 1937, the year this motorcycle was made, but the JF continued unchanged.

Above: The JF Bullet featured a single Amal carburettor and exposed rocker arms and valve springs, the latter being an arrangement that would soon be phased out.

Below: The 499cc single-cylinder Royal Enfield was one of several motorcycles made by the company to bear the Bullet name and one of 20 models in the range.

Above: The exhaust pipes of the JF Bullet were fitted with flattened, triangular silencers of an unusual design.

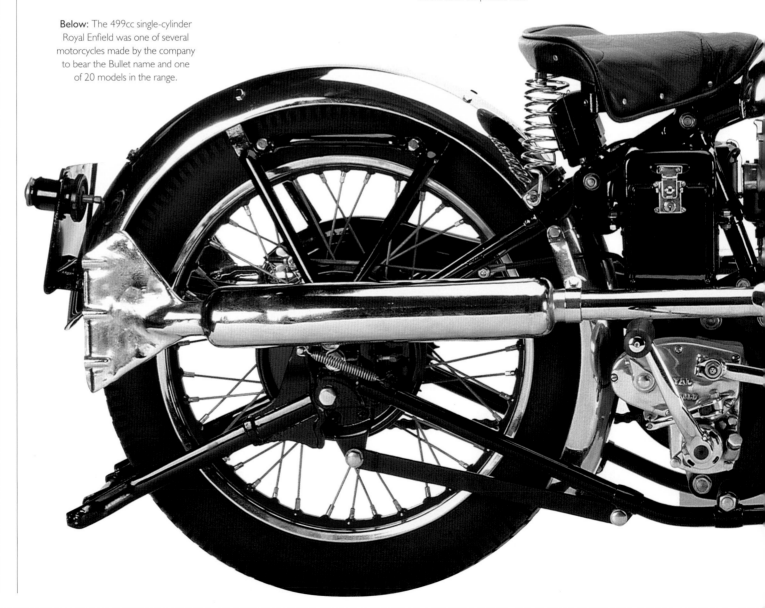

By 1938 there were 20 different models in the range. The war then intervened and Royal Enfield concentrated on manufacturing the 125cc Flying Flea for airborne troops, and the 346cc Model C and CO singles for the Army. The wartime Flying Flea came about as the result of a request from a Dutch company that had sold German DKW motorcycles in Holland prior to World War Two. The Jewish-owned company had its franchise removed by the Nazis and asked Royal Enfield to supply a substitute. The result was a lightweight 125cc two-stroke. When the war started, it was redesigned in order to accompany paratroopers into battle by parachute. Postwar it became part of Royal Enfield's range in civilian colours.

Right: Earlier JF Bullets featured an engine canted forward in the frame. This configuration changed in 1936 when the vertical arrangement illustrated here was adopted.

Above: The overhead-valve JF Bullet featured a four-valve cylinder head and these were operated by cam-driven pushrods. The silencer had been restyled for 1937.

ROYAL ENFIELD 500 TWIN

SPECIFICATIONS
Year: 1951
Engine type: Ohv vertical twin
Engine cycle: Four-stroke
Capacity: 495cc (30.2cu in)
Bore & stroke: 64 x 77mm
Horsepower: 25bhp @ 5500rpm
Top speed: 78mph (125kph)
Compression ratio: 6.5:1
Carburettor: Amal
Transmission: 4-speed
Brakes: F. & R. Drum
Ignition: Coil and points
Frame: Steel cradle
Suspension: F. Telescopic forks. R. Swingarm and shock absorbers
Wheelbase: 54in (1372mm)
Weight: 390lb (177kg)
Fuel: 3.46 gallons (15.73lit)
Oil: 4 pints (2.27lit)
Tyres: 3.25 x 19in

Above: The distinctive logo and the slogan "Made Like A Gun" reflected the fact that The Enfield Cycle Company had supplied machines to the Royal Small Arms factory at Enfield.

ROYAL ENFIELD 500 TWIN (1951)

The success of Triumph's twin introduced before World War Two caused other British motorcycle manufacturers to rush to introduce their own models with the same engine configuration immediately after the war. Royal Enfield was no exception and their machine, introduced in 1948, had a completely new engine, a 495cc overhead-valve vertical twin. The engine was constructed around a single alloy-iron cast crankshaft which was mounted in ball and roller main bearings. The big ends were of the plain type. The engine had two camshafts which were chain-driven. The dynamo was also chain-driven but from the forward camshaft. It had a skew-gear drive to the distributor which housed the points for the coil ignition system. The cylinder barrels were made from alloy while the cylinder heads were cast in iron. The oil pumps were the

standard Enfield items and, in line with Enfield practice, the lubricant was carried in a crankcase sump. The gearbox was bolted to the rear of the engine crankcase and the whole unit fitted in to cycle parts that were almost identical to the single-cylinder Bullets of the time, including the girder forks.

For 1950 the 500 Twin, which unlike Royal Enfield's other motorcycles was never given a name, was modernized by the fitment of telescopic forks. It continued in this form for 1951, the year of this model, until 1958. Other Royal Enfield Twins such as the Meteor models – Meteor, Meteor Minor and Super Meteor – were introduced and produced alongside the 500 Twin for some years. The Constellation, also a vertical twin, appeared in the final year of 500 Twin production.

Below: Because other British manufacturers were offering twins in their ranges, Royal Enfield felt it also needed one. The new engine, a 495cc ohv twin, was introduced in 1948 and endured a decade.

Above: The design of the twin engine followed Royal Enfield's practice of incorporating a crankcase sump into that component to which the gearbox was bolted.

Right: Many of the parts used in the twin were also used in the singles, including the rear frame arrangement, swingarm, shock absorbers and rear drum brake hub.

Below: The Twin's engine used separate cast-iron cylinder barrels, each of which had its own alloy head. The distributor sat behind the engine; ignition was by coil.

Right: Like the remainder of the cycle parts, much of the front end of the Royal Enfield 500 Twin was shared with the smaller capacity single-cylinder machines, such as the 350cc Bullet.

ROYAL ENFIELD BULLET

Specifications
Year: 1954
Engine type: Overhead-valve single
Engine cycle: Four-stroke
Capacity: 346cc (21.1cu in)
Bore & stroke: 70 x 90mm
Horsepower: 18bhp @ 5750rpm
Top speed: 68mph (110kph)
Compression ratio: 6.5:1
Carburettor: Amal
Transmission: 4-speed
Brakes: F. TLS drum. R. Drum
Ignition: Magneto
Frame: Tubular steel loop
Suspension: F. Telescopic forks. R. Swingarm and shock absorbers
Wheelbase: 54in (1372mm)
Weight: 350lb (159kg)
Fuel: 3.25 gallons (14.8lit)
Oil: 4 pints (2.27lit)
Tyres: 3.25 x 19in

Above: The Royal Enfield Bullet had its headlamp mounted in a nacelle which was termed a casquette by the manufacturer. More unusual were the twin sidelights mounted in the same unit.

ROYAL ENFIELD BULLET (1954)

Royal Enfield had used the Bullet name on some of its prewar motorcycles, but the company introduced a new model of the same name in 1948. It caused a sensation on its first outing as it was the first time a swingarm frame had been used in trials competition. The new Bullet was ridden by a Royal Enfield works team during the 1948 Colmore Cup. The road trim version officially appeared in the 1949 Royal Enfield range.

The internals of the engine were carried over from the prewar Model G, although the crankcase was different, as the oil was now carried behind the flywheel compartment. Ignition was by magneto. The transmission bolted to the rear of the crankcase to give semi-unit construction and primary drive was by means of a duplex chain housed in an alloy case. This engine and gearbox assembly was fitted to the frame which featured single top and downtubes. The rear frame loops carried the mounts for the shock absorbers and curved back into the plates on which the swingarm pivoted. Telescopic forks and drum brakes completed the cycle parts.

The machine received favourable reviews and became a stalwart of the

Royal Enfield postwar range. It was gradually upgraded through its long production run; the dynamo gave way to an alternator in 1956 and the magneto to a coil in 1960. The power crept up slightly too, by 1960 the 350cc engine produced 21bhp @ 6500rpm as a result of increased compression ratio. The 1950 model was reported in motorcycle magazines as being capable of 74mph (119kph) and returning over 80mpg (28km/litre). Braking was acceptable, handling was reasonable and maintenance was straightforward, so the machine sold well. The larger 500cc displacement Bullet appeared for 1953 and used mostly the same cycle parts as the 350. The Bullet was available in trials, scrambles and roadgoing trim.

The styling of the machine was given a boost in 1954 when the die-cast casquette headlamp cowl made its appearance. The casquette carried the headlamp, sidelights, speedometer, ammeter and light switch. In the same year the rear-suspension units were also fitted with proprietary brand components which had the effect of increasing suspension movement. Royal Enfield 350cc Bullets were ridden in the 1955 International Six Days Trial (ISDT) by team riders including John Brittain, who won a Gold Medal on one.

Below: The Bullet featured swingarm rear suspension – a fork pivoted behind the gearbox and was damped by a pair of hydraulic rear shock absorbers. The rear wheel could therefore move up and down over bumps.

The gradual upgrades continued, new full-width alloy hubs being introduced for 1956, along with a few changes to the big end and crankshaft bearings of the 350cc engine to make them the same as were used in the 500cc unit. Later the casquette, silencer, petrol tank and front brakes were modified as the Bullet ran into its final years. It was finally discontinued after the appearance of the 1962 models. The name, however, would be used again, this time on a unit-construction 350cc machine.

Above: This is the Bullet in its roadgoing trim, although there were also trials and scrambles versions of the Bullet which were used by the British Team in the 1955 ISDT trial.

Above: The single-cylinder engine displaced 346cc and its long stroke made it suitable for both off-road use and as a reliable commuter bike. The 350cc class was popular in Britain for both these markets.

Above: Royal Enfield used the slogan "Made Like A Gun" to sell its products. However, calling this motorcycle a Bullet was something of a misnomer as it was not a fast machine but rather a steady commuter motorcycle.

Right: The front numberplates were mounted longitudinally on the front mudguard. Such plates were later dropped for road safety reasons.

ROYAL ENFIELD CONTINENTAL GT

SPECIFICATIONS
Year: 1966
Engine type: Single
Engine cycle: Four-stroke
Capacity: 248cc (15.1cu in)
Bore & stroke: 70 x 64.5mm
Horsepower: 26bhp @ 7500rpm
Top speed: 86mph (138kph)
Compression ratio: 9.5:1
Carburettor: Amal
Transmission: 5-speed
Brakes: F. & R. Drum
Ignition: Coil
Frame: Steel cradle
Suspension: F. Telescopic forks. R. Swingarm and shock absorbers
Wheelbase: 52in (1321mm)
Weight: 300lb (136kg)
Fuel: 3.5 gallons (15.9lit)
Oil: 3 pints (1.7lit)
Tyres: F. 3.00 x 18in. R. 3.25 x 17in

Above: The Amal carburettor featured a bell mouth instead of a conventional air cleaner.

ROYAL ENFIELD CONTINENTAL GT (1966)

This 250 became popular as a café racer because of its sleek lines and racetrack-inspired features, such as clip-on handlebars, drum brake cooling discs and race-style seat. It was introduced in November 1964 after a concerted effort by Royal Enfield's management to discover what young motorcyclists wanted at the time. They carried out market research by asking their dealers and apprentices about what youngsters would buy. The result was the Continental GT, basically a stripped-down version of the Crusader Sports.

It used the 250cc Crusader engine and 5-speed gearbox. Race-style parts included the sweptback exhaust, the bell mouth on the carburettor in place of an air cleaner, a plastic tube crankcase breather and of course the rear-set footrests and levers. The clip-on handlebars, fly screen, cooling discs on the front brake hub, humped-back dual seat and fibreglass fuel

tank with its quick-release filler cap completed the appearance of a road-going racer. Royal Enfield drummed up publicity on its introduction by having a team of five riders relay one between John O'Groats and Land's End in less than 24 hours. The Continental GT was reputed to handle well and be capable of 86mph (138kph) and 76mpg (27km/lit).

The Continental GT was, however, an expensive motorcycle, and in August 1965 Royal Enfield contracted its range by deleting four other models in order to concentrate on it. Gradually the remaining models in the Royal Enfield stable were discontinued until production of the Continental also stopped coincident with the closure of Royal Enfield and the sale of the Redditch factory. Times were hard in the contracting British bike industry and the financially struggling company was taken over by Norton-Villiers in 1967.

Right: The Royal Enfield Continental was a genuine attempt to offer a motorcycle of the type that younger customers really wanted.

Right: The café racer styling was evident in the small aero-style screen, clip-on handlebars, race filler cap and long sculpted petrol tank.

Below: One of the café racer styling touches applied to the Continental were the front brake drum trims intended to replicate race-style brake cooling devices.

Above: As befitted its café racer image, the 5-speed Continental GT was genuinely nippy – it could reach 86mph (138kph) and handled well.

ENFIELD INDIA
BULLET

SPECIFICATIONS
Year: 1997
Engine type: Overhead-valve single
Engine cycle: Four-stroke
Capacity: 499cc (30.45cu in)
Bore & stroke: 84 x 90mm
Horsepower: 22bhp @ 5400rpm
Top speed: 78mph (125kph)
Compression ratio: 6.5:1
Carburettor: Mikuni
Transmission: 4-speed
Brakes: F. TLS drum. R. Drum
Ignition: Coil and points
Frame: Tubular steel loop
Suspension: F. Telescopic forks. R. Swingarm and shock absorbers
Wheelbase: 54in (1372mm)
Weight: 370lb (168kg)
Fuel: 3.46 gallons (15.75lit)
Oil: 4 pints (2.27lit)
Tyres: F. 3.25 x 19in. R. 3.50 x 19in

Above: The Enfield India motorcycle concern was started through a licensing agreement that permitted the Madras-based company to produce Royal Enfield Bullets in an Indian factory. It has continued doing so until the present time despite British production being halted.

ENFIELD INDIA 500 BULLET (1997)

It may seem strange to include an Indian-manufactured motorcycle in a book about British bikes, but there is a perfectly good reason. The Indian-produced Enfield Bullet is something of an anachronism in that it is a completely traditional design of 1950s British bike that, by historical accident, is still in production at the beginning of the twenty-first century. During the 1950s the Indian Government made arrangements with Royal Enfield to manufacture their Bullet motorcycle. In 1956 Royal Enfield set up a subsidiary in the Indian city of Madras to produce the 350cc Bullet under licence. This led to the formation of Enfield India Ltd. The Indian factory reproduced the 1955 specification Bullet and continued doing so long after the Redditch-built Bullets were discontinued.

In a complete reversal of the original operation, the Indian-produced motorcycles are now exported around the world. In 1977 the Indian-built machines were imported to Britain for the first time and they have been intermittently available ever since. The Bullet is also exported from India to other European nations and to the USA where it is bought by those who either desire a modern classic bike, who want simple and inexpensive transport, or those who find it an intriguing curiosity. Exports have at times been affected by such diverse factors as labour disputes, tidal waves and floods in India. One strike in the late 1970s closed the factory for a period of four months.

There has been much speculation in the motorcycle press about exactly who buys Enfield India Bullets, and why. Some doubters say smaller-capacity Japanese imports offer both the economy and speed of the Bullet. Others wonder that the cost of a Bullet means that a more sophisticated Japanese bike is almost as affordable. Yet more say that those who want an old British bike would prefer to buy an authentic one rather than a new old bike like this. Despite such scepticism sales have justified the continuing importation of the machines in small numbers. In India, by contrast, the machines are supplied for official use by the Army and police forces in much greater numbers.

The current Bullets have changed slightly from the original 1955 specification. Refinements have been introduced sparingly or when required by law. The motorcycles now feature 12-volt electrics instituted in 1987, an alternator in place of a dynamo, a distributor in place of a magneto and indicator lights as required by law. Subsequently 500cc Bullets have been built in India and exported; these models optionally feature a single disc brake on the front wheel. The Indian-manufactured Bullets are available in three specifications: Standard, Deluxe and Superstar. The latter two feature minor improvements such as chromed panels on the petrol tank.

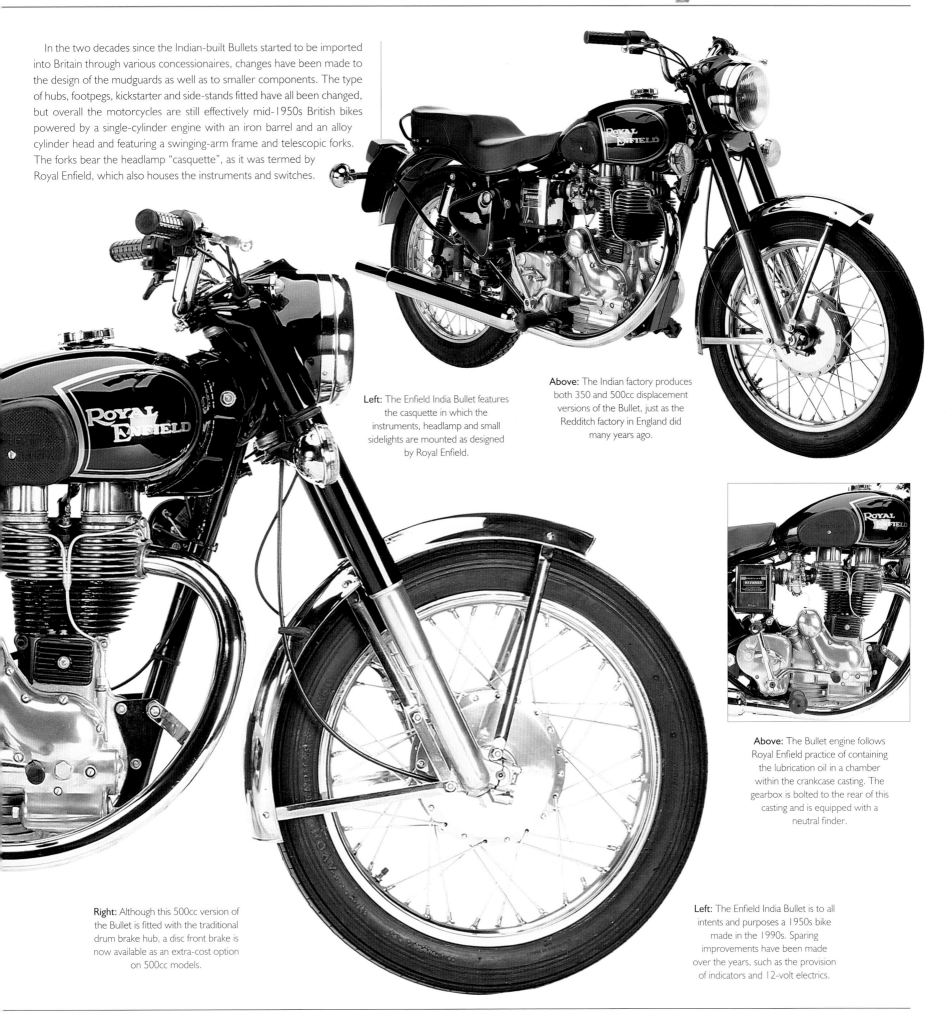

In the two decades since the Indian-built Bullets started to be imported into Britain through various concessionaires, changes have been made to the design of the mudguards as well as to smaller components. The type of hubs, footpegs, kickstarter and side-stands fitted have all been changed, but overall the motorcycles are still effectively mid-1950s British bikes powered by a single-cylinder engine with an iron barrel and an alloy cylinder head and featuring a swinging-arm frame and telescopic forks. The forks bear the headlamp "casquette", as it was termed by Royal Enfield, which also houses the instruments and switches.

Left: The Enfield India Bullet features the casquette in which the instruments, headlamp and small sidelights are mounted as designed by Royal Enfield.

Above: The Indian factory produces both 350 and 500cc displacement versions of the Bullet, just as the Redditch factory in England did many years ago.

Above: The Bullet engine follows Royal Enfield practice of containing the lubrication oil in a chamber within the crankcase casting. The gearbox is bolted to the rear of this casting and is equipped with a neutral finder.

Right: Although this 500cc version of the Bullet is fitted with the traditional drum brake hub, a disc front brake is now available as an extra-cost option on 500cc models.

Left: The Enfield India Bullet is to all intents and purposes a 1950s bike made in the 1990s. Sparing improvements have been made over the years, such as the provision of indicators and 12-volt electrics.

RUDGE ULSTER

SPECIFICATIONS
Year: 1936
Engine type: Ohv single
Engine cycle: Four-stroke
Capacity: 499cc (30.45cu in)
Bore & stroke: 85 x 88mm
Horsepower: 35bhp
Top speed: 87mph (140kph)
Compression ratio: 6.8:1
Carburettor: Amal
Transmission: 4-speed
Brakes: F. & R. Drum
Ignition: Magneto
Frame: Steel cradle
Suspension: F. Sprung girder forks. R. None
Wheelbase: 56in (1422mm)
Weight: 399lb (181kg)
Fuel: 3.5 gallons (15.9lit)
Oil: n/a
Tyres: F. 3.00 x 21in.
R. 3.25 x 20in

Above: The Rudge Ulster's 499cc single-cylinder engine featured a four-valve head. The valves were operated by two pushrods on the right-hand side of the engine.

Right: The Rudge Ulster name came about as a direct result of Graham Walker's record-breaking run in the 1928 Ulster Grand Prix at speeds of more than 80mph (129kph).

RUDGE ULSTER (1936)

The Rudge-Whitworth bicycle factory in Coventry started producing motorcycles in 1911. Their first production machine was a 499cc inlet-over-exhaust configuration machine. In the years after World War One the company produced a 749cc single and a 998cc V-twin. Rudge also built what became known as the multi-gear which was a variable gear that gave up to 21 positions.

In 1923 and 1924 major changes were made to Rudge's range in terms of new engines and new gearboxes. By the 1930s their reputation was established as makers of fine motorcycles, no doubt helped by some considerable racing success. An example of this was Graham Walker's win in the 1928 Ulster Grand Prix, the first time speeds of more than 80mph (129kph) had been achieved in a road race. As Walker was Rudge's sales manager, his victory led to a 499cc sports model being christened the Rudge Ulster for promotional reasons.

In 1930 at the Isle of Man TT Rudge won both Senior and Junior events. The Junior TT was won by riders on machines powered by radial four-valve engines who took the first three places. The Senior TT saw

Rudge machines take first and second places. Rudge intended to cash in on this TT success for sales of the 1931 models. They were thwarted to some degree by the fact that the market for motorcycles was depressed at this time and further hampered by the heavy financial cost of developing the TT-winning machines. Still more development costs had to be borne in redesigning the engines of roadgoing models in order to move the magneto from its position forward of the cylinder to one behind it in the interests of modernity.

The Depression adversely affected Rudge's sales of complete motorcycles and they offered their engines and gearboxes to other manufacturers under the Python name. These engines were used in sev-

Right: The components used in the assembly of the Rudge Ulster were typical of the time and included sprung girder forks, a rigid frame and an overhead-valve single-cylinder engine.

Above: The magneto was positioned forward of the cylinder barrel and its drive enclosed behind the angled alloy cover immediately behind the downward curve of the exhaust.

eral British-made motorcycles and a number of European ones too. Racing remained a priority at Rudge despite indifferent sales and the factory was still successful at it. In 1931 Rudge machines placed first and second in the Lightweight TT, second and third in both Junior and Lightweight TTs in 1932. Sales could not justify the expenditure, however, and the company went in to receivership in March 1933.

A syndicate borrowed the race bikes for the following season and achieved a 1-2-3 sweep in the 1934 Lightweight TT, but this success was not be repeated as the race bikes became obsolete and outclassed by other firms' machines. Trading in receivership kept Rudge in business until late in 1935 when it was realized that sales had not improved sufficiently to improve their position significantly, so Rudge went into liquidation. The firm was acquired by EMI and the works moved to Hayes in Middlesex from Coventry (see also next entry on Rudge Special). The company initially persevered with the same programme of motorcycle production.

Against this uncertain financial background production of the Rudge Ulster continued. It remained a 499cc overhead-valve-engined machine although the pent-roof four-valve head had given way to a radial for 1932, and this had in turn given way to a semi-radial four-valve head for 1933. In this last form it ran on until the outbreak of war in 1939.

Above: The 1936 Ulster was well appointed with instruments including a handlebar-mounted tachometer (left) and speedometer (right), as well as an ammeter fitted in the headlamp shell.

Below: Rear suspension was not usually provided in the 1930s, so the springs fitted below the solo saddle offered the only method of suspension to improve rider comfort.

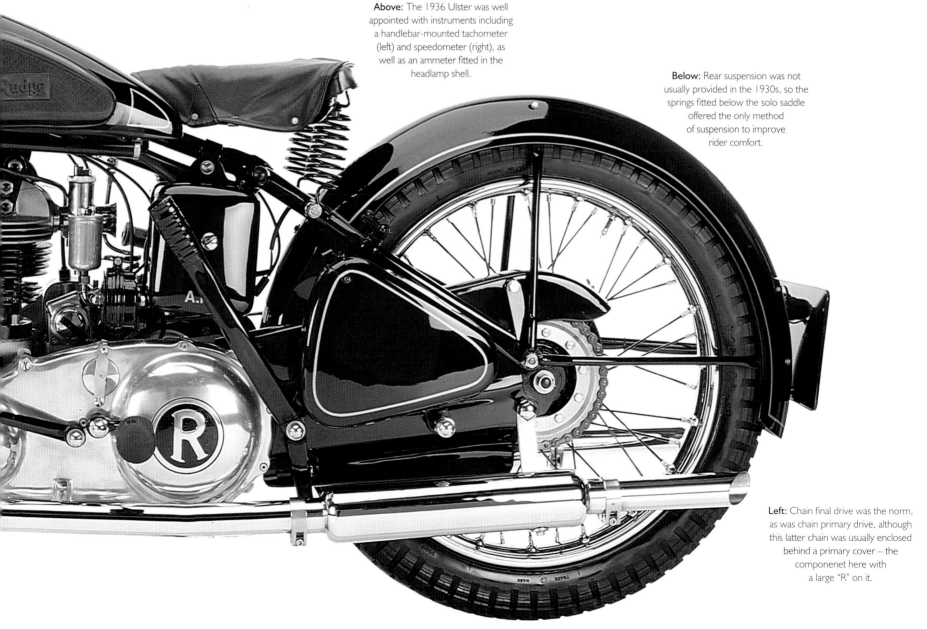

Left: Chain final drive was the norm, as was chain primary drive, although this latter chain was usually enclosed behind a primary cover – the componenet here with a large "R" on it.

RUDGE SPECIAL

SPECIFICATIONS
Year: 1937
Engine type: Ohv single
Engine cycle: Four-stroke
Capacity: 493cc (30.1cu in)
Bore & stroke: 84.5 x 88mm
Horsepower: n/a
Top speed: 70mph (113kph)
Compression ratio: n/a
Carburettor: Amal
Transmission: 4-speed
Brakes: F. & R. Drum
Ignition: Magneto
Frame: Steel cradle
Suspension: F. Sprung girder
forks. R. None
Wheelbase: n/a
Weight: n/a
Fuel: 3.5 gallons (15.9lit)
Oil: n/a
Tyres: 3.25 x 19in

Above: The handlebar-mounted speedometer was calibrated up to a realistic 80mph and incorporated both mileometer and tripmeter. It was made by Smiths, the noted English instrument maker.

Right: Beyond a redesigned cylinder head, the Rudge Special had little about it to make it stand out from the crowd. It was a conventional and docile motorcycle manufactured around the time of Rudge's moves to Hayes, Middlesex.

RUDGE SPECIAL (1937)

Under EMI's control, sales of the Rudge range improved but not to the extent that could justify the size of the Coventry factory. This and the fact that EMI management from Hayes were proving difficult led to the Rudge production lines being shifted to Hayes in Middlesex. Despite the name of this machine – the Rudge Special – it was in fact a standard machine powered by an overhead-valve single-cylinder engine. The Special had a four-valve cylinder head in which the valves were arranged in parallel pairs rather than in the radial configuration of the Ulster models. This difference helped make the Special a more docile motorcycle and one requiring less frequent adjustment of valve clearances. Unusually for the time, the gears were engaged by a left-side, rather than right, foot lever. Some features of the machine including its four-valve head, complex transmission and large brakes contributed to making the Special an expensive motorcycle to buy.

Except for the addition of one motorcycle, the range was almost unchanged for 1938 because of the need to move the plant south. This newcomer was the Sports 250, with a tuned engine and high level exhaust pipe. Despite the upheaval of the move, sales continued at about the same level. An unchanged range was announced for 1939 and production remained steady in order to meet growing demand.

Rudge was also getting involved in the production of Autocycles – motorized bicycles – in conjunction with Norman. This company, an established bicycle manufacturer, was based at Ashford in Kent and it had entered the market in 1939 with two motorized two-wheelers. One was an autocycle known as the Motobyke and the other a 122cc machine called the Lightweight. This latter vehicle was powered by a proprietary Villiers engine and had a 3-speed gearbox. It was constructed around a basic loop frame. Rudge's autocycle used a 98cc Villiers two-stroke engine in a strengthened bicycle-type frame. It was made by Norman in Kent although badged as a Rudge. There were two versions, the Standard and Deluxe which were typical of the era and type of machine featurring rigid forks and drum brakes. The main difference between Standard and Deluxe models was the fitment of engine shields to the latter.

If circumstances had been different, the combined factors of increasing

Above: The valanced front mudguard ended with an unusually styled flared lip on its trailing edge where the mudguard stays joined the mudguard.

Right: The pillion pad mounted on the pinstriped rear mudguard offered a passenger only limited comfort as the machine was devoid of rear suspension.

Below: Sprung saddles such as this were the norm on prewar British motorcycles. Their design and type of mounting suited the sloping tubes of the frame.

sales, lower overheads and the new autocycle product might have enabled Rudge to have survived as a viable motorcycle manufacturer. However, the outbreak of World War Two intervened dramatically. EMI required additional space in their Hayes factory for the production of radar equipment that was vital for the war effort. They perfunctorily shelved motorcycle production in December 1939 in order to create the factory space. Norman also ceased autocycle and motorcycle production for the duration of the war. In 1943 the Rudge company name was sold by EMI to Raleigh Industries when EMI concluded that they would not resume motorcycle production after the war. Raleigh later used the brand name on a range of pedal cycles. Norman did resume motorized two-wheeler production in 1946. Ironically, it too was later acquired by Raleigh Industries, although not until 1960 by which time the company had made a variety of lightweight machines.

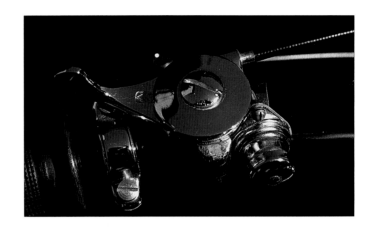

Right: Prewar British bikes relied heavily on traditional engineering. Controls such as these were assembled from numerous components and required chroming and machining. Today, similar components would be manufactured from plastic and alloy.

Below: The fuel tank was of the saddle tank design and curved over the frame's top tube. It was finished in black with gold pinstripes and fitted with rubber knee grips.

Left: The headlight was mounted on brackets forward of the workings of the sprung girder forks and contained some of the instruments and the ignition switch.

Above: The Rudge Special was powered by an overhead-valve 493cc single-cylinder engine with a bore and stroke of 84.5 x 88mm.

SCOTT FLYING SQUIRREL

Year: 1949
Engine type: Twin
Engine cycle: Two-stroke
Capacity: 598cc (36.5cu in)
Bore & stroke: 73 x 71.4mm
Horsepower: 30bhp @ 5000rpm
Top speed: 84mph (135kph)
Compression ratio: n/a
Carburettor: Amal
Transmission: 3-speed
Brakes: F. & R. Drum
Ignition: Coil
Frame: Duplex rigid
Suspension: F. Telescopic forks. R. None
Wheelbase: 57in (1448mm)
Weight: 395lb (179kg)
Fuel: 2.75 gallons (12.5lit)
Oil: n/a
Tyres: 3.25 x 19in

Right: Scott was noted for using water-cooled two-stroke engines in its motorcycles at a time when most manufacturers used air-cooling for both two- and four-strokes.

SCOTT SQUIRREL (1949)

This company was founded by Alfred A. Scott in 1909 in Shipley, Yorkshire and was among the pioneers of the two-stroke motorcycle. The firm enjoyed some Isle of Man TT successes including wins in 1912 and 1913. Most Scott motorcycles were water-cooled and Scott himself is reputed to have had a flair for combining unorthodox ideas with sound and practical engineering. Scott had employed rotary inlet valves, water-cooling and the 180-degree parallel-twin two-stroke in the early years of the twentieth century, long before many of these ideas were adopted by Japanese manufacturers. Scott used the engine as a stressed member in his duplex, triangulated tube frames to enhance handling and he pioneered all-chain-drive and countershaft gears. A.A. Scott relinquished his connection with the company in 1915 and died in 1923 but production of his basic designs continued.

From 1929 Scott produced an air-cooled single as a motorcycle for the smaller-capacity market. Unlike most other British manufacturers of the time, the company did not purchase a Villiers proprietary engine but made its own. It was of a crude design with an iron barrel and alloy head. The number of head bolts had to be doubled in 1930, from three to six, as the smaller number had allowed the cylinder head to warp. The single was equipped with girder forks, a duplex frame and magneto ignition.

The water-cooled two-stroke engine used in the Flying Squirrel was unusual in its design; the flywheel was centrally positioned with twin inboard main bearings, overhung crankpins and crankcase doors to allow access to the engine. The whole was located in a large alloy casting on which sat the block with non-detachable cylinder heads. The engine was made in two capacities, 499cc and 598cc through using cylinders with a common stroke but a change in bore diameter. The fuel tank was positioned atop the triangulated frame and was oval in shape. A number of variants, including sprint and TT replica models of the Flying Squirrel, were offered.

Like other British motorcycle manufacturers, Scott's production was interrupted by the outbreak of World War Two and the company did not make motorcycles for the forces. In 1946 Scott resumed motorcycle production with a version of the Flying Squirrel that was largely unchanged from the prewar machines. It used the same 598cc engine, a water-cooled two-stroke twin with a two-into-one exhaust pipe. The full-width hub drum front brake was new for the postwar machines and these postwar models were generally assembled with Dowty telescopic forks. In 1949 the ignition was changed from magneto to coil, and production looked set to continue for 1950. Market forces were to dictate otherwise, however, as by now the Scott was seen by many potential purchasers as an expensive anachronism. It retailed at a cost not dissimilar to a sporting air-cooled four-stroke twin of the day, but did not offer comparable performance. The company went into voluntary liquidation and the Saltaire, West Yorkshire factory was sold. An engineer and Scott enthusiast bought much of the company's assets and briefly produced motorcycles again between 1956 and 1958.

Right: The typically British sprung saddle offered the only rear suspension on the Yorkshire-built Scott Squirrel.

Above: The Scott Squirrel did not have rear suspension. For this, and other, reasons it was seen by many as an anachronism by the late 1940s.

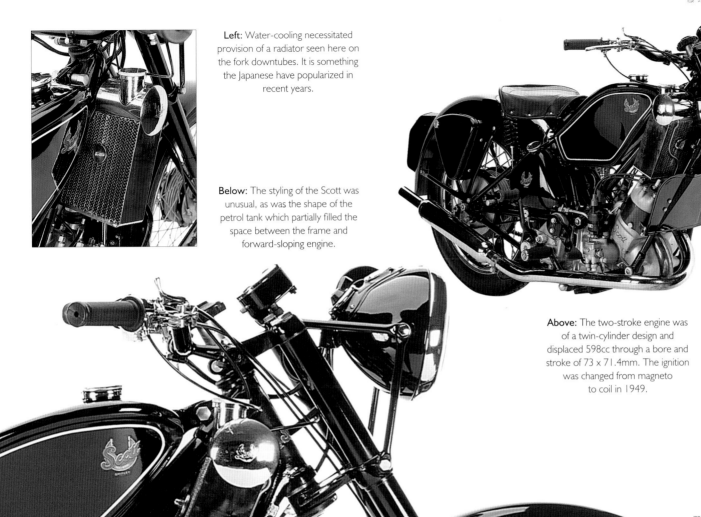

Left: Water-cooling necessitated provision of a radiator seen here on the fork downtubes. It is something the Japanese have popularized in recent years.

Below: The styling of the Scott was unusual, as was the shape of the petrol tank which partially filled the space between the frame and forward-sloping engine.

Above: The two-stroke engine was of a twin-cylinder design and displaced 598cc through a bore and stroke of 73 x 71.4mm. The ignition was changed from magneto to coil in 1949.

Left: When Scott resumed motorcycle production after the war the motorcycles were fitted with Dowty telescopic forks and a full-width hub drum brake.

Above: Although the Scott company failed to manufacture and market water-cooled two-stroke motorcycles successfully in the postwar years, Japanese factories later mass-produced machines of this configuration.

Left: The escalating costs of the Scott Squirrel meant that the machine did not seem to offer customers value for money when compared to the motorcycles offered by other companies at the turn of the decade.

SUNBEAM MODEL 90

SPECIFICATIONS
Year: 1928
Engine type: Ohv single
Engine cycle: Four-stroke
Capacity: 493cc (30.1cu in)
Bore & stroke: 80 x 98mm
Horsepower: n/a
Top speed: 90mph (145kph)
Compression ratio: 7.5:1
Carburettor: Amal
Transmission: 3-speed
Brakes: F. & R. Drum
Ignition: Magneto
Frame: Steel tubular
Suspension: F. Sprung girder forks. R. None
Wheelbase: n/a
Weight: 300lb (136kg)
Fuel: 3.5 gallons (15.9lit)
Oil: n/a
Tyres: 3.25 x 19in

Right: This Sunbeam 90 was built by the Wolverhampton company at a time when they were having considerable Isle of Man TT success including a Senior TT win in 1928.

SUNBEAM MODEL 90 (1928)

The Sunbeam company was founded in 1912 by John Marston who already built bicycles in his Wolverhampton works using the Sunbeam trademark. The first Sunbeam motorcycle was made with a 347cc side-valve engine, a 2-speed gearbox and enclosed primary and final drive chains. Later the company, like many others in the 1920s, used engines from AKD, JAP and MAG and supplied V-twin engined motorcycles. Sunbeam gained a reputation for excellence and innovation and was subsequently acquired by ICI, the chemical company, in 1928.

The Isle of Man TT saw Sunbeam wins in 1920, 1922, 1928 and 1929. The 1920 and 1922 wins were taken by Tommy de la Hay and Alec Bennet respectively, riding side-valve machines. Aboard one of the overhead-valve Model 90 machines, Charlie Dodson won the Senior TT in 1928 despite a crash. He repeated the victory in 1929 and went on to win the French and Belgian Grands Prix later in the year. Sunbeam had introduced overhead-valve machines in 1923 and of these the 500cc displacement model was the most successful. By 1928 this machine featured inlet and exhaust valves set at 90 degrees to one another in the cast-iron head. The domed pistons incorporated full skirts and three piston rings of which the lower one acted as oil scraper ring. Lubrication was dry sump and the double gear pump fed the big end, camshafts, rocker spindles and valve stems as well as scavenging the crankcase. The Sunbeam Model 90 was the last pushrod two-valve-engined machine to win a Senior TT.

While the Model 90 was primarily a racing bike, it was offered in road-going trim with additional features such as a kickstarter, enclosed rear chain and lights. The flat tanks of the first models were dropped for 1929 when the more modern saddle tank was introduced. Versions of this racer were produced until 1935 as the Model 95L.

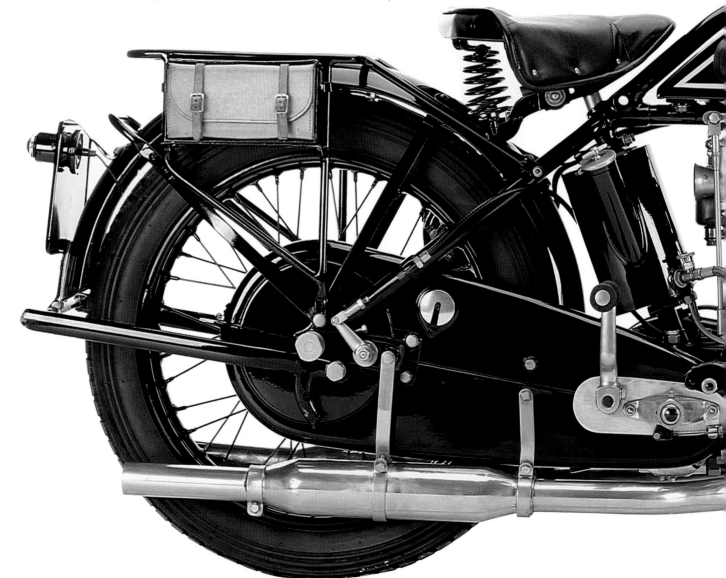

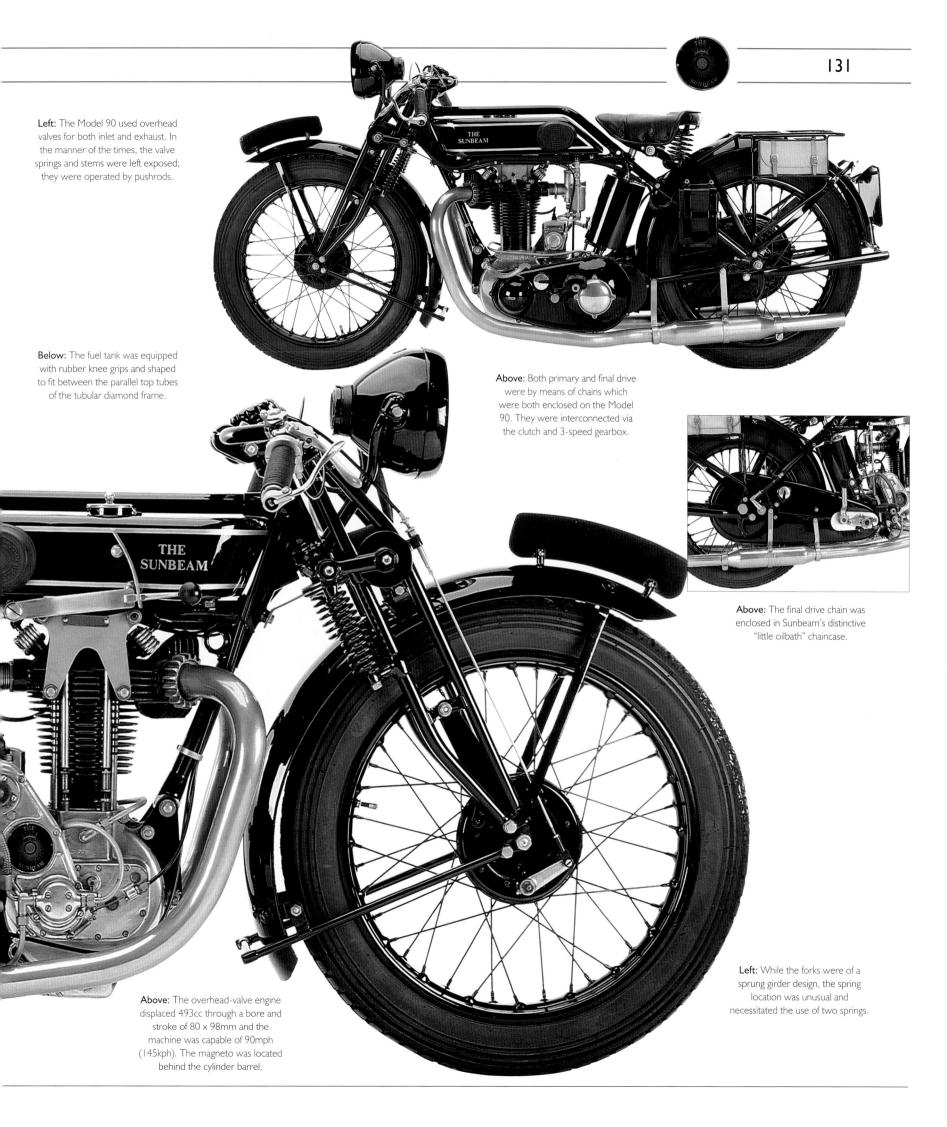

Left: The Model 90 used overhead valves for both inlet and exhaust. In the manner of the times, the valve springs and stems were left exposed; they were operated by pushrods.

Below: The fuel tank was equipped with rubber knee grips and shaped to fit between the parallel top tubes of the tubular diamond frame.

Above: Both primary and final drive were by means of chains which were both enclosed on the Model 90. They were interconnected via the clutch and 3-speed gearbox.

Above: The final drive chain was enclosed in Sunbeam's distinctive "little oilbath" chaincase.

Above: The overhead-valve engine displaced 493cc through a bore and stroke of 80 x 98mm and the machine was capable of 90mph (145kph). The magneto was located behind the cylinder barrel.

Left: While the forks were of a sprung girder design, the spring location was unusual and necessitated the use of two springs.

SUNBEAM S8

Year: 1953
Engine type: In-line twin
Engine cycle: Four-stroke
Capacity: 489cc (29.8cu in)
Bore & stroke: 70 x 63.5mm
Horsepower: 25bhp @ 5800rpm
Top speed: 83mph (134kph)
Compression ratio: n/a
Carburettor: Amal
Transmission: 4-speed
Brakes: F. & R. Drum
Ignition: Coil
Frame: Duplex cradle
Suspension: F. Telescopic forks. R. Plunger frame
Wheelbase: 57in (1448mm)
Weight: 410lb (186kg)
Fuel: 3.25 gallons (14.8lit)
Oil: 4 pints (2.27lit)
Tyres: F. 3.25 x 19in. R. 4.00 x 18in

Above: The ammeter and ignition key switch for the ignition of the Sunbeam S8 were mounted in the side cover of the battery box. The other side was filled by the oil tank.

Right: The Sunbeam S8 was a revised lighter version of the Sunbeam S7. It was introduced in 1949 and production lasted until 1956, although sales were slow because the machine was expensive.

SUNBEAM S8 (1953)

By the late 1920s the roadgoing Sunbeam machines were not faring well in the marketplace against other British makes and the pressure was on to compete. A new range of 250 and 500cc models were introduced in the early 1930s. Times were hard then and Sunbeam's reputation for quality was adversely affected by a management concerned to cut costs. Profits were still not sufficient to satisfy owners ICI, so in 1936 the company was sold to the AJS and Matchless concern in London. After this acquisition Sunbeam came under the AMC umbrella and production moved to London. World War Two then intervened and in 1943 AMC sold the Sunbeam name to BSA. This resulted in a totally new line-up of postwar twins, the 489cc shaft-drive machines.

The Sunbeam S7 and S8 were significant for being truly new postwar British motorcycles. The initial design work was done by Erling Poppe and the S7 motorcycle was introduced in 1947 for the 1948 season with an in-line twin-cylinder engine, 4-speed gearbox, shaft drive to the rear wheel and telescopic forks. While the in-line twin configuration was a

departure from the more common transverse twin, it did facilitate the use of a shaft drive simply because of the direction in which the crankshaft pointed. The engine had the clutch and gearbox bolted to it, the clutch was fitted to the end of the crankshaft. The gearbox was 4-speed and of the indirect type, which enabled the drive shaft to run down one side of the motorcycle. The shaft itself was equipped with a rubber coupling at the front end and a Hardy-Spicer universal joint at the rear. Drive to the wheel was by an underslung worm and the rear brake drum was incorporated into the drive housing. The overhead camshaft engine was innovative too in that it was all-alloy and was of the short-stroke design. The engine and gearbox were fitted to a duplex cradle frame with plunger rear suspension, at the front were telescopic forks. The wheels were both of 16-inch diameter and interchangeable from end to end. These, the hugely valanced mudguards and solo saddle all hinted at the opulent American motorcycle styling of the period.

Some problems with the new design caused improvements to be made during the production run. Erling Poppe had left Sunbeam so BSA staff carried out the development work. The S7 was revised as the S7

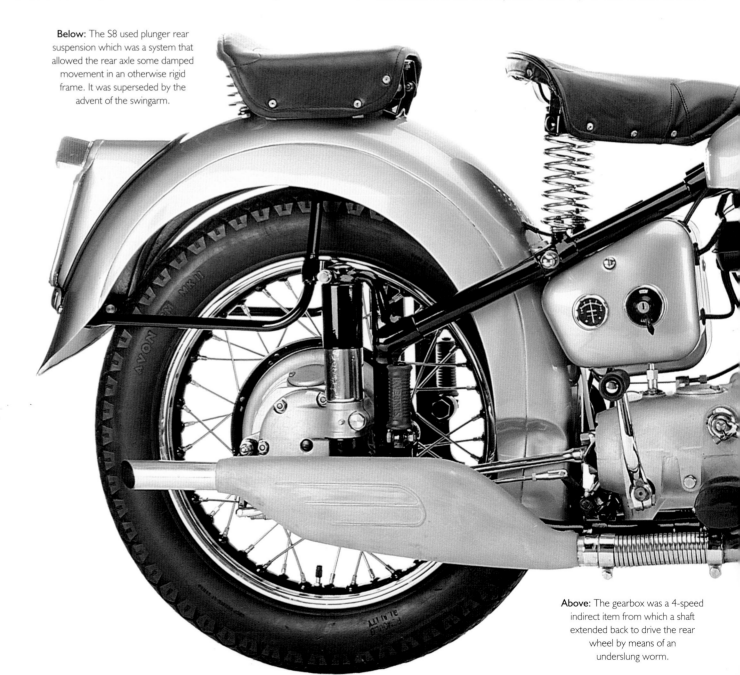

Below: The S8 used plunger rear suspension which was a system that allowed the rear axle some damped movement in an otherwise rigid frame. It was superseded by the advent of the swingarm.

Above: The gearbox was a 4-speed indirect item from which a shaft extended back to drive the rear wheel by means of an underslung worm.

deluxe for 1949 and the S8 was a newly introduced lighter version. From then on both models were produced in limited numbers. Sales were not as impressive as was hoped because both S7 and S8 were expensive machines and offered only average performance with a top speed of around 80mph (129kph). Production of both models lasted until 1956 although machines continued to be available until 1958. This signalled the end of Sunbeam motorcycle production. In the mergers and contraction that characterized the last years of the British motorcycle industry, the Sunbeam name appeared again briefly on some BSA two-stroke scooters but disappeared finally in 1964.

Right: The in-line twin was an unusual configuration for a motorcycle engine, but this layout did facilitate the easy installation of shaft drive to the rear wheel in the fashion of a car.

Below: Much of the styling of the S8 model Sunbeam was conventional and included telescopic forks, a rounded fuel tank, valanced mudguards and a sprung saddle.

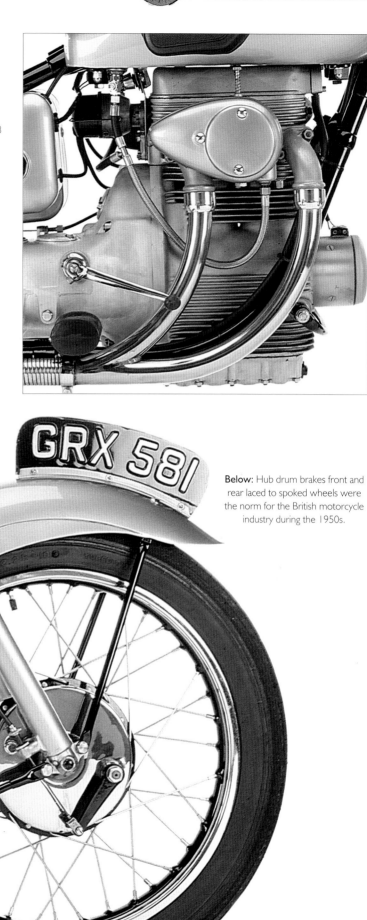

Below: Hub drum brakes front and rear laced to spoked wheels were the norm for the British motorcycle industry during the 1950s.

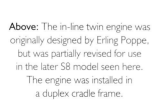

Above: The in-line twin engine was originally designed by Erling Poppe, but was partially revised for use in the later S8 model seen here. The engine was installed in a duplex cradle frame.

TRIUMPH 500CC

SPECIFICATIONS

Year: 1908
Engine type: Side-valve single
Engine cycle: Four-stroke
Capacity: 476cc (29.05cu in)
Bore & stroke: 84 x 86mm
Horsepower: 3hp @ 1500rpm
Top speed: 40mph (64kph)
Compression ratio: 4:1
Carburettor: Triumph patent
Transmission: Single-speed
Brakes: F. None. R. Rubber block
Ignition: Magneto
Frame: Steel diamond
Suspension: F. Sprung forks. R. None
Wheelbase: 49in (1245mm)
Weight: 250lb (113kg)
Fuel: n/a
Oil: n/a
Tyres: 26 x 2.25in

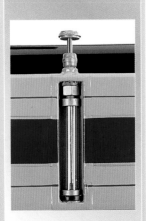

Above: The tank-mounted hand pump for transferring lubrication oil from the tank to the engine.

TRIUMPH 500 (1908)

The Triumph marque is one of Britain's most famous motorcycle makes and one with a long history. The company was founded by Siegfried Bettman in 1885 to sell bicycles. In 1887 Bettman was joined by Maurice Schulte and the two Germans established themselves near Coventry to manufacture bicycles. By 1897 they began to experiment with motorized bicycles and by 1902 had made a motorcycle powered by a 220cc Minerva engine. Later they used Belgian Fafnir and English JAP engines until Schulte designed the company's first powerplant.

The first Triumph engine was made in 1905. It was of a side-valve design and developed 3.5hp. The engine had mechanically operated valves actuated by tracks machined into timing gears which meshed with a pinion on the end of the crankshaft. Main bearings were of the ball type. A B&B carburettor was fitted and the ignition was normally by battery and coil, although a magneto was available as an option. This engine was manufactured in two displacements, 499cc and 547cc.

The matter of front suspension was next addressed by the fledgling Triumph company. They designed a rocking fork assembly which was controlled by a horizontal fork and introduced this on their machines from 1906, along with a stronger frame design. These improvements went a long way to establishing the brand as one that offered reliability and sound design. The fact that motorcycles could be reliable helped the motorcycle industry survive as, after a bout of initial enthusiasm, the public's infatuation with motorcycles had waned. Triumph's production increased exponentially: the company made 250 motorcycles in 1905 and 3,000 in 1909. Triumph's popularity was boosted by their taking part in the 1907 Isle of Man TT – the first ever – and by registering a win in the following year's TT. Jack Marshall rode the Triumph to second place in 1907 and to the win in the single-cylinder class in 1908; he also set the fastest lap time in the latter year.

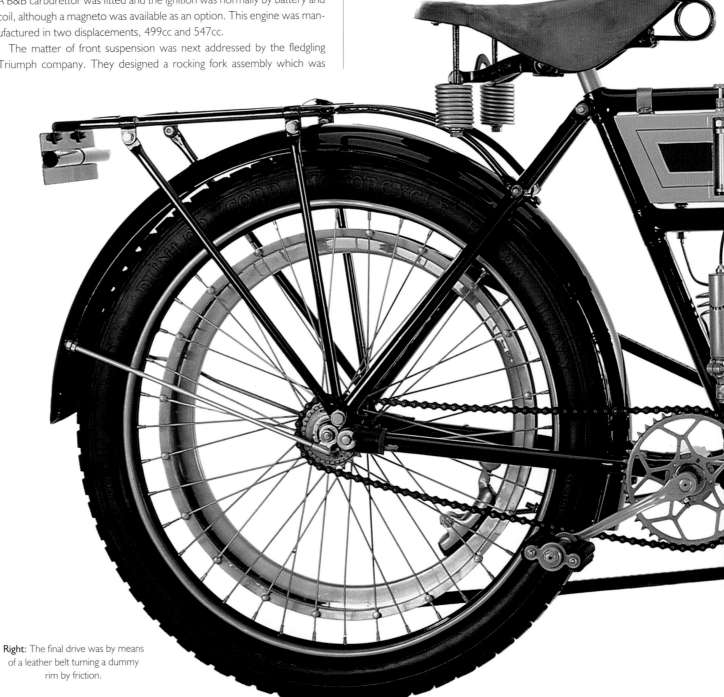

Right: The final drive was by means of a leather belt turning a dummy rim by friction.

By 1908 Triumph was using its own design of twin barrel carburettor, as seen on this machine. It was also experimenting with various types of transmission in order to give more than a single speed. One system was a variable pulley that required the rider to screw the pulley in or out to change the ratio. This necessitated stopping and adjusting the drive belt and was found to be particularly tedious in hilly areas. The next system tried was a Sturmey-Archer 3-speed hub similar to a pedal cycle component, but strengthened to suit the power of an internal combustion engine. This was not wholly successful either and it would be a number of years before Triumph could offer a functional gearbox and clutch.

New for 1910 was another model, a sports TT motorcycle intended for racing with a short wheelbase and no pedals. The tourer was a more sedate machine with pedals and a long wheelbase. The Triumph motorcycle then stayed almost unchanged until 1914 when a 225cc single with a 2-speed gearbox but no clutch was introduced. Later in the same year Triumph introduced the model H which was a 500cc machine with a 3-speed gearbox, clutch and kickstarter. Around 30,000 of these were supplied to the British Army for World War One and earned the accolade of "Trusty". The Model H sold well in civilian colours in the post-war boom for motorcycles and formed the basis for an expanded Triumph range.

Below: In the early days of motorcycling there was no generally accepted layout for the various hand and foot controls, so manufacturers tried numerous layouts to their own specification. Triumph used long levers mounted into the handlebar ends.

Above: The means of providing front suspension for a motorcycle was also open to experimentation, but it usually involved coil springs, such as here.

Above: Early motorcycles used a total-loss lubrication system that involved the rider pumping lubricant into the engine from where it was lost to the atmosphere via the exhaust.

TRIUMPH SPEED TWIN

SPECIFICATIONS
Year: 1938
Engine type: Parallel twin
Engine cycle: Four-stroke
Capacity: 499cc (30.45cu in)
Bore & stroke: 63 x 80mm
Horsepower: 26bhp @ 6000rpm
Top speed: 93mph (150kph)
Compression ratio: 7.2:1
Carburettor: Amal
Transmission: 4-speed
Brakes: F. & R. Drum
Ignition: Coil and points
Frame: Tubular steel cradle
Suspension: F. Sprung girder forks. R. None
Wheelbase: 54in (1372mm)
Weight: 353lb (160kg)
Fuel: 3.5 gallons (15.9lit)
Oil: 5 pints (2.8lit)
Tyres: F. 3.00 x 20in. R. 3.50 x 19in

Above: The Speed Twin had a panel in the top of the petrol tank that held the switches and supplementary instruments. The speedo was mounted on the handlebars.

Right: The prewar Speed Twin became the benchmark by which other motorcycles would be judged in the postwar years. Its success meant that other manufacturers would introduce parallel-twin-powered motorcycles to their respective ranges.

TRIUMPH SPEED TWIN (1938)

The first parallel vertical twin from Triumph was designed by Val Page, announced in 1933 and manufactured until 1936. In that year Triumph's car and motorcycle producing factories went separate ways. Jack Sangster of Ariel bought Triumph and put Edward Turner in charge of the Coventry factory. Turner designed the overhead-valve parallel twin of 499cc which appeared in the Speed Twin of 1937. This engine would form the basis of many Triumph motorcycles right up until the 1980s, powering bikes such as the Daytona, Bonneville, Tiger and Thunderbird. The Speed Twin, however, was the first production machine to use Edward Turner's new parallel-twin engine. It used cycle parts from Triumph's range of singles and was immediately popular, sparking the trend towards vertical twins which was followed by all the major British manufacturers in the postwar years.

The new engine was designed to be as simple as possible. It was based on a vertically split aluminium crankcase in which the crankshaft was mounted on ball races. The crankshaft was built up from three component parts and designed to give a 360-degree crankshaft layout. Turner favoured this configuration as it gave even firing intervals, which allowed a standard magneto ignition, gave an even exhaust note, eased carburation and minimized vibration by the standards of the day. Alloy connecting rods with removable end caps were used and to these were fitted hollow gudgeon pins and conventional solid skirt pistons with three piston rings, one of which was an oil scraper. Compression ratio was 7.2:1 and the cylinder barrels were cast as one from iron.

The gear-driven camshafts were mounted in the crankcase, diagonally fore and aft of the crank itself. The pushrods were contained in tubes that ran from the crankcase to the bottoms of the rocker boxes. The cylinder head which carried both inlet and exhaust valves at 90 degrees to each other was also cast from iron. The inlet ports were parallel to facilitate use of a single carburettor, while the exhaust ports were splayed to enable the twin exhaust pipes to clear the frame downtube and run down either side of the motorcycle. The spark plug bores were splayed so as to point the

Right: As rear suspension had not become commonplace on motorcycles in the prewar years, rider and pillion were offered some comfort through the provision of a sprung saddle and pillion pad.

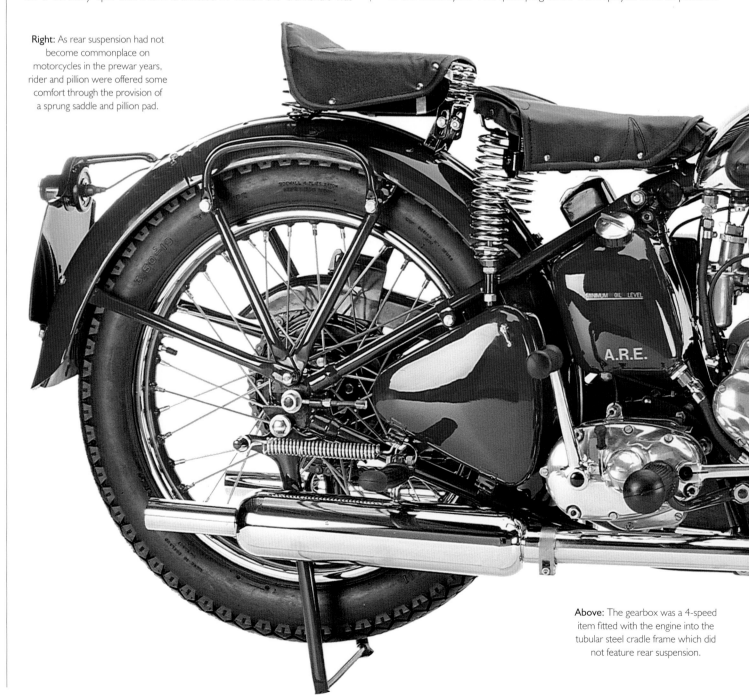

Above: The gearbox was a 4-speed item fitted with the engine into the tubular steel cradle frame which did not feature rear suspension.

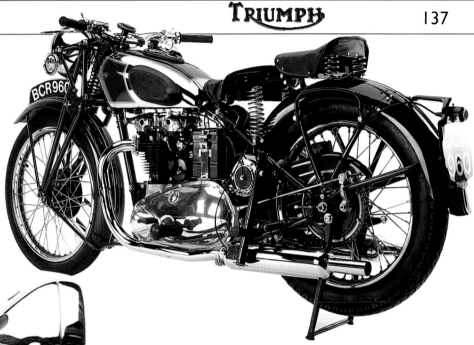

Right: Both primary and final drive was by means of a chain, although the former is concealed behind the elliptical primary cover seen above and behind the exhaust pipe.

Left: The speedo was mounted over the handlebars. The sporting aspirations of the Speed Twin were revealed by the fact that it was graduated up to 120mph.

plugs out laterally. The valves ran in cast-iron guides and had dual valve springs. The valves operated by rockers which were contained in a pair of alloy rocker boxes that ran across the cylinder head. Valve-timing gear was enclosed in the alloy case on one side of the engine while the primary drive was in the other. The whole engine was lubricated by a dry-sump system. The magdyno was mounted behind the cylinders and gear-driven. Transmission was 4-speed and the clutch was actuated by a pushrod that ran through the gearbox mainshaft. The clutch lever was mounted on the handlebars and the right foot changed gear. The engine and gearbox assemblies were fitted into cycle parts that were almost all derived from the Tiger 90.

The rigid frame was made from steel tubes brazed into forged lugs to a full cradle design. Sprung girder forks and a sprung saddle offered a degree of comfort to the rider, while items such as the mudguards and petrol tank were chosen to make the complete Speed Twin look a well-proportioned motorcycle. Finished in Amaranth Red, the motorcycle was an immediate sales success as a result of the judicious combination of engineering, styling, performance and price.

Above: The Speed Twin used the first incarnation of the twin-cylinder engine that was to become so famous for Triumph and to endure into the 1980s.

Left: The speedometer was driven from the front wheel hub and the cable can be clearly seen extending up from the hub in front of the girder forks to the speedo behind the headlamp shell.

TRIUMPH TIGER 100

SPECIFICATIONS
Year: 1939
Engine type: Ohv twin
Engine cycle: Four-stroke
Capacity: 499cc (30.45cu in)
Bore & stroke: 63 x 80mm
Horsepower: 34bhp
@7000rpm
Top speed: 100mph (161kph)
Compression ratio: 8:1
Carburettor: Amal
Transmission: 4-speed
Brakes: F. & R. Drum
Ignition: Magneto
Frame: Steel cradle
Suspension: F. Sprung girder
forks. R. None
Wheelbase: 54in (1372mm)
Weight: 365lb (166kg)
Fuel: 4 gallons (18.2lit)
Oil: 8 pints (4.55lit)
Tyres: F. 3.00 x 20in.
R. 3.25 x 19in

Above: Triumph's distinctive logo used as a tank badge. It is fitted in the centre of the painted panel on the otherwise chromed petrol tank, as was the fashion in the immediate pre- and postwar years.

TRIUMPH TIGER 100 (1939)

The Tiger 100 was the sports version of the Triumph Speed Twin. It was announced in 1939. The compression ratio had been raised for the new machine and a few changes were made to the internals. The appearance of the Tiger 100 closely matched that of the single-cylinder Tiger 70, 80 and 90 models of various displacements. The numerical designation approximated to the machine's top speed. The petrol tanks were chromed and further embellished with silver painted panels outlined in black. The wheels and mudguards also had the silver and black finish. Few changes were needed or made for the following year's production.

Triumph was one of several marques to attempt to win the prestigious Maudes Trophy in 1939. In March of that year the Auto Cycle Union (ACU) selected two Triumph 500cc machines, a Tiger 100 from a Sheffield dealer and a Speed Twin from a dealer in Biggleswade. Then, in accordance with the rules of the event, the bikes were checked at the factory and dispatched on their round trip to John O'Groats in Scotland, Land's End and thence Brooklands in England. The route was shortened slightly because of snow in Scotland which meant that the machines had to cover slightly in excess of 1,800 miles (2,900km) prior to a six-hour run around the Brooklands circuit. Apart from a couple of minor mechanical problems and a puncture, the two Triumph twins performed well and in November the ACU confirmed that Triumph had won the Trophy. Unfortunately events on the world stage had moved on by then, to the extent that the Maudes Trophy was of little significance.

With the large-capacity parallel twins proving a success, Edward Turner started to design a smaller-capacity twin to add to the range. The Tiger 85 was to be a 350cc twin that closely resembled the Tiger 100 in style and finish. The engine and cycle parts were to feature much that was new, and it was planned to announce the new model in the autumn for the following year's range, as was normal practice. The problem was that the Tiger 85 was to be announced in September 1939 for 1940 sales. The new machine was announced in parts of the motorcycle press but production of the machine was cancelled due to the outbreak of World War Two.

On the outbreak of war the British quickly standardized its motorcycle requirements and took a single model type from each British factory. Prior

to Triumph's Coventry works being destroyed in the Blitz, it supplied numbers of the 3HW to the British Army. The 3HW was a military version of the prewar Tiger 80 single. The company were working on a military 350cc twin, the 3TW, based on what was to be the Tiger 85 when they were bombed out of their Coventry factory in 1940. They moved to Meriden where their factory was to become famous in the postwar years. The 3TW was temporarily forgotten about in the midst of war, but much of it reappeared in the postwar years as the TRW. Production of Triumph motorcycles was resumed in 1944 when the new factory was complete.

Below: The Triumph Tiger 100 was one of two models of Triumph motorcycle that helped the company win the prestigious Maudes Trophy. Sadly by the time news of the win was public, the outbreak of war overshadowed it.

Above: The Tiger 100 was the sports version of the Speed Twin with a higher compression engine, although its appearance closely matched that of the single-cylinder Tiger 70, 80 and 90 models.

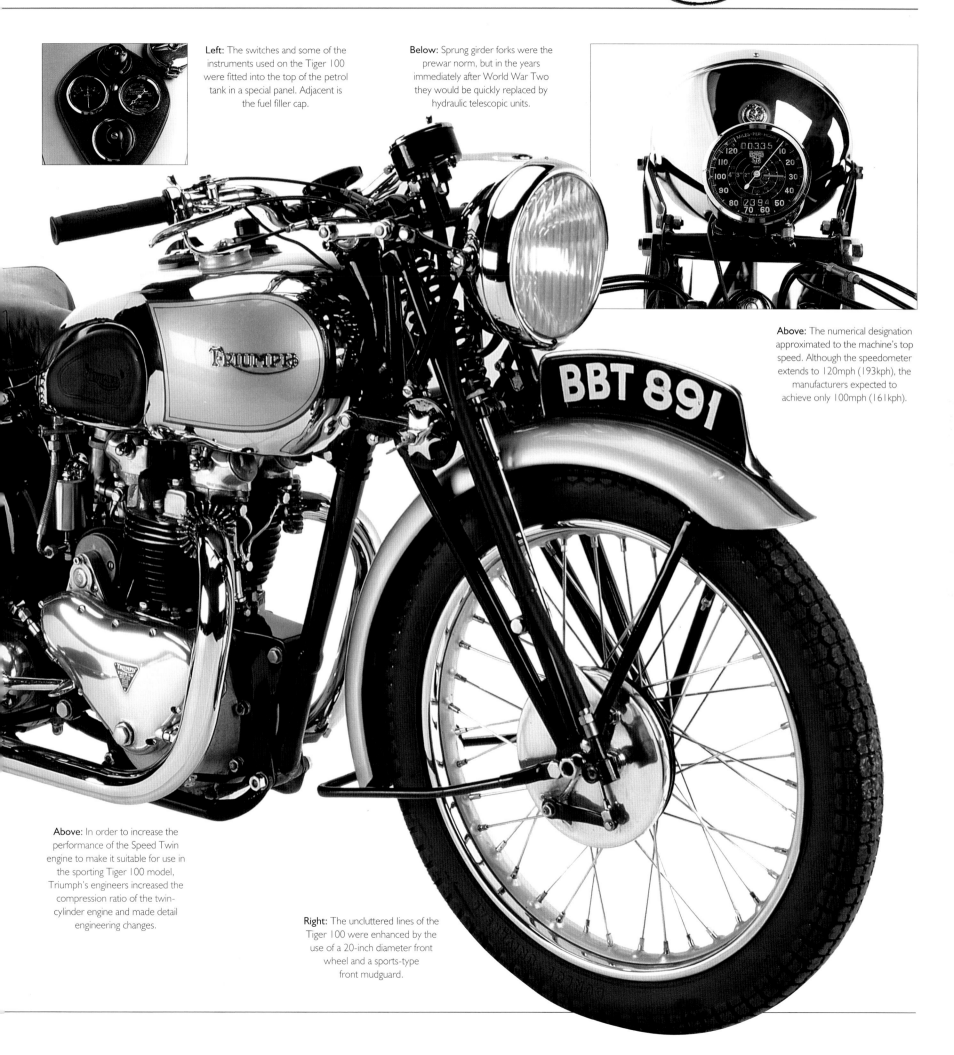

Left: The switches and some of the instruments used on the Tiger 100 were fitted into the top of the petrol tank in a special panel. Adjacent is the fuel filler cap.

Below: Sprung girder forks were the prewar norm, but in the years immediately after World War Two they would be quickly replaced by hydraulic telescopic units.

Above: The numerical designation approximated to the machine's top speed. Although the speedometer extends to 120mph (193kph), the manufacturers expected to achieve only 100mph (161kph).

Above: In order to increase the performance of the Speed Twin engine to make it suitable for use in the sporting Tiger 100 model, Triumph's engineers increased the compression ratio of the twin-cylinder engine and made detail engineering changes.

Right: The uncluttered lines of the Tiger 100 were enhanced by the use of a 20-inch diameter front wheel and a sports-type front mudguard.

TRIUMPH 5T SPEED TWIN

SPECIFICATIONS
Year: 1950
Engine type: Vertical twin
Engine cycle: Four-stroke
Capacity: 499cc (30.5cu in)
Bore & stroke: 63 x 80mm
Horsepower: 27bhp @ 6300rpm
Top speed: 85mph (137kph)
Compression ratio: 7.0:1
Carburettor: Amal
Transmission: 4-speed
Brakes: F. & R. Drum
Ignition: Magneto
Frame: Steel cradle
Suspension: F. Telescopic forks. R. None (Sprung hub option)
Wheelbase: 55in (1397mm)
Weight: 365lb (166kg)
Fuel: 4 gallons (18.2lit)
Oil: 8 pints (4.55lit)
Tyres: F. 3.25 x 19in. R. 3.50 x 19in

Above: The well-equipped rider of the 1950s could even check on the time of day by glancing at a handlebar-mounted stopwatch such as this.

Above: The speedometer, ammeter and ignition switch were all positioned in the headlamp nacelle giving the rider a clear view of them.

TRIUMPH 5T SPEED TWIN (1950)

After the cessation of hostilities at the end of World War Two, Edward Turner lost no time in reorganizing the Meriden factory for civilian production of Triumph motorcycles. Within a short period both the Speed Twin and Tiger 100 reappeared, the only immediately obvious upgrade to both models being the fitment of telescopic front forks. The new forks were similar to those developed during the war and were hydraulically damped in both directions; they reduced unsprung weight considerably. The new design gave suspension travel of 6.25in (15.9cm), the tubes slid on a lower mild-steel bush coated with white metal and an upper bush made from Tufnol (a proprietary material). Felt rings acted as reservoirs of oil to keep the fork stanchions lubricated. Fork springs of different rates were used for the 350cc solo, 500cc solo and 500cc sidecar models.

Smaller changes to the twins included fitting a separate dynamo in front of the cylinders where it was gear-driven from the exhaust camshaft. The lubrication system within the engine was improved. For example, the rocker box lubrication was taken from the scavenge return line thereby ensuring a steady supply of warm oil. The front wheel was reduced to 19 inches in diameter and the speedo drive was transferred to the rear wheel. The Speed Twin in this form first appeared in 1946 and ran on

unchanged into 1947 because in the aftermath of the war there were still considerable shortages of materials. A sidestand was available as an option, as was a sprung rear hub. This latter component had been designed by Edward Turner and offered limited rear suspension through a sprung wheel spindle. In this form the sporting and good-looking Speed Twin was popular with motorcyclists.

A number of changes were made to the Speed Twin for the 1949 season and these were as usual announced in the October of the preceding year. The tank-top instrument panel was deleted and the headlamp nacelle that was to become a long-running Triumph design feature was introduced. It enclosed the top of the forks and handlebar clamp, the bars emerged from it through rubber grommets. The instruments, a speedometer and ammeter, and switches were located in the top of the nacelle unit and the headlamp in its face. The oil pressure gauge was discontinued and the speedometer was now driven from the gearbox. The air filter supplied by Vokes was installed alongside the battery and a larger dynamo was installed.

At this time a new model based on the 500cc twin was announced to supplement the range. It was the TR5 Trophy, so called because three works riders had competed in the 1948 International Six Days Trial and won individual Gold Medals and the Team award. The Trophy was an

Right: Apart from the sprung hub, the Speed Twin was otherwise devoid of rear suspension, relying on a sprung saddle for the rider and telescopic forks at the front.

Right: The Triumph Speed Twin was fitted with the sprung-hub rear suspension system which offered limited rear suspension through the use of a sprung wheel spindle.

instant success as club riders could commute aboard the bike and then compete on it at weekends. The lucrative American market was demanding a larger-capacity twin and in September 1949 Triumph unveiled the 650cc Thunderbird. The larger displacement engine was derived from the 500cc engine, and in a motorcycle otherwise made up of Speed Twin parts, it was shown at a public demonstration at the Montlhéry race circuit outside Paris. On this circuit three Thunderbirds were ridden 500 miles (805km) at over 90mph (145kph) (see also Thunderbird entry on page 144). The Speed Twins for 1950 were altered slightly and due to shortages of nickel were marketed with painted fuel tanks and partially redesigned gearboxes. Both the Thunderbird and the Speed Twin would remain in production with Triumph through the decade.

Above: The parallel twin engine displaced 499cc as a result of a bore and stroke of 63 x 80mm. It went on to become the engine for the legendary Bonneville.

Left: The styling of the Speed Twin was modern and streamlined for its time, with the chrome trims on the sides of the headlamp nacelle and those on the sides of the fuel tank projecting a modern and stylish image.

Right: The front brake was a single-leading-shoe unit to which was laced a 19-inch diameter wheel rim. The wheel was fitted between the telescopic fork legs.

TRIUMPH TRW

SPECIFICATIONS
Year: 1952
Engine type: Side-valve parallel twin
Engine cycle: Four-stroke
Capacity: 499cc (30.45cu in)
Bore & stroke: 63 x 80mm
Horsepower: 18bhp @ 5000rpm
Top speed: c.70mph (113kph)
Compression ratio: 6.0:1
Carburettor: Solex Type 26
Transmission: 4-speed
Brakes: F & R. Drum
Ignition: Magneto
Frame: Tubular steel
Suspension: F. Telescopic forks. R. Rigid
Wheelbase: 53in (1346mm)
Weight: 340lb (154kg)
Fuel: 3 gallons (13.64lit)
Oil: 4 pints (2.27lit)
Tyres: F. 3.25 x 19in. R. 4.00 x 19in

TRIUMPH TR5 TROPHY

SPECIFICATIONS
Year: 1954
Engine type: Vertical twin
Engine cycle: Four-stroke
Capacity: 499cc (30.5cu in)
Bore & stroke: 63 x 80mm
Horsepower: 25bhp @ 6000rpm
Top speed: 95mph (153kph)
Compression ratio: 6.0:1
Carburettor: Amal
Transmission: 4-speed
Brakes: F. & R. Drum
Ignition: Magneto
Frame: Steel cradle
Suspension: F. Telescopic forks. R. None
Wheelbase: 53in (1346mm)
Weight: 304lb (138kg)
Fuel: 2.5 gallons (11.4lit)
Oil: 6 pints (3.4lit)
Tyres: F. 3.00 x 20in. R. 4.00 x 19in

TRIUMPH TRW (1952)

The Triumph TRW can trace its roots back to the Blitz (the German bombing campaign aimed at Great Britain) in the opening months of World War Two. Triumph had been planning to produce a 350cc twin for the British Army until they were blitzed out of their Birmingham premises. With the destruction of the factory went prospects for the 3TW as it was known. For the remainder of the war Triumph produced 350cc singles based on their prewar models.

Later, once the company had moved to Meriden, Warwickshire, Bert Hopwood drew up designs for a new side-valve twin, the 5TW, with a 500cc engine. It did not go into production, but it provided the basis for the postwar prototype military machine, the TRW, and was displayed for military appraisal in 1946. However, the war was now over and there was a glut of surplus military motorcycles. Not surprisingly, an order was not forthcoming. In July 1948 a slightly redesigned TRW appeared and it sold in small numbers to the British Army, and in sufficient numbers to foreign armies, to ensure a production run that lasted into the 1960s.

The final TRW engine was a 500cc side-valve with a vertically split crankcase carrying both crankshaft and gear-driven camshaft which was situated forward of the cylinders. The cylinder block was cast from alloy and had cylinder liners pressed in. The valve chest was sited in front of the cylinders and featured pressed-in guides. The cylinder head was a single casting. The cycle parts were conventional – a telescopic front end and rigid frame typical of Triumphs of the day.

Above: The military provenance of the TRW engine meant that ease of maintenance and reliability took precedence over out-and-out performance.

Above: The Triumph TRW was an unusual machine built by the company for military evaluation. It used a twin-cylinder engine.

Above: A specially shortened frame with high ground clearance was designed to accommodate the Trophy's ohv twin-cylinder engine.

Left: A 20-inch diameter front wheel and 19-inch rear helped increase the ground clearance of the 500cc Triumph twin for off-road use. A sprung saddle offered some suspension.

Left: The Triumph Trophy was so called because a British team on Triumph twins won the 1948 International Six Days Trial.

Above: The gearbox was a 4-speed item fitted with the engine into the tubular cradle frame, which was made from steel and did not feature rear suspension.

TRIUMPH TR5 TROPHY (1954)

Triumph motorcycles had been used in many International Six Days Trials over the years, but the ISDT of 1948 led to an entirely new model. Yorkshireman Allan Jefferies was the team captain for the 1948 event which was held in Italy. The team won the major Trophy, generally referred to as "the Trophy" in order to distinguish it from the less important "Vase". The Vase also went to Great Britain in 1948, as did the manufacturer's team prize with the help of Jim Alves on his Triumph and Triumph's other riders who were similarly mounted. This success was the first of a series of wins for Great Britain and Triumph who won the ISDT in the three following years. The competition was held in Wales in 1949 and 1950 and returned to Italy for the 1951 event.

As a result of the first success a new model based on the 500cc twin was announced to supplement the range. It was the TR5 Trophy named after the most important of the ISDT prizes. The Trophy was based on the parallel-twin engine but featured the alloy cylinder barrel and cylinder head spawned from the wartime Triumph-engined electricity generator. The Trophy engine was fitted with standard camshafts, low compression pistons and a single carburettor which combined to produce 25bhp @ 6000rpm. The frame was based on the standard Triumph item but redesigned slightly to incorporate a short downtube and short wheelbase. The Trophy was a popular machine and suited tuning; either up to ISDT tune where, with 7.5:1 pistons, riders could achieve almost 100mph (161kph) or down to works trials spec with 4.5:1 compression ratio to give torque at low revs which is essential for slow-speed use off-road.

TRIUMPH 6T THUNDERBIRD

SPECIFICATIONS
Year: 1955
Engine type: Vertical twin
Engine cycle: Four-stroke
Capacity: 649cc (39.6cu in)
Bore & stroke: 71 x 82mm
Horsepower: 34bhp @ 6300rpm
Top speed: 96mph (154.5kph)
Compression ratio: 7:1
Carburettor: Amal
Transmission: 4-speed
Brakes: F. & R. Drum
Ignition: Coil and points
Frame: Steel cradle
Suspension: F. Telescopic forks.
R. Swingarm and shock absorbers
Wheelbase: 55.75in (1416mm)
Weight: 385lb (175kg)
Fuel: 4 gallons (18.2lit)
Oil: 6 pints (3.4lit)
Tyres: F. 3.25 x 19in.
R. 3.50 x 19in

Right: The Triumph Thunderbird was famed for many things, not least of which was it being the mount of Marlon Brando, starring as Johnny of the Black Rebels MC in the classic film *The Wild One*.

TRIUMPH T20 TIGER CUB

SPECIFICATIONS
Year: 1955
Engine type: Ohv single
Engine cycle: Four-stroke
Capacity: 199.5cc (12.17cu in)
Bore & stroke: 63 x 64mm
Horsepower: 10bhp @ 6000rpm
Top speed: 70mph (113kph)
Compression ratio: 7:1
Carburettor: Amal
Transmission: 4-speed
Brakes: F. & R. Drum
Ignition: Coil
Frame: Steel cradle
Suspension: F. Telescopic forks.
R. Plunger frame
Wheelbase: 49in (1245mm)
Weight: 218lb (99kg)
Fuel: 2.62 gallons (11.9lit)
Oil: 2.25 pints (1.28lit)
Tyres: 3.00 x 18in

TRIUMPH 6T THUNDERBIRD (1955)

As a model the Triumph 6T Thunderbird enjoyed a long production run as part of the history of the 649cc Triumph Twin. Introduced in 1949, this model survived until 1966 although this production run was divided into three distinct periods; 1949–1954, 1955–1962 and 1962–1966 because of the way the machine was progressively upgraded. The initial launch of the Thunderbird in September 1949 was at the Montlhéry track near Paris. It was intended that three examples of the new model would be ridden to the circuit near Paris, tested around it at over 90mph (145kph) until 500 miles (805km) had been covered and then ridden back to Meriden.

Triumph staff undertook a practice run with the bikes disguised with Tiger 100 tanks. The Montlhéry circuit is banked in parts and the riders found that at around the 400-mile (644km) mark the tyres were worn through to the canvas on one side. This meant that the riders had to modify their riding styles in order to keep the motorcycles more upright. Subtle adjustments to throttle cables were made so that with the throttle on the stop, the Thunderbirds were not running flat out, but nevertheless in excess of the 90mph (145kph) lower limit demanded by the publicity stunt. In the actual event five riders would ride in relay on the circuit.

The three Triumphs with the optional sprung hub were ridden out to Montlhéry for the actual event, and once there began the test at 9.15 am. Things went according to plan until near lunchtime when Len Bayliss

coasted machine number three into the pits with a split petrol tank. This had to be changed and this unavoidable delay for repairs cost the team 15 minutes. Later Allan Jefferies brought the same bike in as the chainguard had rattled loose. A total of 316 laps of the circuit equated to 500 miles (805km) and the three machines achieved an average running speed in excess of 90mph (145kph). Two achieved the average in excess of 90 mph (145kph) including stops. The machine that had needed a new tank averaged 86.07mph (138.5kph) including stops. So another Triumph legend was born.

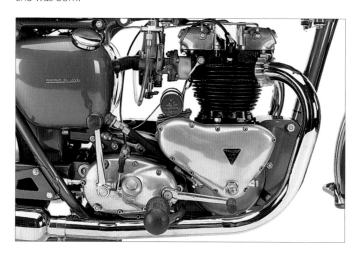

Above: The 650cc Thunderbird was proven when three machines were taken on an endurance run to France and then lapped around the famous Montlhéry race circuit until they had covered 500 miles (805km).

Below: The Thunderbirds made from 1955 onwards featured a swingarm and shock absorbers, which provided better rear suspension than the earlier optional sprung-hub device.

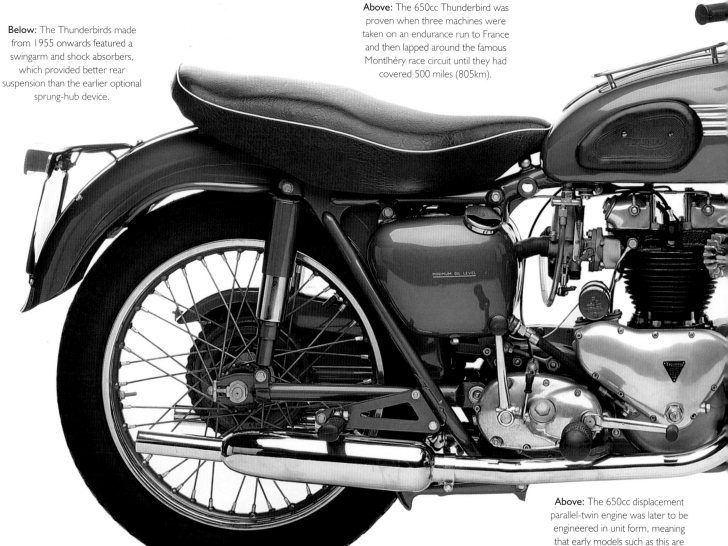

Above: The 650cc displacement parallel-twin engine was later to be engineered in unit form, meaning that early models such as this are referred to as pre-unit Triumphs.

Above: The four-stroke engine was developed to avoid the cost of Triumph having to develop their own two-stroke engine or buy in Villiers units.

Above: The Tiger Cub was to all intents and purposes a small "big bike" and it promoted brand loyalty to Triumph by getting youngsters started on machines of that marque.

Above: The Triumph T20 Tiger Cub was a successful lightweight four-stroke motorcycle with a 4-speed unit gearbox to which this gear indicator was fitted.

TRIUMPH T20 TIGER CUB (1955)

Triumph unveiled a new lightweight motorcycle in November 1952 at the Earl's Court, London motorcycle show. It was known as the Triumph T15 Terrier and was powered by a 150cc single-cylinder engine. Edward Turner intended that it would appeal to younger buyers who would in time, it was reasoned, move up to a larger displacement twin. The new model featured a four-stroke engine chosen by Turner to avoid having to use bought-in Villiers engines like so many other manufacturers and so risk losing Triumph's identity. This expedient avoided the cost of designing a two-stroke engine specifically for Triumph. The ohv Terrier had a 4-speed unit gearbox, telescopic forks and a plunger frame. It was a success and for 1954 Triumph introduced a larger displacement version: the 200cc T20 Tiger Cub, which was unveiled at the Earl's Court show in November 1953.

The Tiger Cub featured a number of detail improvements over the earlier model, most notably to the electrical system. The Tiger Cub was supplied in the sprung-plunger frame although this was changed to a swingarm and shock absorbers for 1957. The Cub became far more popular than the Terrier and remained in production until 1968. Following its introduction in 1954, the 1955 Cub, the year of this machine, was altered only in the smallest of details. A few more changes were made for the 1956 models including an improved engine lubrication system and a slightly strengthened petrol tank.

One area where the Tiger Cub had considerable competitive success was in off-road events. Triumph marketed a T20C model, the C suffix of course designating the machine as a "competition" one. The trials Cub was like many such machines of the day still closely based on the roadster but with the addition of lighter, smaller mudguards and a higher exhaust pipe that gave better ground clearance. During the 1960s Triumph also experimented with various sports Cub models.

TRIUMPH 5T SPEED TWIN

SPECIFICATIONS
Year: 1956
Engine type: Vertical twin
Engine cycle: Four-stroke
Capacity: 499cc (30.5cu in)
Bore & stroke: 63 x 80mm
Horsepower: 27bhp @ 6300rpm
Top speed: 92mph (148kph)
Compression ratio: 7.0:1
Carburettor: Amal
Transmission: 4-speed
Brakes: F. & R. Drum
Ignition: Coil
Frame: Steel cradle
Suspension: F. Telescopic forks. R. Swingarm and shock absorbers
Wheelbase: 55.75in (1416mm)
Weight: 380lb (172kg)
Fuel: 4 gallons (18.2lit)
Oil: 6 pints (3.4lit)
Tyres: F. 3.25 x 19in. R. 3.50 x 19in

Above: This Speed Twin sports another style of handlebar-mounted watch – evidently a popular accessory in the 1950s.

TRIUMPH SPEED TWIN (1956)

The Speed Twin was modified for 1952. A crankshaft-mounted Lucas alternator was fitted as part of improving the motorcycle, but this necessitated changes to both the crankshaft and chaincase. It also meant that the motorcycle needed a new wiring loom and the fitting of a rectifier for voltage control and coil ignition. The next big change came in 1955 when all Triumph's twin-cylinder motorcycles were upgraded with the introduction of frames with swingarm rear suspension.

In 1957 the Triumph tank badge was changed to the famous chrome grille emblazoned with the word Triumph. At the same time the Speed Twin was fitted with a full-width hub front brake. But by now the Speed Twin was being overshadowed by other, more sporting, models in Triumph's range, such as the Tiger 100 and T110. Attention was also focused on the streamliner which had been run on Bonneville Salt Flats in Utah and which was displayed at the 1956 Earl's Court Show standing on a layer of Bonneville salt that had been shipped over specially with the

machine. A unit-construction 350cc Triumph was announced early in 1957, and slightly more than a year later the Speed Twin and TR5 Trophy were dropped from the range, to be superseded by the unit-construction 500cc machines. The biggest news, however, which featured a machine relying on a non-unit construction engine and gearbox, was just about to break. It was the Triumph Bonneville, added to the new model lists at the last minute, but announced in 1958 for the 1959 range.

Left: Triumph's range of twin-cylinder machines were redesigned in 1955 to accommodate swingarm rear suspension.

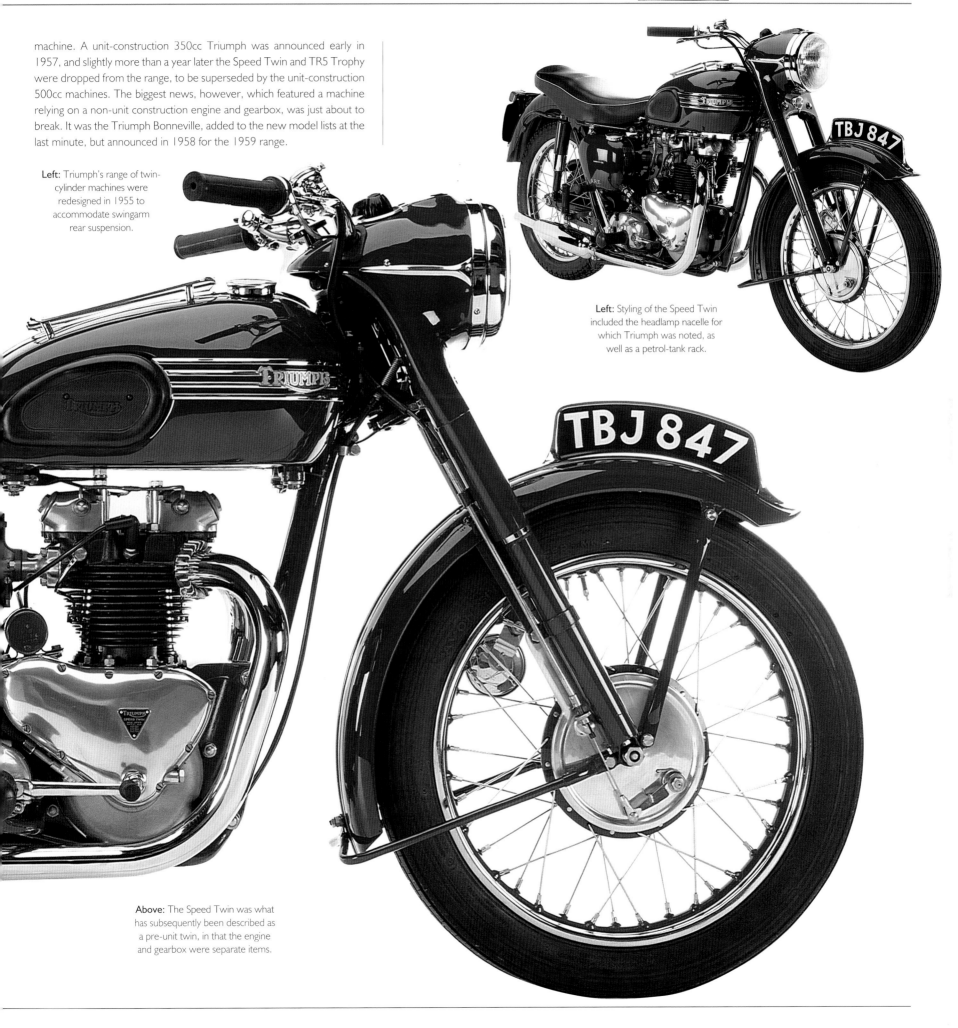

Left: Styling of the Speed Twin included the headlamp nacelle for which Triumph was noted, as well as a petrol-tank rack.

Above: The Speed Twin was what has subsequently been described as a pre-unit twin, in that the engine and gearbox were separate items.

TRIUMPH 3TA

SPECIFICATIONS
Year: 1958
Engine type: Parallel twin
Engine cycle: Four-stroke
Capacity: 349cc (21.3cu in)
Bore & stroke: 58.25 x 65.5mm
Horsepower: 18.5bhp @ 6500rpm
Top speed: 80mph (129kph)
Compression ratio: 7.5:1
Carburettor: Amal
Transmission: 4-speed
Brakes: F. & R. Drum
Ignition: Coil
Frame: Steel cradle
Suspension: F. Telescopic forks. R. Swingarm and shock absorbers
Wheelbase: 52.75in (1340mm)
Weight: 340lb (154kg)
Fuel: 3.5 gallons (15.9lit)
Oil: 5 pints (2.84lit)
Tyres: 3.25 x 17in

Right: Triumph's 3TA and later the 5TA featured a distinctive rear mudguard which was soon nicknamed the "bathtub" because of its resemblance to an old-style bath turned upside-down.

TRIUMPH 3TA (1958)

Triumph announced a new motorcycle for 1957; it was a four-stroke twin but differed from what had gone before in a number of ways. Not least of these was the fact that it was of unit construction, in other words the engine crankcase and gearbox were both integral parts of a pair of castings divided vertically. The new engine had a displacement which put it in the 350cc class, an engine size largely ignored by Triumph since the 1940s. The motorcycle in which this new engine was fitted was called the Twenty-One in celebration of the 21 years since the motorcycle-producing part of the Triumph company had been sold to Jack Sangster. It also was a reference to the displacement of the engine expressed in inches as was the norm in the US market.

The engine was a mix of the new and the conventional: barrels and head were bolted on as normal and the crankshaft assembly was in accordance with Triumph practice. The crankcases though were new, the right crankcase half also incorporated much of the gearbox shell meaning that the primary drive centres were fixed. The twin was supplied with fuel and air mixture by a single Amal Monobloc carburettor, while two exhaust pipes were fitted in the manner of the larger displacement twins.

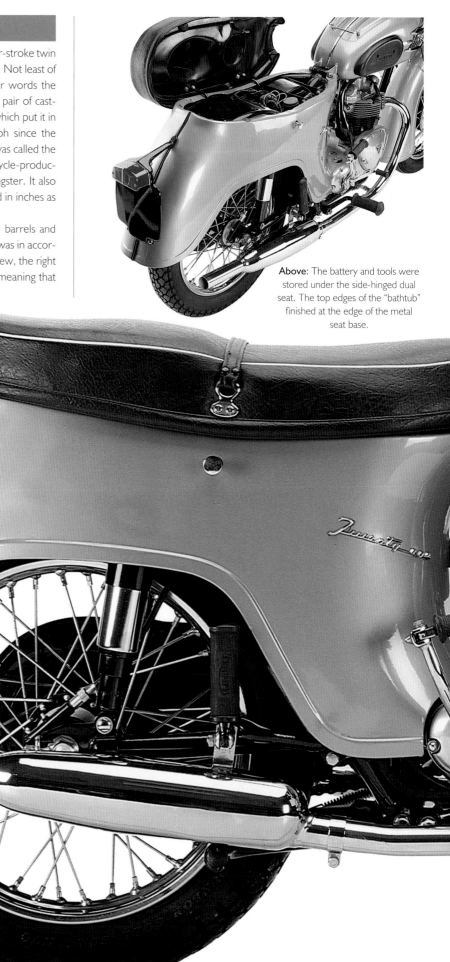

Above: The battery and tools were stored under the side-hinged dual seat. The top edges of the "bathtub" finished at the edge of the metal seat base.

The styling of the new machine was a radical departure from Triumph's norm. While at the front a headlamp and switches mounted in a nacelle could be found, the rear was completely restyled. The front mudguard was redesigned to complement the rear. Through use of two large steel pressings, the rear of the machine was almost fully enclosed. The two panels were supported by the frame tube and acted both as a seat base and as a large, wide mudguard that covered the top of the shock absorbers. The two panels were jointed vertically along the centre line of the machine. This styling was soon nicknamed the "bathtub" design but it was sufficiently popular for Triumph to introduce a 500cc version in 1958 which was known as the 5TA. It was also powered by a unit-construction engine.

Below: The 3TA was also known as the Triumph Twenty-One which was a reference to the displacement of the 350cc parallel twin in cubic inches. It also celebrated 21 years of motorcycle production under the direction of Jack Sangster.

Above: A small gear indicator was situated on top of the inner casing of the gearbox. The engine was built using a cast-iron block and a light-alloy head.

Above: The 3TA engine was constructed around a new design, the unit-construction type. The gearbox and crankcase were largely cast as one, meaning that the primary drive centres were fixed.

TRIUMPH T120 BONNEVILLE

SPECIFICATIONS
Year: 1959
Engine type: Vertical twin
Engine cycle: Four-stroke
Capacity: 649cc (39.6cu in)
Bore & stroke: 71 x 82mm
Horsepower: 46bhp @ 6500rpm
Top speed: 110mph (177kph)
Compression ratio: 8.5:1
Carburettor: Amal
Transmission: 4-speed
Brakes: F. & R. Drum
Ignition: Coil and points
Frame: Steel cradle
Suspension: F. Telescopic forks. R. Swingarm and shock absorbers
Wheelbase: 55.75in (1416mm)
Weight: 404lb (183kg)
Fuel: 4 gallons (18.2lit)
Oil: 6 pints (3.4lit)
Tyres: F. 3.25 x 19in. R. 3.50 x 19in

TRIUMPH T120 BONNEVILLE (1959)

In the autumn of 1958 Triumph Motorcycles announced their 1959 model range including, at the last minute, the machine that was to become a legend within the British motorcycle industry and far beyond. It was the T120 Bonneville, named in recognition of Triumph's successes on the Bonneville salt flats of Utah, USA. Johnny Allen had piloted a Thunderbird-engined streamliner to 214.4mph (345kph) in 1956 to take the American Motorcyclist Association's land speed record, while in 1958 Bill Johnson had clocked 147mph (237kph) on a Tiger 110.

The new bike was basically a tuned T110. The engine was fitted with a higher performance alloy head that featured twin splayed ports and twin Amal carburettors. A one-piece forged crankshaft and cast-iron flywheel was used. The styling was typical of Triumphs of the time including such elements as the one-year-only headlamp nacelle and valanced mudguards. Less typical was the tangerine and pearl grey finish. This and its

Above right: This style of headlamp nacelle was used by Triumph on other motorcycles, but only for a single year on the Bonneville. It contains the instruments.

Above: The first Bonnevilles are now described as pre-unit, as they were built before Triumph switched to unit construction which featured crankcases with integral gearboxes.

high performance meant that the Bonneville was the talk of the 1958 Earl's Court Show in London.

The high performance cylinder head and higher performance camshafts enabled the new machine to produce 4bhp more than the T110 Thunderbird. This performance stretched both the brakes and the single downtube frame to their limits. Early Bonnevilles were noted for weaving at speed which caused Triumph to experiment with duplex frames before settling on a single larger-diameter frame tube for the unit-construction twins introduced in 1963. The Bonneville was redesigned for 1960 with more sporting looks that included a large chromed head-lamp and smaller unvalanced mudguards. The legend was born and, as a model, it would endure until the absolute end of Triumph parallel-twin production under Les Harris in the 1980s.

Above: The Triumph Bonneville, new for 1959, created a sensation in the autumn of 1958, not least because of its unusual tangerine and pearl grey paint finish.

Above: The Triumph Bonneville was, at its inception, basically a tuned Triumph T110. It was named to commemorate exploits on the Bonneville salt flats in Utah, USA.

TRIUMPH T120 BONNEVILLE

SPECIFICATIONS

Year: 1968
Engine type: Vertical twin
Engine cycle: Four-stroke
Capacity: 649cc (39.6cu in)
Bore & stroke: 71 x 82mm
Horsepower: 47bhp @ 6700rpm
Top speed: 110mph (177kph)
Compression ratio: 9:1
Carburettor: Amal
Transmission: 4-speed
Brakes: F. & R. Drum
Ignition: Coil and points
Frame: Steel cradle
Suspension: F. Telescopic forks. R. Swingarm and shock absorbers
Wheelbase: 55in (1397mm)
Weight: 363lb (165kg)
Fuel: 4 gallons (18.2lit)
Oil: 6 pints (3.4lit)
Tyres: F. 3.00 x 19in. R. 3.50 x 18in

TRIUMPH T120 BONNEVILLE (1968)

By 1968 the Triumph Bonneville had been considerably refined. The Triumph company had to offer motorcycles that would compete with both BSA and Norton. After the latter's introduction of the Featherbed frame in 1952 and BSA's welded duplex frame for the A10 of 1954, Triumph were forced to improve the handling of the Bonneville. A series of changes were made; the steering head angle was altered in 1961, and again in 1966, while improvements were made to the swingarm pivot in 1963 and 1968. The fork suspension travel was increased in 1965 and further improved with new fork valves for 1968. As a result, the 1968 T120 was a better-handling and better-looking Bonneville than its 1959 and 1960 brethren.

The reputation of the Bonneville gained a further massive boost in the Isle of Man Production TT of 1969. This event had been introduced in 1967 and saw riders race round the 37.73-mile (60.72km) mountain circuit three times. It was an important event for manufacturers in terms of

Right: By 1968 the styling of the Bonneville had naturally evolved, but it was clearly still the same sport model as the 1959 bike seen on the previous pages.

sales for the forthcoming year. Malcolm Uphill had entered the 1969 race on a race-prepared 60bhp 650cc Bonneville fitted with a full fairing and a pair of Dunlop K81 tyres. On his first lap he went through the speed trap located outside The Highlander pub at 100.09mph (161.07kph). The second lap was faster and, sure of a win, Uphill eased back slightly to average a tantalizing 99.99mph (160.91kph) for the race. This feat was noted in several ways; Dunlop, for example, marketed a new tyre, the TT100, Uphill saw his name written in the history books and Triumph saw the reputation of the Bonneville considerably enhanced.

Left: Compare this engine with that of the Bonneville on pages 150-151 to see the difference between pre-unit and unit construction.

Below: The 1959 style of headlamp nacelle was soon replaced by a single chrome headlamp shell, and the instruments were mounted above the handlebars.

Above: The later Bonneville was stopped by a twin-leading-shoe front drum brake. This was superseded in turn by a disc brake system.

Above: The Bonneville relied on a 650cc parallel-twin engine fitted with twin carburettors for its motive power. By 1968 the engine was being built in unit form.

TRIUMPH T100T DAYTONA

SPECIFICATIONS
Year: 1969
Engine type: Overhead-valve parallel twin
Engine cycle: Four-stroke
Capacity: 490cc (29.9cu in)
Bore & stroke: 69 x 65.5mm
Horsepower: 39bhp @ 7400rpm
Top speed: 113mph (182kph)
Compression ratio: 9:1
Carburettor: Twin Amals
Transmission: 4-speed
Brakes: F. TLS drum. R. Drum
Ignition: Coil and points
Frame: Tubular steel
Suspension: F. Telescopic forks. R. Swingarm and shock absorbers
Wheelbase: 54.5in (1384mm)
Weight: 338lb (153kg)
Fuel: 2.2 gallons (10lit)
Oil: 5.8 pints (3.3lit)
Tyres: F. 3.60 x 19in. R. 4.10 x 18in

Above: The Triumph logo appeared in cast form in a number of variations on the theme. Their shape and size made them popular with Rockers as belt buckles which proclaimed a loyalty to the Meriden brand.

TRIUMPH DAYTONA T100T (1969)

Triumph had won the Daytona 200 race in Florida in 1962 but lost to Harley-Davidson in 1963, 1964 and 1965, so they were eager to reclaim the honours in 1966. Race T100/R motorcycles were shipped from England to the Florida venue for the works riders who included Gary Nixon, Dick Hammer and Buddy Elmore. They found that the new race-bikes were fast but fragile, and during practice in the week leading up to the race breakdowns were common. The bearings in the new engines were not holding up, causing the engines to lose oil pressure. Gary Nixon switched to a US-prepared Triumph but Hammer and Elmore stuck with the English-prepared machines. Hammer qualified second fastest but Texan Elmore only qualified 46th fastest as he lost oil pressure in his engine. Elmore's mechanic, Dick Bender, had to work quickly to rebuild the engine before the race from the parts of the other blown-up engines.

During the race Hammer's Triumph engine failed, but Elmore steadily worked his way up the field from 46th. By lap 2 he was in 19th place, by lap 4 he was in 11th and by lap 8 he was in 4th place. He passed race leader Gary Nixon during lap 22, but while in the pits allowed Nixon to regain the lead. On the 32nd lap Elmore passed Nixon again and stayed ahead to win the 53-lap race. Bender's built-from-parts engine had done the job and set a new average speed record of 96.582mph (155.43kph). Triumph came back to Daytona for 1967 with Nixon and Elmore taking 1st and 2nd places respectively.

The March 1966 Daytona 200 won by Buddy Elmore gave the Triumph Daytona its name. The new motorcycle was introduced in the 1967 Triumph range. While the first Daytona models were described as being "directly evolved" from the race-winning Tiger 100, this claim may have been somewhat economical with the truth. The Daytona certainly looked remarkably similar to the Triumph Tiger of previous years with the addition of a second carburettor. It also relied on a single-leading-shoe front brake and, although improved, the frame was not "entirely new" as claimed either. The frame was a considerable improvement on the previous type with a downtube of increased diameter, a lower centre of

Right: The T100T Daytona was powered by a unit-construction 490cc version of Edward Turner's parallel-twin-cylinder engine, essentially a Trophy engine that was fitted with twin Amal carburetors.

Above: The kickstart and gearshift were on shafts that protruded from the gearbox end cover while the oil tank was located under the seat forward of the rear mudguard.

gravity, a lower overall height and more rigid swingarm pivot mounting point. These modifications enhanced the handling of the 500cc Triumph considerably.

By 1969, the year of this machine, the front brake had been upgraded to the altogether more effective 8-inch twin-leading-shoe unit that is typical of the BSA/Triumph range of the era. The bottom end of the engine had been improved through the use of different bearings for the crankshaft. The 500cc Daytona in this form was one of the most powerful 500cc motorcycles ever produced in Britain. It was capable of 68mph (109kph) in second gear, 88mph (142kph) in third gear and had a top speed in excess of 110mph (177kph) in fourth gear.

Above: The Daytona was a modified version of the bikes used to win the prestigious Daytona 200 mile race. It is no exaggeration to say that the win went to Triumph as a result of the unstinting efforts of works mechanic Dick Bender.

Right: The later production versions of the Triumph Daytona were equipped with the full-width hub twin-leading-shoe drum brakes of eight inches (203mm) diameter.

Above: Triumph's parallel twin was a compact and neat engine especially in unit form. The ignition contact breaker points are concealed behind the circular cover on the timing case, while the coils are just visible under the tank.

TRIUMPH X75 HURRICANE

SPECIFICATIONS

Year: 1973

Engine type: Vertical triple

Engine cycle: Four-stroke

Capacity: 740cc (45.16cu in)

Bore & stroke: 67 x 70mm

Horsepower: 58bhp @ 7250rpm

Top speed: 105mph (169kph)

Compression ratio: 9:1

Carburettor: Triple Amals

Transmission: 5-speed

Brakes: F. TLS drum. R. Drum

Ignition: Coil

Frame: Duplex tube cradle

Suspension: F. Telescopic forks. R. Swingarm and shock absorbers

Wheelbase: 60in (1524mm)

Weight: 444lb (201kg)

Fuel: 2 gallons (9.09lit)

Oil: n/a

Tyres: F. 3.25 x 19in. R. 4.25 x 19in

Below: When first shown, the Hurricane created a sensation as it was unlike anything previously made by a British motorcyle manufacturer, seemingly owing its design influences to American choppers.

TRIUMPH X75 HURRICANE (1973)

The American market was extremely important to British motorcycle manufacturers from the end of World War Two onwards. Importers of British machines had to sell their bikes into a market that was very different from the British set-up and so they had bikes produced specifically for their markets – in some cases specifically for the East and West coasts of America, as they often had representatives on each coast. The concept of the "factory custom" motorcycle was introduced in the USA in 1970 by the last surviving US domestic motorcycle manufacturer, Harley-Davidson. The company unveiled what it christened the Super Glide, a landmark machine that started the trend for factory-produced "customs". The idea had been kickstarted by the film *Easy Rider* which introduced the chopper style of bike to mainstream American motorcyclists. Inevitably other manufacturers felt that they needed to compete in this new market.

Triumph was no exception and, despite the problems the company were facing in England, it came up with the X75 Hurricane. The machine was styled by the US designer Craig Vetter from Illinois, USA. Surprisingly the Hurricane was unveiled at the Earl's Court motorcycle show in London but unsurprisingly it created a sensation. The styling definitely drew its influences from choppers although it was not as radical-looking as many of them. Hints of dirt-track bike styling could also be discerned.

The basis of the Hurricane was the BSA triple-cylinder engine mounted in the Triumph Trident frame which was fitted with slightly overlength forks. The three exhaust pipes curved out of the engine and ran down the right side of the machine with the three megaphone silencers fanning upwards by the rear wheel. The steel fuel tank was concealed behind a fibreglass moulding that flowed from the headstock back into the short dual seat and down into the sidepanels. The front and rear mudguards were standard chromed Triumph triple items that looked completely in keeping with the styling. Wide handlebars with a fair amount of rise in them were fitted. The wheels were spoked with alloy rims; although the Trident now had a disc front brake, the Hurricane retained the conical drum front hub and brake.

The Hurricane was reportedly comfortable to ride at speeds of up to 70mph (113kph) although it had a large turning circle. The finish was unusual for Triumph: the fibreglass bodywork was painted orange but featured a pair of yellow stripes running the length of the tank and sidepanels. Clearly the machine was designed for cruising around town rather than sporting riding. It inevitably drew criticism from those dismissive of chop-

Right: The styling of the Triumph Hurricane was partially carried out by Craig Vetter. The lines of the motorcycle flow from front to rear.

Right: The three exhaust pipes were unorthodox but stylish, running down the right side of the bike before fanning out in three separate silencers.

pers, and was undeniably expensive when new, but it remains an enduring example of one of the early factory customs.

The Hurricane was only produced in limited numbers because of its high retail price and the financial and labour relations problems experienced by Triumph in the early 1970s. Although the Hurricane used the BSA engine, it bore the Triumph name because, by the time the machine was ready to be marketed, BSA had collapsed. Trident production relied on input from both the BSA Small Heath plant and the Triumph Meriden plant, and the workers' blockade which began in the autumn of 1973 made it a difficult period for the production of motorcycles in general, not just for expensive, limited-edition machines such as this.

Above: The Hurricane looked sensational from almost any angle. It was long, low and sleek and was among the earliest of the "factory customs".

Left: The Hurricane had a 3.25 x 19in front tyre fitted to a rim that was laced to the standard twin-leading-shoe front brake hub.

Above: The fuel tank was a steel canister hidden within the fibreglass moulding that ran from the headstock back into the sidepanels on each side of the dual seat.

TRIUMPH T160 TRIDENT

SPECIFICATIONS
Year: 1975
Engine type: Vertical ohv triple
Engine cycle: Four-stroke
Capacity: 740cc (45.16cu in)
Bore & stroke: 67 x 70mm
Horsepower: 58bhp @ 7250rpm
Top speed: 119.5mph (191kph)
Compression ratio: 9.5:1
Carburettor: Triple Amals
Transmission: 5-speed
Brakes: F. Single disc. R. Disc
Ignition: Coil
Frame: Duplex tube cradle
Suspension: F. Telescopic forks. R. Swingarm and shock absorbers
Wheelbase: 59in (1499mm)
Weight: 518lb (235kg)
Fuel: 4.8 gallons (21.82lit)
Oil: 6 pints (3.4lit)
Tyres: 4.10 x 19in

Above: By 1975 the famous Triumph logo was appearing on fewer machines as a result of the contraction of the British bike industry.

Right: Many of the components used in the construction of the Trident were common to the Bonneville including such parts as the rear light assembly. The swingarm of the rear suspension was lengthened an inch (25mm) between the T150 and T160 models.

TRIUMPH T160 TRIDENT (1975)

The roadgoing Triumph (and BSA) triples had an enviable racing pedigree with Daytona 200 and Isle of Man TT wins to their credit. However there were initial problems with the design of the Triumph triple, and designer Doug Hele had to iron them out for the race bikes that were ridden by the likes of Dick Mann and John Cooper. The engine was derived from the 500cc Triumph twin with, to put it in simple terms, another half an engine grafted on to it, which made it relatively complex and costly to produce.

The Trident triple appeared first in 1968 as the T150, but this model was later upgraded. The final version of the triple was the T160 of 1974 and this was produced until 1976. It would have undoubtedly been manufactured for longer but for the collapse of parent company Norton-Villiers-Triumph. The T160 was longer, lower and sleeker than its predecessor and the frame was derived from the Production TT-winning Slippery Sam racers. The T160 incorporated all the features of the T150 and boasted an electric starter before this was commonly available. The starter turned the engine through a ring gear on the clutch. The T160 was fitted with

Above: Trident was a clever name for a three-cylinder motorcycle and Norton-Villiers-Triumph put it on the sidepanels of their triples – both the T150 and T160 (seen here).

Above: The Trident had the classic lines of a 1970s sports bike. The tank with its two-tone paint scheme and long flowing lines is nothing short of elegant.

Left: The three-cylinder engine needed three exhaust pipes, but in the interests of styling and balance Triumph produced a system with two pipes siamesed into one for the centre cylinder. Each of these merged with the pipes for the outer cylinders before the silencer.

Below: The mid-1970s were a time when new technology was being used in conjunction with the traditional. The wheels were designed to use traditional spokes and rims, but the hubs were made to carry disc brakes which were being popularized by Japanese imports.

a US-style left-foot gear change, unlike the T150, because of the importance of American sales.

The T160 was a classic design of sports bike with swept back handlebars that followed the line of a long sleek tank that reached back into a long low seat. Power came from the three-cylinder engine mounted across the frame, its crankshaft spaced the con rods at 120 degrees to one another which gave the engine a distinctive exhaust note. The overhead-valve engine was designed with four main bearings, two plain, one roller

and one ball. The two plain bearings were located between the con rods. Vibration was reputed to be minimal although the handlebars were rubber-mounted to reduce any vibration being transmitted to the rider's hands. The transmission, the same unit as used in 650 and 750 Triumph twins, was 5-speed. The T160 was capable of 48mph (77kph) in first, 67.5 (109kph) in second, 88.5 (142kph) in third, 104 (167kph) in fourth and 120 (193kph) in top. With these ratios the Trident achieved 37 miles per gallon (13km/lit) for all-round use. Primary and final drive were by means of a chain.

On the T160 models the cylinders were inclined forwards to increase weight distribution and the redesigned frame meant that the seat was lower than before, while the engine was an inch (25mm) higher for improved ground clearance. The swingarm was lengthened by an inch and the forks shortened through the simple expedient of using shorter springs. These various modifications to the T150 made the T160 an altogether better motorcycle that was more comfortable to ride and which handled better. The exhaust pipe for the centre cylinder had two pipes siamesed together immediately in front of the engine, one pipe ran to each silencer both to preserve a symmetrical appearance and to balance the exhausts. The wheels were of the traditionally spoked type but the hubs were designed to accept brake discs, as disc brakes and calipers were superseding the drum type especially for front brakes, and particularly on competitors' machines, such as the Honda CB750 Four.

The T160 Trident was manufactured wholly at Small Heath because of the difficult industrial relations situation facing the NVT – Norton-Villiers-Triumph – group. T150 Tridents and BSA Rocket 3s relied on input from both companies' factories. Engines were made at Small Heath by BSA and frame and final assembly work took place at Triumph's Meriden plant. The Meriden blockade meant that the Trident production could not continue, so the NVT group had to retool the Small Heath factory to produce Tridents. The first motorcycles were not completed until 1974.

Above: The three-cylinder engine achieved good balance which minimized vibration through spacing the con rods at 120 degrees to each other. The engine was constructed unit-fashion with a 5-speed gearbox.

TRIUMPH T140D

SPECIFICATIONS

Year: 1979

Engine type: Overhead-valve parallel twin

Engine cycle: Four-stroke

Capacity: 744cc (45cu in)

Bore & stroke: 76 x 82mm

Horsepower: 51bhp

Top speed: 96mph (154kph)

Compression ratio: 7.9:1

Carburettor: Twin Amals

Transmission: 5-speed

Brakes: F. Single disc. R. Disc

Ignition: Coil

Frame: Duplex steel cradle

Suspension: F. Telescopic forks. R. Swingarm and shock absorbers

Wheelbase: 56in (1422mm)

Weight: 413lb (187kg)

Fuel: 2.8 gallons (12.7lit)

Oil: 4 pints (2.27lit)

Tyres: F. 4.10 x 19in. R. 4.10 x 18in

Above: While the Triumph logo appeared on the sides of T140D petrol tanks, it was in a smaller form than on earlier twins.

Right: By the late 1970s drum brakes were almost completely superseded by the disc and hydraulic caliper seen at the back of this Bonneville mounted to the wheel and installed behind the swingarm and shock absorber of the rear suspension.

TRIUMPH T140D BONNEVILLE (1979)

During the 1970s the British motorcycle industry entered a period of decline that saw a number of companies merge or cease production. Triumph became part of a group that comprised BSA, Norton Villiers and Triumph. This group produced Nortons in Wolverhampton, and Triumphs at Meriden, while BSA supplied engines for the famous Triumph Trident from the Small Heath plant. The contraction of the British motorcycle industry continued apace and in 1973 management took the decision to close the Meriden plant.

This decade of turbulent labour relations was about to witness an unprecedented development in the engineering industry. The Meriden workforce occupied the plant and staged a sit-in to protest at the news that the plant would close. The workers strove to form a co-operative. The sit-in lasted for 18 months and was resolved mainly by a change of government when the Labour party won the 1974 General Election. The co-operative then finally became a reality and Triumph Bonnevilles made by Triumph Motorcycles (Meriden) Ltd went into production, while NVT went on to produce the Norton Commando.

Bonnevilles started coming off the Meriden line again in the latter part of 1974 in the wake of the workers' sit-in. The workers earned a set wage and managed to keep the factory going principally because of the demand for Triumphs in the USA which accounted for 70 percent of sales. As well as the Bonneville, the co-operative also made the TR7RV, a single carburettor version of the 750 based on the same displacement parallel vertical twin. Sadly the co-operative failed in 1983 after struggling valiantly against the odds (and always desperately short of funds) to develop new mod-

els such as the water-cooled, twin-overhead-camshaft vertical twin which got as far as the prototype stage.

The co-operative Bonnevilles were gradually upgraded as time and money allowed and legislation necessitated. For 1978, Amal Mark II concentric carburettors were fitted to the Bonneville, the engine breathing was revised and the cylinder head was redesigned with parallel inlet ports. All these features were aimed at enabling the engine to comply with American emissions legislation. For 1979 came the T140D with cast alloy wheels, a stepped seat and an all-over black finish with gold pinstripes. It was available in European and American specification models. Differences between the two centred on the types of handlebars and tanks fitted.

As the company was only building one basic motorcycle – the various models differed only in terms of details such as type of petrol tank and number of carburettors fitted – for a time the co-operative fared reasonably well. Triumph motorcycles remained popular despite the Japanese invasion and were the best seller in the 750cc class in the UK. The machine won the prestigious *Motor Cycle News* "machine of the year" title in 1979. Between then and the closure of the plant, Triumph would offer a trail bike, the Tiger Trail; a touring model, the Bonneville Executive; an electric start model, the TSS; and a factory custom, the TSX. Prototypes of a faired machine, the TS8-1, and a low rider, the Phoenix, were also developed, as were the smaller capacity reincarnations of Daytona and Thunderbird models with a displacement of 599cc.

Below: The commonality of parts across the Meriden co-operative's motorcycles – US and European Bonnevilles as well as single carburettor Tigers and twin carburettor Bonnevilles – made production somewhat easier.

Below: The T140D was an updated version of the Bonneville offered in both European and US specifications. It is the latter that is seen here; the main differences are in the style of petrol tank and shape of handlebars fitted.

Above: The cast alloy wheels, stepped dual seat and distinctive black and gold finish were part of a styling package new for 1979 and aimed at the important US export market.

Left: The cast alloy wheels were of a seven-spoke design, while the integral cast hub facilitated the mounting of a disc brake.

Above: So that Triumph motorcycles would conform to the emissions regulations of some US states, Triumph switched to the use of a pair of Amal Mark II concentric carburettors fitted, as normal, behind the cylinder barrels.

TRIUMPH T140V JUBILEE BONNEVILLE

SPECIFICATIONS

Year: 1977
Engine type: Overhead-valve parallel twin
Engine cycle: Four-stroke
Capacity: 744cc (45.4cu in)
Bore & stroke: 76 x 82mm
Horsepower: 50bhp @ 7000rpm
Top speed: 111mph (179kph)
Compression ratio: 7.9:1
Carburettor: Twin Amals
Transmission: 5-speed
Brakes: F. Single disc. R. Disc
Ignition: Coil and points
Frame: Tubular steel
Suspension: F. Telescopic forks. R. Swingarm and shock absorbers
Wheelbase: 56in (1422mm)
Weight: 443lb (201kg)
Fuel: 4 gallons (18.2lit)
Oil: 4 pints (2.27lit)
Tyres: F. 3.25 x 19in. R. 4.00 x 18in

Above: The Triumph logo long featured the characteristic R that underlined the logo and joined it together.

TRIUMPH T140V JUBILEE BONNEVILLE (1977)

In 1977 the Triumph co-operative at Meriden was producing 300 motorcycles per week after the Government and the GEC group had stepped in to assist the company. 1977 was also the year of the Silver Jubilee of Queen Elizabeth II's accession to the throne of the United Kingdom in 1952. At the suggestion of Lord Stokes, the former British Leyland Chairman and adviser to the co-operative, Triumph produced a limited-edition motorcycle to commemorate this occasion. The Jubilee model was to be based on the existing oil-in-frame Bonneville and be built in limited numbers with a special finish. It was a clever marketing ploy at a time when Triumph was striving to put the effects of the long strike and sit-in behind it. The co-operative had sought to modernize the Bonneville, by such means as changing the gear shift to the left side of the machine to conform with US regulations and incorporating a rear disc brake. In 1976 there were two models in the Triumph range, the T140V Bonneville with twin Amal carburettors and the TR7RV Tiger with a single Amal.

The Jubilee Bonnevilles for 1977 had a European specification tank, a left-foot gear change, Girling gas shock absorbers and disc brakes front and rear. Only 2,400 Jubilee models were made, 1,000 for the UK, 1,000 for the USA and 400 for other export markets. The Bonnevilles were primarily finished in silver with red, white and blue details. The wheel rims were painted in a similar scheme. Both of the motorcycle's side panels carried a Union Jack with Silver Jubilee 1977 and Limited Edition badges, and the words "Silver Jubilee" were added to the logo on the back of the dual seat.

Left: Triumph Bonnevilles featured the logo on the vinyl of the dual seat, but the limited edition Silver Jubilee models were also marked as such.

Above: Both sidepanels on the Silver Jubilee Bonnevilles featured an additional badge below the normal Bonneville 750 one. This featured a Union Jack and recorded the date of the Queen's Silver Jubilee.

Above: The Silver Jubilee Bonnevilles were made by the workers' co-operative at Meriden. The carried the words "Made In England" proudly on the downtube.

Above: The "Jubilee Bonnie" was a sensible marketing ploy by the co-operative as it attempted to get over the effects of the sit-in and exploit the American market with a machine specifically revised for it.

TRIUMPH T140ES BONNEVILLE

SPECIFICATIONS

Year: 1981
Engine type: Overhead-valve parallel twin
Engine cycle: Four-stroke
Capacity: 744cc (45.4cu in)
Bore & stroke: 76 x 82mm
Horsepower: 50bhp @ 7000rpm
Top speed: 111mph (179kph)
Compression ratio: 7.9:1
Carburettor: Twin Amals
Transmission: 5-speed
Brakes: F. Twin disc. R. Disc
Ignition: Coil and points
Frame: Tubular steel
Suspension: F. Telescopic forks. R. Swingarm and shock absorbers
Wheelbase: 56in (1422mm)
Weight: 443lb (201kg)
Fuel: 4 gallons (18.2lit)
Oil: 4 pints (2.27lit)
Tyres: F. 3.25 x 19in. R. 4.00 x 18in

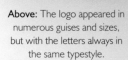

Above: The logo appeared in numerous guises and sizes, but with the letters always in the same typestyle.

TRIUMPH BONNEVILLE ROYAL (1981)

The Bonneville Royal was another limited-edition Triumph motorcycle marking an important date for the British Royal Family. It commemorated the wedding in 1981 of HRH Prince Charles, Prince of Wales to Lady Diana Spencer. Only 250 examples of this motorcycle, based on the electric-start 750cc Bonneville, were made. It featured cast spoked Morris Alloy wheels and a twin disc front end, as well as the chrome petrol tank. This was the first Triumph motorcycle to have such a tank since Edward Turner had stopped fitting them in 1950.

At the beginning of the 1980s Triumph were clearly aware of the need to market their motorcycles actively in order both to compete with the Japanese manufacturers, and to take account of fashions within motorcycling in both domestic and export markets. Using components such as the cast alloy wheels from the Royale and redesigned sidepanels, the company produced the TSX. Overall the TSX bore a resemblance to the Japanese factory customs that were proving so popular in the USA in the early 1980s. Bright graphics on the tank and sidepanels and metallic paint completed the package.

At the time of the liquidation of the Meriden co-operative an eight-valve TSX – the TSX-8 – was being planned using the Weslake-designed heads that had appeared on the Triumph TSS of 1983. Following the closure of the Meriden works, Bonnevilles were again briefly produced. Between 1985 and 1988 they were manufactured by L.F.Harris in Devon under licence from John Bloor who had bought the assets of the company Triumph Motorcycles (Meriden) Ltd.

Above: The Bonneville Royal of 1981 celebrated the wedding of Prince Charles and Lady Diana Spencer. The limited edition motorcycle had a chromed petrol tank but otherwise was largely a stock 1981 Bonneville.

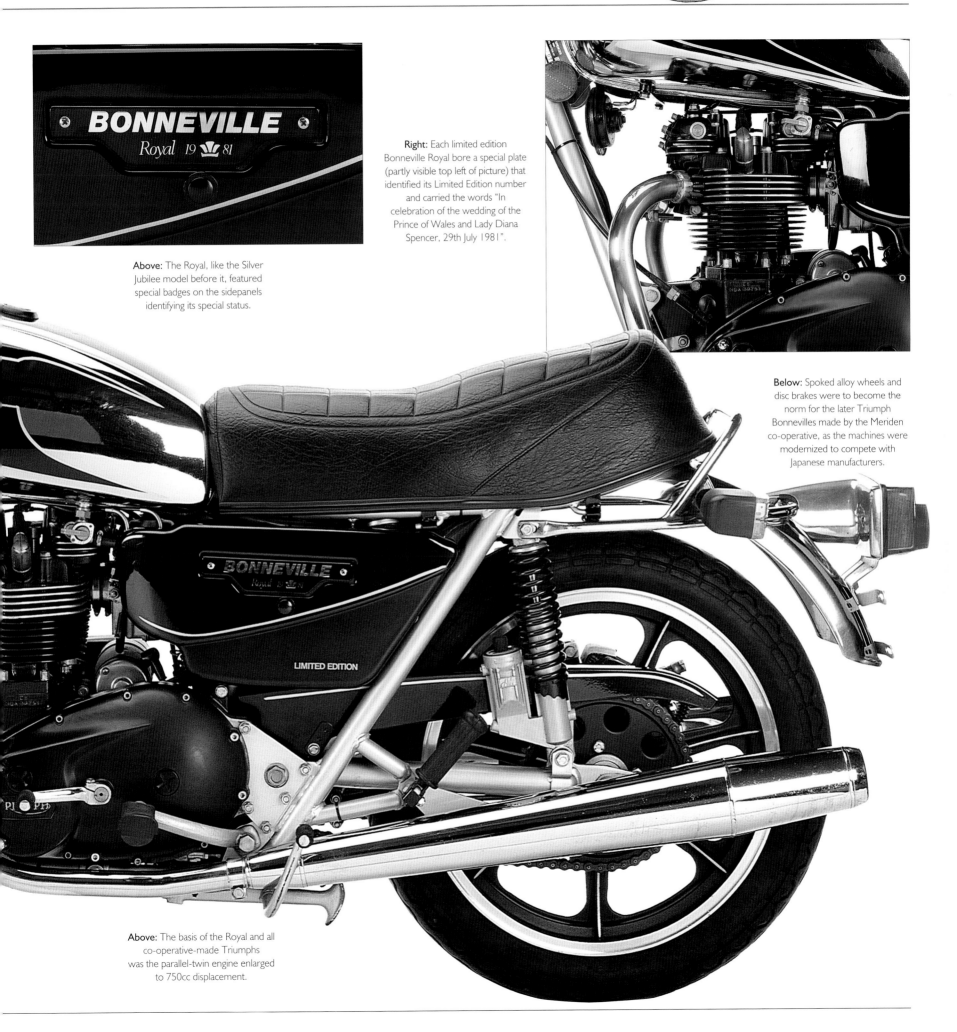

Above: The Royal, like the Silver Jubilee model before it, featured special badges on the sidepanels identifying its special status.

Right: Each limited edition Bonneville Royal bore a special plate (partly visible top left of picture) that identified its Limited Edition number and carried the words "In celebration of the wedding of the Prince of Wales and Lady Diana Spencer, 29th July 1981".

Below: Spoked alloy wheels and disc brakes were to become the norm for the later Triumph Bonnevilles made by the Meriden co-operative, as the machines were modernized to compete with Japanese manufacturers.

Above: The basis of the Royal and all co-operative-made Triumphs was the parallel-twin engine enlarged to 750cc displacement.

TRIUMPH T509 SPEED TRIPLE (1996)

When the brave but ill-fated co-operative at Meriden closed and its assets were auctioned by the receivers, John Bloor, a Midlands industrialist, acquired the famous marque. He licensed the rights to build Bonnevilles to Les Harris for a five-year period while he started to develop a new range of Triumph motorcycles. Work started on a new factory in Hinckley, Leicestershire in 1985. The new range of six motorcycles was unveiled at the Cologne motorcycle show in Germany in 1990.

The Trophy 1200 was a sportsbike in the style of the Japanese superbikes of the era. It featured a high-performance liquid-cooled four-cylinder engine, a full fairing, as well as alloy wheels, disc brakes and an alloy swingarm. The new model Triumphs sported names that had been made famous by the original Triumph concern, but which were in keeping with the new models. The new Trident was based on a triple-

cylinder engine and was available in a 750cc displacement as the original Trident had been. It was also made in a displacement of 900cc. Apart from being a much more modern bike than the original, the new Triumph differed in that the engine was liquid-cooled. It featured three Mikuni carburettors, digital ignition and electric start. The remainder of the machine was technologically up-to-date featuring cast wheels – 17in front and 18in rear – disc brakes front and rear, a monoshock rear suspension system and adjustable forks.

The Speed Triple came slightly later; its name is derived from the pre-war Triumph Speed Twin but it was adapted in order to reflect the triple-cylinder engine used in this motorcycle's construction. The Speed Triple was designed as a sports roadster and found a place on race tracks in a competition series designed especially for it. These bikes proved enormously popular and swiftly re-established the Triumph as a premier marque in the industry.

TRIUMPH T509 SPEED TRIPLE

SPECIFICATIONS
Year: 1996
Engine type: Liquid-cooled triple
Engine cycle: Four-stroke
Capacity: 885cc (54cu in)
Bore & stroke: 76 x 65mm
Horsepower: 97bhp @ 9000rpm
Top speed: 130mph (209kph)
Compression ratio: 10.6:1
Carburettor: 3 flat slide CV
Transmission: 6-speed
Brakes: F. Twin discs. R. Disc
Ignition: Electronic
Frame: Steel cradle
Suspension: F. Telescopic forks. R. Monoshock swingarm
Wheelbase: 58.7in (1490mm)
Weight: 460lb (209kg)
Fuel: 4 gallons (18lit)
Oil: n/a
Tyres: F. 120/70 ZR 17. R. 180/55 ZR 17

Above: Triumph's three-cylinder engine, 1990s-style. Note how even the logo has been subtly modified for a more modern look.

Right: Rising rate monoshock suspension has become the norm for sportsbikes and is concealed behind the sidepanels. Single-sided swingarms and three-spoke alloy wheels are also the norm.

Below: The Speed Triple looks lean and quick. It is responsive, handles well, and has quickly found a ready market.

Above: While most sports bikes of the last couple of decades have both a speedometer and tachometer, the appearance of a temperature gauge reflects the arrival of liquid-cooled motorcycle engines.

Above: The Triumph T509 Speed Triple uses a modern and innovative version of the twin-spar alloy frame from which the engine hangs. The Triumph design is of an unusual section.

TRIUMPH T595

SPECIFICATIONS
Year: 1997
Engine type: Dohc triple
Engine cycle: Four-stroke
Capacity: 956cc (58.28cu in)
Bore & stroke: 79 x 65mm
Horsepower: 112bhp @ 9200rpm
Top speed: 160mph (257kph)
Compression ratio: 11.2:1
Carburettor: Sagem EFI
Transmission: 6-speed
Brakes: F. Twin discs. R. Disc
Ignition: Electronic
Frame: Alloy twin spar
Suspension: F. Telescopic forks. R. Rising rate monoshock
Wheelbase: 56.7in (1440mm)
Weight: 436.5lb (198kg)
Fuel: 3.96 gallons (18lit)
Oil: n/a
Tyres: F. 120/70-17. R. 190/50-17

TRIUMPH T595 DAYTONA (1997)

Through the 1990s the trend for sportsbikes was increasingly towards higher performance and enhanced handling. The large Japanese factories all offered sportsbikes of comparable performance, as did Italian Ducati. The range of liquid-cooled triple-cylinder Triumphs initially introduced in 1990 were well-engineered, worthy motorcycles but they were not cutting-edge sportsbikes in global terms. John Bloor's Triumph Motorcycle company was a well-established motorcycle manufacturer by the middle of the decade and for 1997 it unveiled a sportsbike, the T595, designed to compete with the likes of the Honda Fireblade and Ducati 916.

The Triumph T595 was a liquid-cooled triple-cylinder-engined motorcycle with fuel injection to enhance performance while meeting increasingly stringent emission regulations in all Triumph's export markets worldwide. In order to increase performance Triumph kept the overall weight of the motorcycle as low as possible, and managed to save around 22lb (10kg) in redesigning the engine itself. The

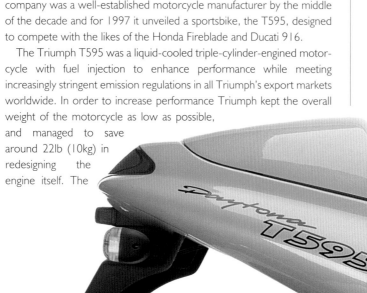

Right: In the 1990s tyres have been considerably developed and become much wider in order to enhance the handling performance of a superbike.

Above: The distinctive lines of the T595 Daytona ensured that it was a sensation when first shown to the motorcycling public. It further established the new Triumph company's market position.

chassis was redesigned to be on a par with that of the Honda Fireblade and Ducati 916, but to appear very different. The frame was constructed from oval-section alloy tube to a twin-spar design. Twin-spar frames have become the norm for sportsbikes in the 1990s and the engine hangs below the main frame members. The suspension at each end, rising rate monoshock rear and 45mm telescopic forks at the front, was fully adjustable. The brakes and forks were Japanese-developed items from Nissin and Showa respectively. The geometry of the frame and forks was such that the rake and trail (24 degrees/86mm) meant that the T595 was fast-steering but balanced by a long wheelbase (56.7in/1440mm). The fairing and bodywork were distinctive and stood out from its foreign rivals.

Above: Use of a fairing such as this enables the manufacturer to build a motorcycle with many of the components associated with liquid cooling hidden away. Other components, such as the lights, become an important element in the overall shape.

TRIUMPH TIGER

SPECIFICATIONS
Year: 1996
Engine type: Liquid-cooled dohc triple
Engine cycle: Four-stroke
Capacity: 885cc (54cu in)
Bore & stroke: 76 x 65mm
Horsepower: 84bhp @ 8000rpm
Top speed: 130mph (209kph)
Compression ratio: 10.6:1
Carburettor: 3 Mikuni flat slide CV
Transmission: 6-speed
Brakes: F. Twin discs. R. Disc
Ignition: Electronic
Frame: Steel cradle
Suspension: F. Telescopic forks. R. Monoshock swingarm
Wheelbase: 61in (1550mm)
Weight: 460lb (209kg)
Fuel: 5.3 gallons (24.1lit)
Oil: n/a
Tyres: F. 110/80/19. R. 140/80/17

TRIUMPH THUNDERBIRD

SPECIFICATIONS
Year: 1997
Engine type: Liquid-cooled dohc triple
Engine cycle: Four-stroke
Capacity: 885cc (54cu in)
Bore & stroke: 76 x 65mm
Horsepower: 70bhp @ 8000rpm
Top speed: n/a
Compression ratio: 10:1
Carburettor: 3 Mikuni flat slide CV
Transmission: 5-speed
Brakes: F. Single disc. R. Disc
Ignition: Electronic
Frame: Steel monoshock
Suspension: F. Telescopic forks. R. Adjustable monoshock
Wheelbase: 61in (1550mm)
Weight: 485lb (220kg)
Fuel: n/a
Oil: n/a
Tyres: F.110/80/18. R. 160/80/16

Right: The styling of the Triumph Tiger is typical of current off-road bikes with long-travel suspension front and rear and high ground clearance. To enhance this, the exhaust pipe runs high above the wheel and immediately below the dual seat.

TRIUMPH TIGER (1996)

The popularity of desert "raids" such as the legendary Paris–Dakar race led to the development of a new style of motorcycle. These machines were usually based around large-displacement engines and combined aspects of racing motorcycles with some from off-road competition motorcycles. Their purpose was to enable them to compete in long-distance races that covered a mixture of roads, tracks and deserts. To this end they had large fuel tanks, long-travel suspension, used off-road tyres and had high ground clearance. As is often the case the style of the race bikes spawned a fashion for similarly styled roadsters. Most of the Japanese factories offered such machines in the form of the Tenere, Super Tenere, Africa Twin and others, while the European factories, including BMW, Cagiva and Gilera, also made variations of this type of motorcycle.

Triumph introduced their version in 1994 but instead of using a name that called to mind the deserts of North Africa, they chose one from Triumph's past. The Tiger had won considerable competition success for Meriden in the past and was a name with a connection to the wilder parts of the globe.

Design work had started in 1991 with the intention of making the new Tiger very different from the other motorcycles in the Hinckley Triumph range. The new design included a large-capacity fuel tank made from nylon that extended forward into the twin headlamp fairing to replicate the desert-race styling and keep the weight forwards. The fairing and fuel tank flowed into the seat and sidepanels from which the high level exhaust pipe appeared to emerge below a luggage rack. To ensure good ground clearance long-travel suspension components were fitted to the steel frame in which the liquid-cooled three-cylinder engine was fitted.

Above: The Triumph Tiger combines race replica and off-road styling popularized by events such as the Paris–Dakar desert raid.

Above: The liquid-cooled double-overhead-camshaft triple engine is fitted to the tubular steel cradle frame and protected during off-road use by a steel bash plate.

Right: While several of Triumph's machines are based around a common three-cylinder engine, the unit fitted to the Thunderbird has more chromed parts.

Below: The Triumph Thunderbird is a nostalgically styled motorcycle, as its name suggests. History has been carefully recreated though the use of a traditionally shaped tank with old-style tank badges. The dual seat, grab rail, silencers and spoked wheels all echo the past.

Left: The entire front end and handlebar arrangement is nostalgic with separate clocks and a chromed headlamp bezel.

Above: The Thunderbird was introduced by Triumph as the fashion for retro machines developed. It combines old styling with new technology, such as disc brakes and a liquid-cooled engine.

Left: The Triumph Tiger has a small fairing (in which the dual headlamps are mounted) that flows into the lines of the large-capacity fuel tank. The model name is writ large on the sides of the fairing of this unique motorcycle.

Right: Long-travel forks with the axle mounted forward of the fork tubes are clearly motocross-inspired, while the mudguard and road-type tyre are more sportsbike in styling.

TRIUMPH THUNDERBIRD (1997)

One trend in motorcycle styling that became particularly popular during the 1990s was that for "retro" machines. These were modern motorcycles that took their styling cues from the motorcycles of twenty and thirty years earlier. The "new" Thunderbird, as it was often referred to, was styled in a way that conjured up images of the old parallel-twin-powered machine. It actually used a version of the three-cylinder water-cooled Triumph engine. The old-time styling in the new Thunderbird can be recognized in the rounded fuel tank with nostalgic tank badges, a traditional dual seat over a rear mudguard, old-style lights and traditional paint colours. The Thunderbird was popular because of the Triumph brand heritage and suited the trend towards 1990s retro bikes. Its choice of name followed Triumph's policy of using old model names on brand new motorcycles. It was introduced to immediate acclaim from the press and public in 1994.

The Triumph company built on the success of their nostalgic Thunderbird with another machine in similar style, the Adventurer 900. This was more of a cruiser-styled motorcycle than the Thunderbird, even though it was based around the same liquid-cooled triple and monoshock frame. The Adventurer had high pullback handlebars, nostalgic tank badges and a solo seat over a custom-styled rear mudguard. Many of the engine parts were chromed and the exhaust pipes were typically English megaphones. Both the Thunderbird and Adventurer were partially designed to appeal to important export markets including America. Production at the Hinckley, Leicestershire factory was increased dramatically as the machines went on sale in the USA.

VELOCETTE MODEL K

SPECIFICATIONS
Year: 1925
Engine type: Ohc single
Engine cycle: Four-stroke
Capacity: 348cc (21.2cu in)
Bore & stroke: 74 x 81mm
Horsepower: n/a
Top speed: 65mph (105kph)
Compression ratio: n/a
Carburettor: B & B
Transmission: 3-speed
Brakes: F. & R. Drum
Ignition: Magneto
Frame: Steel diamond
Suspension: F. Side-sprung
girder forks. R. None
Wheelbase: n/a
Weight: 260lb (118kg)
Fuel: n/a
Oil: Dry sump
Tyres: 2.75 x 21in

VELOCETTE MODEL K (1925)

The company, initially known as Taylor-Gue, was a cycle-manufacturer which began by manufacturing motorcycle frames for another company, Ormonde, which soon folded. Taylor-Gue bought out Ormonde's interests and started production of their own motorcycles under the Veloce name in 1905. By 1910 a 276cc four-stroke motorcycle was in production. This machine was advanced for its day as it featured wet-sump lubrication and a unit-construction engine and gearbox although the latter item was only 2-speed. In 1913 a two-stroke model of 206cc displacement was introduced and christened the Velocette. This was the name which was to be used on all subsequent machines.

The Model K first appeared in 1925 and was the first Velocette with an engine designed by one of the Goodman family which ran the company.

(John Taylor, one of the founders of Taylor-Gue, originally Johannes Gutgemann, an emigré from Germany, had changed his name again in 1911 to Goodman.) Subsequently three generations of the family were to control the Velocette firm. The Model K was also the first four-stroke offered by the company since 1916 when the company had switched to making components for Rolls-Royce armoured cars for the remainder of World War One. The Model K engine had a cast-iron cylinder barrel and cast-iron head with a lapped joint constructed without a head gasket.

Through the late 1920s a number of Isle of Man TT victories went to Velocette using the Goodman overhead-camshaft engine. This 348cc ohc unit was developed into a range of models, namely the KSS, KTT and KTP (see overleaf). These models in slightly modified form were the basis of Velocette's range, along with the 248cc MOV, for several years. The MSS, a 495cc model, was introduced in June 1935 (see pages 176-177).

Below: The lines of the Velocette Model K were sporting – the sprung seat maintained the line created by the frame top tube, while it curved down underneath the seat to join the rear axle.

Left: The overhead-valve engine had exposed valve springs and rockers that were operated by a pushrod contained in a metal tube.

Right: The Model K was attractively engineered down to the smallest details. This is a valve stem cover on one of the wheel rims.

Above: The Model K used an overhead-valve 348cc engine; it was the first four-stroke made by the company since 1916 when production had been switched to war work for Rolls-Royce.

Above: The trade name Velocette first appeared on a two-stroke motorcycle in 1913. It went on to establish itself as one of the great names in British motorcycle history.

VELOCETTE KTT MK VI (1936)

The KTT model was one of a range of three machines with similar designations based on the works race model of 1928. The Mark I KTT was closest to the race bike – a production racer on sale to the public. The KSS was similar and was marketed as a sports roadbike. Finally there was the KTP which featured coil ignition and a dynamo in place of the magneto. Otherwise the machines were similar, all using a 348cc overhead-camshaft engine. The KTT became the KTT Mk II for 1931 with an improved engine. This practice became the norm so that any year's improvements were signified by a different suffix. This system meant that by 1936 the KTT had developed into the Mk VI.

As the Mark IV the KTT had acquired a new cylinder head and hairpin valve springs. The machine was updated to its Mark V form and announced in April 1935. While the displacement stayed at 348cc and the configuration was still overhead camshaft, the barrel was reduced in length and positioned further into the larger crankcase. Long studs were used to assemble both head and barrel to the crankcase. The gearbox was retained unchanged and the two major assemblies were fitted to an all-new cradle frame. The final result was a racebred motorcycle with

Right: The Model K Velocette was powered by the first engine to be designed by a member of the Goodman family, which would control the firm for three generations.

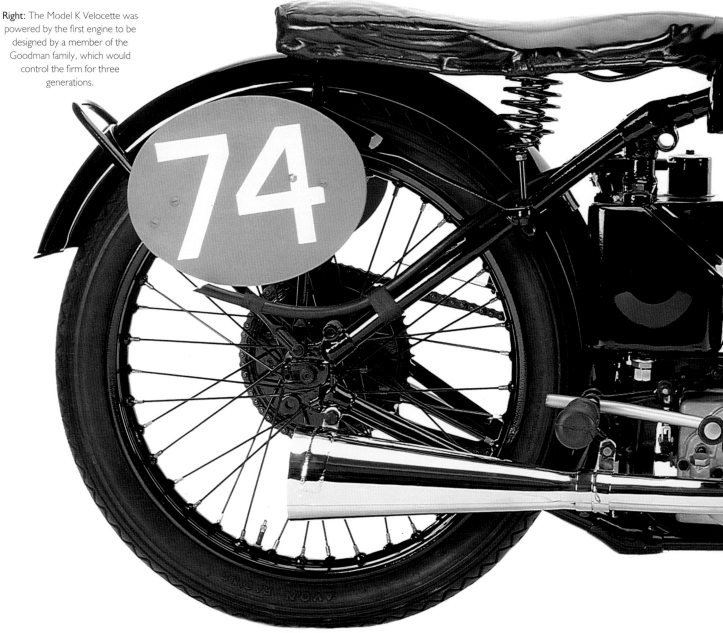

Left: The 348cc engine used in the KTT series of motorcycles was an overhead camshaft design. It utilised a race-type Amal carburettor and magneto ignition.

Below: The KTT Mk VI used 21-inch diameter wheels front and rear, although later the trend for road-race bikes was to smaller diameter wheels, often of 19-inch diameter.

race-type carburettor, magneto ignition, open exhaust pipe and a left-side oil filler cap to suit Isle of Man TT pits – the Goodman family that ran Velocette were fanatical about motorcycle racing.

1936 brought the Mk VI KTT which was essentially a KSS cylinder head fitted to the Mk V engine. Fewer than ten of these machines were built for racing. One was victorious at the Manx Grand Prix of that year in a frame that was to become the basis of the Mk VII. The 1939 Mk VIII was the final version and featured a swinging-arm rear suspension set-up based on air suspension and oil damping. The outbreak of war then saw the company switch to general engineering contracts, although they did supply some motorcycles to the military during the conflict. Production of the company's black and gold machines resumed after the war with a range similar to that of 1939.

Left: A KTT Mk VI such as this won the Manx Grand Prix of 1936. The war interrupted Velocette's racer production.

Above: The KTT Mk VI was a race bike and, devoid of lights, it used sprung girder forks for suspension at the front.

VELOCETTE MSS

SPECIFICATIONS
Year: 1954
Engine type: Ohv single
Engine cycle: Four-stroke
Capacity: 499cc (30.45cu in)
Bore & stroke: 86 x 86mm
Horsepower: 25bhp
Top speed: 82mph (132kph)
Compression ratio: n/a
Carburettor: Amal
Transmission: 4-speed
Brakes: F. & R. Drum
Ignition: Magneto
Frame: Steel tubular
Suspension: F. Telescopic forks.
R. Swingarm and shock absorbers
Wheelbase: 53.75in (1365mm)
Weight: 385lb (175kg)
Fuel: 3 gallons (13.6lit)
Oil: 4 pints (2.27lit)
Tyres: 3.25 x 19in

Above: The 3-gallon tank of the MSS was the same unit as was fitted to the ohc 350cc Velocette MAC.

Right: The Velocette MSS featured rear shock absorbers that were adjustable through slotted top mounts which allowed the shock absorbers to be moved fore and aft.

VELOCETTE MSS (1954)

During the years of World War Two, Veloce Ltd, the company which made Velocettes, partially refitted their factory with new machinery in order to carry out work for military contracts. Veloce turned this machinery to motorcycle manufacture after the cessation of hostilities. There had been a Velocette MSS of 1938 derived from the racing 350 MAC, but the war intervened and it was Velocette MAC (WD) motorcycles that were produced for the duration of the conflict, although not in the numbers that military BSAs and Nortons were. The first postwar Velocette MSS appeared in 1946 as an overhead-valve single-cylinder motorcycle of 495cc displacement with a bore and stroke of 81 x 96mm. It was closely based on the prewar single-cylinder-engined Velocettes with a rigid frame and girder forks and was popular for use with a sidecar. Production was discontinued during 1948 and the company turned its attention to the innovative LE models. The second postwar MSS was unveiled in 1954 in a redesigned form.

The new version of the MSS was also a single-cylinder motorcycle but with a new engine. This one had a bore and stroke of 86 x 86mm which gave a displacement of 499cc. The new machine was considerably faster than its predecessor. The engine was cast from alloy and had an iron cylinder liner fitted. A feature unique to the MSS in Velocette's range was that the cylinder head featured hairpin valve springs for the overhead valves. The rocker box was a separate component and the rockers were contained in split housings. The valve lifter was positioned in the crankcase. The MSS cycle parts were similar to those used in the construction of the sprung Velocette MAC, a 350cc single. The frame was of the swinging-arm rear suspension type and featured adjustable rear shock absorbers. The adjustment was in the top mountings and allowed the shock absorbers to pivot fore and aft. A stepped dual seat topped what was otherwise an utterly conventional, if not dated, British motorcycle of the mid-1950s.

The MSS stayed in production for 1955 and Velocette also made a scrambles version of the MSS in that year. The scrambler used a tuned

Right: The Velocette MSS of 1954 was the second version of the ohv single-cylinder motorcycle to be made in the postwar years.

Below: The advent of widespread use of rear suspension allowed for the fitment of unsprung dual seats to motorcycles as here.

Above: The transmission was a separate assembly, in this case a 4-speed gearbox with, as was the norm for the time, a foot-pedal kickstarter.

MSS engine with a TT carburettor and different exhaust pipe. The cycle parts were slightly modified and alloy mudguards, a bash plate and smaller fuel tank were fitted. Both models remained in production for 1956, although the rigid MAC was discontinued. In its place came another variant of the scrambler, an endurance model fitted with lights in order to make it road-legal. The MSS remained popular as a sidecar machine especially with the motorcyclists who preferred a single-cylinder-engined motorcycle to a twin. The arrival of the Viper and Venom sports models in 1956 in many ways overshadowed the more staid MSS which continued in production through 1957 and 1958. New for 1959 was a glass-fibre enclosure around much of the engine, gearbox and sides of the machine. In this form the range of four Velocette singles continued into the 1960s.

Above: The MSS is seen here in roadgoing trim. Later a scrambles version was offered which included an engine bash plate and knobbly tyres, as well as a different exhaust, carburettor and tuned engine.

Above: The overhead-valve single-cylinder engine displaced 499cc achieved through a bore and stroke of 86 x 86mm. It produced 25bhp and was capable of more than 80mph (129kph).

VELOCETTE LE MARK III

SPECIFICATIONS
Year: 1959
Engine type: Side-valve twin
Engine cycle: Four-stroke
Capacity: 192cc (11.7cu in)
Bore & stroke: 50 x 49mm
Horsepower: 8bhp @ 6000rpm
Top speed: 55mph (89kph)
Compression ratio: n/a
Carburettor: Amal
Transmission: 4-speed
Brakes: F. & R. Drum
Ignition: Coil
Frame: Monocoque
Suspension: F. Telescopic forks. R. Trailing fork
Wheelbase: 51.25 (1302mm)
Weight: 250lb (113kg)
Fuel: 1.25 gallons (5.7lit)
Oil: 1.75 pints (1lit)
Tyres: 3.00 x 19in

VELOCETTE THRUXTON

SPECIFICATIONS
Year: 1967
Engine type: Ohv single
Engine cycle: Four-stroke
Capacity: 499cc (30.5cu in)
Bore & stroke: 86 x 66mm
Horsepower: 41bhp @ 6200rpm
Top speed: 105mph (169kph)
Compression ratio: 9:1
Carburettor: Amal
Transmission: 4-speed
Brakes: F. & R. Drum
Ignition: Magneto
Frame: Steel cradle
Suspension: F. Telescopic forks. R. Swingarm and shock absorbers
Wheelbase: 53.75in (1365mm)
Weight: 375lb (170kg)
Fuel: 4.5 gallons (20.5lit)
Oil: 4 pints (2.27lit)
Tyres: F. 3.00 x 19in. R. 3.25 x 19in

VELOCETTE LE MARK III (1959)

Velocette sprang a real surprise in 1949 with the introduction of the LE model. It featured a 149cc horizontally opposed side-valve twin engine with water-cooling. The machine incorporated a 3-speed hand-change gearbox and extensive weather protection. The LE was an attempt to capture a segment of the mass-market for basic transportation for everyone in the manner that the Italian scooter manufacturers were to exploit so successfully. Unfortunately the Velocette was somewhat ahead of its time and never really managed to establish itself in this market.

The LE was a radical motorcycle for its day and a remarkable achievement for the Goodman family who possessed considerably less resources than rival companies such as Triumph and BSA. It had numerous novel features including a monocoque frame, adjustable pivoted-fork rear suspension, hand-lever starting and a hand-change transmission. The horizontally opposed twin-cylinder engine, which featured water-cooling and shaft drive, was a departure in engineering style for the company too.

The LE was introduced in 1949 but by 1952 had been improved by increasing its displacement from 149cc to 192cc. In 1951 the Velocette range consisted only of the MAC and the LE. The MAC was a traditional overhead-valve single-cylinder motorcycle and two versions of it were produced for 1953. The MSS was then reintroduced in revised form and later in scrambler trim, while the LE was upgraded through the fitting of larger diameter wheels. With other minor upgrades, such as the provision of an external oil filter, production of the Mark II LE ran on until 1958 when the LE III made an appearance. This was the Mark III version of the LE with a 4-speed gearbox, foot gearshift and kickstart. The instruments were moved from their position in the top of the legshields to the headlamp cowl. The Mark II and Mark III versions were manufactured alongside one another in 1958, but after this year only the Mark III was available.

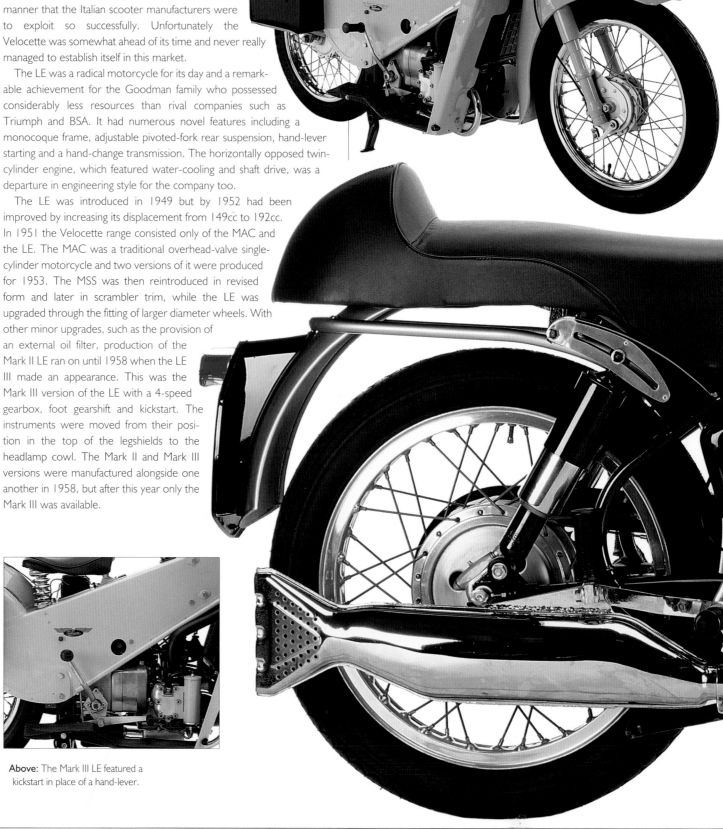

Above: The Mark III LE featured a kickstart in place of a hand-lever.

Left: The Velocette LE was an unusual machine based around a shaft-drive water-cooled flat-twin engine of 192cc displacement and a monocoque frame. It incorporated leg shields in an attempt to offer the rider a degree of weather protection. In many ways it was ahead of its time.

Below: The Velocette Thruxton Venom got its name in celebration of Velocette's racing success at the Thruxton, Hampshire circuit. It was the last sports bike made by the company.

VELOCETTE THRUXTON VENOM (1967)

In the middle of the 1950s Velocette introduced the Viper and Venom models, of 349cc and 499cc displacement respectively. Both were high-performance sports bikes and they were followed by other derivatives including the Viper and Venom Clubman, and later still the Thruxton Venom. The Venom Clubman was derived from the MSS; the Thruxton Venom was named after the famous Hampshire race circuit on which a series of production-machine marathons were run. The Thruxton was introduced in 1965, ironically in the very year that the 500-mile race left Thruxton to take place on the Castle Combe race circuit in Wiltshire. Location did not matter though, the Velocette machines still dominated the 500cc class.

The Thruxton Venom featured as standard a number of race-type components that had to be purchased separately in order to make the Clubman Venom a competitive racer. These included an Amal GP carburettor, a 10:1 compression piston, hairpin valve springs, close-ratio gears, a racing-style seat, clip-on bars and alloy wheel rims. The GP carburettor was angled steeply upwards and to provide sufficient clearance for it the rear corner of the fuel tank had to be cut away. The cycle parts comprised a strengthened version of Velocette's motocross forks and a steel cradle frame. The single-cylinder engine had a cast-iron barrel topped with an alloy cylinder head. In this form the Thruxton was noted as being free-revving and relatively vibration-free. More importantly, performance was on a par with the BSA Gold Star.

In 1967, the year this machine was manufactured, a Thruxton Venom was ridden to an Isle of Man TT victory. Despite this success, the Thruxton Venom represented, in many ways, Velocette's swansong. The company closed in 1971, having ceased production of the Thruxton Venom in 1970.

Left: The Velocette Thruxton Venom was typical of sports bikes of its time with a racing-style dual seat, racing filler cap, alloy mudguards, drum brakes front and rear and short, flat handlebars.

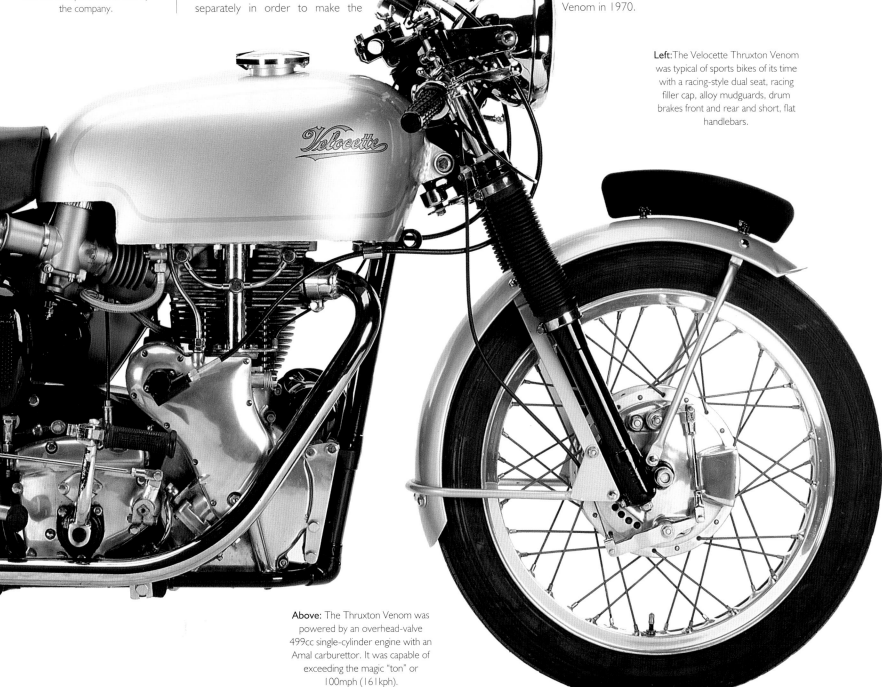

Above: The Thruxton Venom was powered by an overhead-valve 499cc single-cylinder engine with an Amal carburettor. It was capable of exceeding the magic "ton" or 100mph (161kph).

VINCENT-HRD

SPECIFICATIONS

Year: 1935
Engine type: Ohv single
Engine cycle: Four-stroke
Capacity: 498cc (30.4cu in)
Bore & stroke: 84 x 90mm
Horsepower: n/a
Top speed: 92mph (148kph)
Compression ratio: n/a
Carburettor: n/a
Transmission: 4-speed
Brakes: F. & R. Twin drum
Ignition: Magneto
Frame: Tubular steel
Suspension: F. Sprung girder
forks. R. Sprung frame
Wheelbase: n/a
Weight: 385lb (175kg)
Fuel: 3.25 gallons (14.8lit)
Oil: n/a
Tyres: F. 3.00 x 20in.
R. 3.25 x 19in

Above: Philip Vincent bought the H.R.D. trademark from Howard R. Davies who had also manufactured quality motorcycles.

Right: Once Philip Vincent had been joined by Phil Irving, the company began to manufacture engines of its own design which were introduced in 1935.

VINCENT-HRD (1935)

Philip C. Vincent was a graduate of Cambridge University where he had studied Mechanical Science. He had formed a low opinion of many of the engineering practices and features of motorcycles of the 1920s and so he decided to build his own. His first machine incorporated a Swiss MAG engine, a Moss gearbox, Webb forks and featured rear suspension through a pivoting triangular rear frame section. The triangular frame pivot was located behind the gearbox while the springs which permitted movement were mounted under the saddle. As this experimental machine was a success Vincent decided to expand into full-time motorcycle production and purchased the established HRD name from OK Supreme.

One of the reasons that Philip Vincent wanted to use the HRD brand name was because his philosophy about motorcycles was similar to that of Howard R. Davies, the founder of the HRD marque. He too intended to build limited numbers of high quality sporting motorcycles. The HRD marque was well known as Howard Davies had won and placed in a number of Isle of Man TT races before and after World War One on machines of his own construction. By 1930 Vincent-HRD had a reputation as makers of high quality, high class, handbuilt motorcycles. Ironically they were criticised by some for fitting rear suspension to their machines simply because it was considered avant garde at the time.

The new company used proprietary engines from Rudge and JAP initially but later began to manufacture engines of Vincent's own

Below: On its introduction the Vincent sprung-frame rear suspension was criticised by some for being too avant garde.

Left: As at the rear, Vincent used a front wheel an inch taller than many other manufacturers when he fitted a 20-inch item.

Right: The earlier Vincent-HRDs used the conventional sprung girder design of forks, although a distinctive front hub with two brake drums was fitted.

Left: The HRD Vincent trademark displayed on the side panel of the 500cc single-cylinder motorcycle.

Left: Vincent favoured tall wheels and tyres and used a 19-inch diameter rear wheel when many companies used an 18-inch wheel.

Above: Vincent and Irving designed their own engine after problems with proprietary units at the 1935 Isle of Man TT races.

design. The company offered small numbers of 490cc and 600cc side-valve and overhead-valve JAP-engined machines for touring and racing respectively. In 1930 it sold 36 motorcycles and in 1931 it sold 48. The range of motorcycles was widened to include Rudge Python-engined machines which were fitted to a redesigned frame. The Australian engineer Phil Irving joined Vincent-HRD in 1931 and the combined efforts of Vincent and Irving led to the development of the V-twins for which the Vincent marque is best remembered. First though came experiments with commuter two-strokes with Villiers and JAP engines.

Vincent experienced problems with JAP engines in the Isle of Man TT of 1934 and found Rudge engines difficult to source, so the company opted to manufacture its own engine. These engines included a number of innovative design features. They were introduced in 1935 and became the basis of all future Vincent engines. One notable feature was the arrangement of the valves which were operated by splayed pushrods running parallel to the valve stems. The camshaft was positioned high in the engine to facilitate this. In Philip Vincent's opinion, this design and the use of double valve guides was considerably better practice than that of the company's competitors. The new engine was unveiled at the Olympia, London Motorcycle Show in October of 1935. It was installed in three models of motorcycle, the Meteor, Sports Comet and Racing TT model; all three were supplied with the sprung frame and twin drum brakes front and rear. Vincent stopped using proprietary engines after 1935 and all their 1936 models had Vincent's own engine which had been refined in details. Road models were equipped with a Miller Mag-Dyno. There were five models in the 1936 range, a Comet Special and TT road model were added to the line. The 1937 range consisted of four singles and a V-twin which grabbed the headlines although it would come to even greater prominence after the war. The singles continued in production until 1939 when the company, in common with many other manufacturers, went over to war work.

VINCENT BLACK SHADOW SERIES C (1949)

Above: The Vincent-H.R.D. badge featured the figure of the winged Roman god Mercury.

Right: The Series C Vincents featured front and rear suspension that was redesigned from the Series B units. Once proven, the Series B models were dropped.

The first Vincent V-twin – the 998cc Rapide – was announced in 1937. The design was arrived at by using two of the high camshaft single-cylinder engines on a single common crankshaft. It is reputed that Phil Irving, Vincent's Australian engineer and designer, had the idea of a V-twin after seeing two engineering drawings of singles overlapping one another. Philip Vincent was attracted to the idea as he had approved of the concept of the V-twin ever since he had ridden a McEvoy Anzani machine as an undergraduate. This story may be apocryphal but the result was a fast motorcycle with the 47-degree V-twin engine fitted to a slightly longer than standard single-cylinder frame. There were problems with the clutch because of the power of the V-twin engine, but the basic idea was proven. Vincent wanted to build a sports motorcycle that was faster than a Brough Superior but as the company stopped motorcycle production in late 1939, further developments had to wait until after the war.

Phil Irving and Philip Vincent redesigned the Series A Vincent Rapide during the war years and reintroduced it in redesigned form in 1945 as the Series B Rapide. Significant changes had been made to the motorcycle including a major redesign of the engine. The angle between the cylinders had been increased to 50 degrees to suit available magnetos better. The primary drive and clutch mechanism were redesigned. The latter item was designed to have a self-servo action whereby engine torque forced a pair of pivoted shoes into contact with the clutch drum. The wheelbase of the Series B had been shortened by using the engine and gearbox as a structural member which was suspended below a box-section top tube that doubled as an oil tank. Other details that met with approval were items such as the easily adjustable final drive chain and infinitely adjustable riding position.

The postwar Vincent-HRD Rapide was correctly advertised as the "world's fastest standard motorcycle" and it went into production in 1946. Subsequently a faster version, the Black Shadow, was introduced in early 1948 and this had a top speed in excess of 120mph (193kph). A racing version, the Black Lightning, was also made and these two models had some of their alloy engine parts anodized and stove-enamelled black. The Black Shadow was capable of more than 120mph (193kph) through an increased compression ratio and use of larger carburettors.

The Series C variants of the motorcycles were announced for 1949 and while the engines were the same as those in Series B models, the front forks were upgraded by the fitment of what Vincent described as

Girdraulics – a hydraulically damped girder design – while the springing of the rear suspension was damped. The racing version, the Black Lightning, was produced without lights, kickstart or stands, and with TT carburettors and unbaffled exhaust pipes.

It was inevitable that machines designed with performance as a primary consideration would achieve success in competition. In Britain George Brown rode a succession of Vincent V-twins to numerous short-circuit, hillclimb and sprint victories. Most notable was his world record run of 1947 on a Vincent nicknamed Gunga Din. Later he used a more modified machine named Nero and subsequently a supercharged one, Super Nero. Many of the experimental ideas in Gunga Din were incorporated in the Black Shadow production machines. Rollie Free pushed the American speed record over the 150mph (241kph) mark on the salt flats of Bonneville near Wendover in Utah in 1948. He rode a Black Lightning and lay prone along the motorcycle wearing nothing but swimming trunks to reduce drag.

Right: The Black Shadow was the roadgoing model while the racing version, in a higher state of tune, was dubbed the Black Lightning.

Above: The fact that Vincents were intended to be sporting motorcycles is emphasised by the speedometer which is calibrated up to 150mph.

Above: The 1949 Black Shadow had H.R.D. cast into the timing cover of the engine and painted on the side of the fuel tank. On later machines this would read Vincent.

VINCENT RAPIDE SERIES C

SPECIFICATIONS
Year: 1952
Engine type: V-twin
Engine cycle: Four-stroke
Capacity: 998cc (60.9cu in)
Bore & stroke: 84 x 90mm
Horsepower: 45bhp @ 5700rpm
Top speed: 110mph (177kph)
Compression ratio: 6.5:1
Carburettor: Amal
Transmission: 4-speed
Brakes: F. Twin drum. R. Drum
Ignition: Magneto
Frame: Tubular steel
Suspension: F. Girdraulic forks.
R. Sprung frame
Wheelbase: 56.5in (1435mm)
Weight: 455lb (206kg)
Fuel: 3.5 gallons (15.9lit)
Oil: 6 pints (3.4lit)
Tyres: F. 3.00 x 20in.
R. 3.50 x 19in

Above: The hinged rear mudguard facilitated removing the rear wheel to repair punctures or change tyres.

Right: The Series C Vincents were so described because of the new type of front forks used – Girdraulics – which differentiated them from the earlier Series B models.

VINCENT RAPIDE SERIES C (1952)

The Series C Vincents were announced in 1949 and listed alongside the Series B models. The major differences to the Rapides and Black Shadows centred on the type of suspension fitted, most noticeably in the type of forks. Vincent and Irving considered telescopic forks to be inadequate for solo motorcycles and worse for sidecar outfits. In upgrading their motorcycles they opted for a redesigned girder type fork which they described as the Girdraulic. These forks, designed not to twist and so impair handling, were based around a pair of forged alloy blades linked to the headstock by forged links and braced below the bottom link pivot. This was mounted via an eccentric bush which allowed adjustment of the trail for either sidecar or solo use. These bushes also acted as the upper mounts for the pair of long spring units which provided suspension. By mounting them on the eccentric adjusters, the springs were under greater load when used for sidecar work. Damping was by a separate hydraulic unit mounted conventionally between the fork links. At the rear the friction dampers were replaced with a hydraulic unit and new springs.

Once the new systems were proven, the Series B models were dropped and only Series C models were built from 1951 onwards. Production continued until 1955 when the Series D models were announced. These were fully enclosed mod-

els with a deeply valanced front mudguard and a single moulding which ran around the remainder of the machine below the line of the seat. A hinged portion at the rear allowed access to the rear wheel. A windscreen and handlebar fairing were also fitted. Underneath this bodywork was a slightly modified Vincent V-twin motorcycle. Changes included a switch to Amal Monobloc carburettors, coil and points ignition, a single rear suspension unit and smaller diameter wheels. The Rapide was renamed the Black Knight and the Shadow renamed the Black Prince. The new models excited great interest when first displayed, but serious problems with the manufacture of the bodywork led to the production of Series D machines to Rapide and Black Shadow specifications and completely without bodywork.

The "open" Series D models assembled without bodywork had a tubular subframe to carry the dual seat but otherwise retained the new engineering features of the Series D models. The mudguards were as

Above: The Series C models were upgraded from the Series B by the provision of hydraulic dampers under the seat in place of the friction dampers previously fitted.

those used on Series C models. This stop-gap measure kept the firm going, but as a small-scale motorcycle manufacturer making expensive sports motorcycles, the financial situation was precarious. At an Owners' Club dinner in Cambridge in 1955 Philip Vincent announced an end to motorcycle production once outstanding orders had been completed.

The postwar exception to the company's range of sports motorcycles was its production of the Firefly, a 48cc two-stroke motorcycle developed by Miller, the electrical components company. Vincent also did a deal with the German firm, NSU, to import the NSU Quickly 49cc two-stroke-moped. The sales of mopeds such as this soon led to the demise of the clip-on cycle motor. A few machines were also made and listed as NSU-Vincents; these utilized a number of German-made components and a similar number of British ones, in order to comply with various trading restrictions of the time.

Above: In the construction of Vincents, like Broughs before them, quality of workmanship, engineering and finish were paramount.

Right: The ammeter allowed the rider to check that the battery was being charged while the engine was running, especially important when the lights were on.

Above: Vincent motorcycles were essentially sports bikes handbuilt in limited numbers at a time when other manufacturers were concentrating on the mass commuter market.

VINCENT COMET

SPECIFICATIONS
Year: 1953
Engine type: Ohv single
Engine cycle: Four-stroke
Capacity: 499cc (30.45cu in)
Bore & stroke: 84 x 90mm
Horsepower: 28bhp @ 5800rpm
Top speed: 88mph (142kph)
Compression ratio: n/a
Carburettor: Amal
Transmission: 4-speed
Brakes: F. Twin drum. R. Drum
Ignition: Magneto
Frame: Steel tubular
Suspension: F. Girdraulic forks.
R. Sprung frame
Wheelbase: 55.75in (1416mm)
Weight: 400lb (181kg)
Fuel: 3.75 gallons (17lit)
Oil: 5 pints (2.84lit)
Tyres: F. 3.00 x 20in.
R. 3.25 x 19in

Above: Vincent motorcycles used this quirky rear stop light as a matter of course for some years.

Right: While early Vincent V-twins were derived from a pair of Vincent singles, the later singles, such as this postwar Comet, were derived from the V-twin engine with the rear cylinder removed.

VINCENT COMET (1953)

The line of Vincent V-twins were derived from the single-cylinder Vincent Comet because the V-twin was a combination of two single-cylinder engines. The V-twin was redesigned by Irving and Vincent during the war years and subsequently – in reciprocal fashion – the postwar single was derived from the new V-twin. In 1949 the Vincent company produced a single-cylinder machine by leaving the front cylinder canted forwards as in the twin and by replacing the rear cylinder with a cast alloy frame member and adding some gearbox plates to facilitate the use of a Burman 4-speed gearbox. The crankcase was slightly redesigned and the dynamo was driven from the timing gears. Two models were listed: these were designated the Series B Meteor and the Series C Comet. The Meteor had a solo seat but otherwise the single-cylinder models followed the styling of the V-twins closely.

Another single was added to the range for 1950; it was the Grey Flash built for racing. In the manner of the Black Lightning, the Grey Flash had no lights or other road equipment. There were three models of Grey Flash listed. After the Series B Vincents including the Meteor were discontinued, only the Series C singles remained in production as the Comet

Left: Vincents were quality motorcycles and close attention was paid to details such as this rear wheel spindle and chain adjuster.

and various Grey Flash models. The range was further reduced for 1952 when the Grey Flash was discontinued leaving the Comet as the only single-cylinder Vincent. Along with the two roadgoing V-twins, the Comet remained in production through 1953 – the year this machine was made – and 1954, the year that saw the introduction of the diminutive Firefly model. Sales of the Comet were always small simply because many buyers viewed the single-cylinder machine as a poor relation of the V-twin. This was despite race successes with the likes of George Brown and John Surtees in the saddle of Grey Flash machines.

When Vincent planned to move on to the enclosed Series D models, the single-cylinder machine was intended to remain in the range. The Comet was to be renamed the Victor and it would feature the slightly smaller-diameter wheels and other modifications to the cycle parts of the V-twins. (It is interesting that Royal Enfield later named one of their motorcycles the Meteor and BSA one of their off-road machines the Victor.)

Only one example of a Vincent Victor with a glass-fibre enclosure was built for the Earl's Court, London Motorcycle Show of 1954. At this show it is reported that the styling of the enclosed Vincents attracted favourable comment but that the quality of some of the moulding attracted an

Right: Vincents used an unusual system of rear suspension that involved the shock absorbers being mounted under the front of the dual seat and which allowed the rear section of the frame to pivot.

Above: The Comet used a 4-speed Burman gearbox. Both primary and final drive were by means of chains.

amount of criticism. Philip Vincent was particularly concerned about the quality of his products and changed the supplier of the mouldings, which led to a delay in starting production. When Series D models were supplied without their bodywork, a single Series D Comet was made, although this was later fitted with bodywork for a show. During the mid-1950s production of Vincent motorcycles eventually came to a halt after a period of co-operation with the German NSU company and fulfilment of all outstanding orders.

Left: Smiths, as automotive instrument manufacturers, supplied their products to the majority of British motorcycle makers, including Vincent.

Above: To increase front braking capability Vincents were fitted with an unusual twin drum system that was incorporated into the front hub.

Above: The V-twin engine was modified to make a single-cylinder unit. The space for the rear cylinder was covered with a cast alloy rear frame member. The dynamo was driven from the timing gears and a 4-speed Burman gearbox was used.

Left: Vincents used what the manufacturers described as Girdraulic forks which were, in essence, hydraulically damped girder forks.

Above: Vincent's brand name was cast into the primary cover of the engine in both V-twin and single-cylinder configuration machines.

GLOSSARY

Air cooling Engine cooling reliant on air passing over the finned cylinder barrels and heads.
Air intake Where the engine allows the entry of air to the carburettor, usually through a filter.
Automatic inlet valve Inlet valve operated by the suction of the engine. Superseded by mechanically actuated valve.

Belt drive Leather or rubber belt used for final drive on a motorcycle.
BHP Brake horsepower, a standard measure of an engine's output.
Big end The eye of the conrod that encircles the crankshaft and contains a bearing surface.
Bore Diameter of cylinder barrel.
Bush The place in which the end of a shaft rotates used in place of a roller bearing.

Cambox The enclosure for the camshaft.
Camshaft Shaft that opens and closes inlet and exhaust valves.
Carburettor Device for producing and regulating petrol and air fuel mixture.
Chain drive A chain used for primary and/or final drive on a motorcycle.
Coil An electrical winding that provides the High Tension (HT) current for the ignition circuit.
Combustion chamber Shaped area within an engine where compressed fuel/air mixture is ignited.
Compression ratio The amount of compression of the fuel/air mixture.
Conrod A contraction of connecting rod which describes the component that connects the piston to the crankshaft.
Countershaft The shaft within the gearbox that rotates in the opposite direction to the mainshaft.
Crankcase The castings containing the crankshaft and main bearings.
Crankpin The pin that connects flywheel and conrods where an engine does not use a cast crankshaft such as in a single or twin-cylinder engine.
Cylinder The casting in which the piston moves up and down during compression and exhaust strokes of the engine cycle.
Cylinder head The top of the cylinder, usually a separate component which in overhead-valve models contains the valves.

Displacement The volume displaced by the movement of the piston within the cylinder barrel.
Distributor Ignition component that allows high tension electrical current to flow to the spark plug(s).
DOHC Double-overhead-camshaft type engine.
Druid forks A proprietary design of sprung girder forks.
Dry-sump lubrication A system where an engine has two oil pumps; one supplies oil to the engine from the oil tank, while the other returns it to the tank.
Dynamo The electrical component that charges the battery while the engine is running.

Final drive The drive from the gearbox to the rear-wheel sprocket, usually, but not always, by means of a chain.
Flywheel The weight positioned on the crankshaft that ensures it continues to spin between firing strokes.

Four-stroke An engine powered by the induction, compression, ignition, exhaust cycle.
Flat twin A motorcycle engine with two horizontally opposed cylinders.

Girder forks Front forks that through their sprung parallelogram design provide suspension for a motorcycle.

IOE Inlet over exhaust, the valve configuration of some engines.

Little end The end of the conrod connected to

the gudgeon pin within the piston and containing a bearing surface.

Magneto An ignition component that produces high tension electrical current for the spark plugs. Largely superseded by coil ignition and later electronic ignition.
Main bearings The bearings in which the crankshaft rotates.
Manifold The pipes which carry fuel/air mixture to or exhaust gases from the engine during the combustion cycle.
Moped A motorcycle of less than 50cc displacement.

Nacelle A stylised headlamp housing situated around the fork yokes; Triumph coined the word nacelle while Royal Enfield described the unit as a casquette.

OHC Overhead-camshaft type engine.
OHV Overhead-valve type engine in which inlet and exhaust valves are incorporated in the cylinder head.

Piston The component which moves up and down the bore of the cylinder in the induction and exhaust phases of the four-stroke cycle of the internal combustion engine.

Plunger Type of rear suspension where rear wheel spindle moves up and down.
Pressure plate The clutch plate that operates in conjunction with the friction plates.
Primary drive The drive from the engine to the gearbox, usually by means of a chain.
Pushrods The rods that operate the inlet and exhaust valves on engines where the camshaft is incorporated in the crankcase.

Rocker box The component that encloses the rockers and valve springs on an overhead-valve engine.
Rotary valve A type of inlet and exhaust valve often used in two-stroke engines and cylindrical in shape.

Saddle tank A petrol tank that hangs over the top tube of a motorcycle frame in the manner of a saddle.
Shock absorber Also referred to as a damper because it damps rear suspension movement.
Side-valve Type of engine where inlet and exhaust valves are located in the side of the cylinder, also known as a flathead.
SLS Single-leading-shoe drum brake, the normal arrangement for the brake pads within a drum brake hub.

Stroke The distance that the piston moves up and down in the cylinder barrel. Cylinder displacement is calculated by multiplying the square of the radius of the barrel by Pi (π) and multiplying this figure by the stroke.
Supercharger A component that relies on forced air induction to enhance an engine's performance.
Swinging arm, swingarm Also referred to as a pivoted fork, a type of rear suspension where the rear wheel is positioned in a pivoting fork.

TLS Twin-leading-shoe drum brake, a high-performance drum brake.

Two-stroke An internal combustion engine that relies on the up and down movement of the piston to open and close the inlet and exhaust valves.

Wankel A rotary engine devised by Felix Wankel.
Wet sump A motorcycle engine that carries its lubricating oil within the engine rather than in a separate oil tank.

INDEX

> introduction

I changed my career direction in college to graphic design because of white space. Not because I liked it, but because I was terrified of it. You see, I was a fine arts painting major and the thought of blank canvases staring me in the face for the rest of my life drove me to do what I do now. But white space in graphic design offers a different set of challenges. As graphic designers we are supposed to present a message by putting something into that white space, but visual communication is as much about taking out as it is about putting in. What really pointed me in this new direction in the early 1970s was an eight-by-eight white hardbound book titled *The Push Pin Style*. It was full of inspirational work by Milton Glaser, Seymour Chwast, San Antupit, and a whole bunch of other guys whose names I couldn't, and still can't, pronounce. Much of that work utilized white space effectively as evidenced by Glaser's well-known Bob Dylan poster. Much like Marcel Duchamp's cut paper silhouette it uses white space juxta-posed to a black space to create a striking image. But, unlike Gla-ser's poster, Duchamp's example used white space as a positive shape rather than a negative space.